The Media and Models of Masculinity

The Media and Models of Masculinity

Mark Moss

LEXINGTON BOOKS
Lanham • Boulder • New York • Toronto • Plymouth, UK

Published by Lexington Books
A wholly owned subsidiary of The Rowman & Littlefield Publishing Group, Inc.
4501 Forbes Boulevard, Suite 200, Lanham, Maryland 20706
www.rowman.com

Estover Road, Plymouth PL6 7PP, United Kingdom

British Library Cataloguing in Publication Information Available

The hardback edition of this book was previously cataloged by the Library of Congress as follows:

Library of Congress Cataloging-in-Publication Data

Moss, Mark.
The media and the models of masculinity / by Mark Moss.
p. cm.
Includes bibliographical references and index.
1. Men in mass media. 2. Masculinity. 3. Men -- Identity. I. Title.
P94.5.M44M67 2011
305.310973--dc22
2010053235

ISBN: 978-0-7391-6625-3 (cloth : alk. paper)
ISBN: 978-0-7391-6626-0 (pbk. : alk. paper)
ISBN: 978-0-7391-6627-7 (electronic)

♾™ The paper used in this publication meets the minimum requirements of American National Standard for Information Sciences Permanence of Paper for Printed Library Materials, ANSI/NISO Z39.48-1992.

Printed in the United States of America

This book is dedicated to the memory of my father, William Moss

Contents

Preface

A number of years ago I was having my car serviced and in the waiting room there was a magazine with David Brooks' "The Return of the Pig" folded over. The article, which detailed the rise or rebirth of boorish behavior in men, was amusing and accurate. I chuckled at what Brooks had written and thought about the various ways that the media had portrayed men. There were numerous versions to think about. I put the ideas away and walked to a bookstore not far from the service center. At the bookstore I noticed a number of books targeted toward boys, in particular, *The Dangerous Book for Boys*, and similarly titled offerings. Again, I began to think about concepts that structured and defined a mediated version of masculinity. Those ideas have come to the fore in the following pages. Yet they have been tempered and molded over the past few years by viewing and reading about the nature of contemporary masculinity as defined by the media.

In the summer of 2009, it seemed that every newspaper, Website, and magazine featured an article about the upcoming season of *Mad Men*. The Matthew Weiner–produced, and often –written, drama, airing on various cable stations but originating in the United States on AMC, was a throwback look at the workings of an advertising agency in the late 1950s and early 1960s. Glaringly, it put the spotlight on a variety of politically incorrect practices that seemed to pervade the office environment of the times: drinking, smoking, and sexual harassment being the main attractions. The story lines were intriguing, crisply written, intelligent, and very appealing to a select audience. In one sense it was television at its best— very good watching. In another sense it highlighted extreme depictions of masculinity from a variety of angles. The Cary Grant–like sartorial polish and handsomeness of the main character, played by Jon Hamm; the sophisticated elegance of an era where men wore suits, ties, and hats seemed to appeal to many men and women who discussed the show on chat lines, blogs and, appropriately, at the water cooler. The show's fictional and historical associations are quite relevant to this work. It was during the 1950s that so much of what influenced mediated masculinity matured and morphed into the archetypes of today. From Hugh Hefner and the Kinsey studies to stylized icons, the 1950s, in fact and fiction, have come to exert an enormous influence on contemporary masculinity. This is why this work constantly references this era.

Add to *Mad Men* a slew of shows such as *Entourage, Two and a Half Men*, as well as movies as diverse as *Sideways* and *The Last Samurai*, the films of Guy Ritchie, experiments such as *Queer Eye for the Straight Guy* and *Monster Garage*, and what is presented is an eclectic array of media offerings that dictate the variety of ways a man can be deemed masculine and secondly, that reinforce the notion that the media is enormously powerful in conveying accepted and acceptable models of masculinity. The contrasts that the media present are significant and diverse; they range from the juice-head immaturity of the guys on *The Jersey Shore*—all very concerned about their appearance—to the chic gawkiness of the man/boys populating *The Big Bang Theory*.

At the turn of the twentieth-century most middle class men took as their models the roles that were played by successful men in business, sports, and government. Newspapers in particular, but books and magazines as well, provided templates of comparison and pictures of masculinity for men to aspire. Beyond that, most of the modeling came from men that they would have seen in person, on the street, or at work. The examples of masculine style and deportment were finely tuned and only few templates existed. A little over a hundred years later the offerings from the media were much more diverse and enormously fertile. No longer were the static guides confined to a few examples. The media has provided numerous examples for men to model themselves on and yet, despite this diversity most spring from a few key types.

Over the past thirty years a number of studies have appeared that focus on masculinity—from a variety of perspectives—but at no time has such intense a selection of media and multiplicity of content been available. From sophisticates to boors to laughable fathers, the assortment of masculine stereotypes available from all media is truly impressive. This book attempts to survey the models of masculinity presented by the media in its many different forms. It emphasizes the dominant and pervasive impact that the media have had upon defining and signifying masculine roles. There is a grand assortment of influences, some original and some derivative, which have inspired and influenced men over the past decades which cause men to act, dress, and literally "be" a particular kind of man.

The political evolution of men has waxed and waned over this same period. During times of enormous economic and personal distress, men have attempted to recapture places for themselves that tried to distinguish their place in a changing society. For those thrust out of jobs that have been a part of their culture and heritage, the blow has been particularly potent. For others, once king-of-the-world types, soul searching accompanies a series of retrenchments.

In a variety of cases men are responding to the various messages sent through marketing channels and embodied in the diverse portraits painted through characters on television, in film and peppered throughout the media. This work looks at this process.

Introduction

That said, I do have certain qualities consistent with metrosexuality, including a taste for expensive home furnishings, La Prairie skin products, and heirloom tomatoes. It's crazy, I know, but I prefer well-made objects to those of lesser quality. Go figure.[1]

There may have been a day when men wore only white boxer shorts or whatever their wives or girlfriends or mothers bought for them. It is possible that at one time men simply didn't care about their underwear. Today, however, underwear is much more than a piece of underclothing; underwear is a consumerist symbol of masculinity just as lingerie is a consumerist symbol of femininity.[2]

The quotes above are quite funny to those "in the know." They are meant to be humorous but there is a fair degree of seriousness in the observances. Many men have no idea what is being referred to; underwear, tomatoes, and skin products may be irrelevant to their lives. But, many men *will* be aware of the references. Some may snicker while others may feign a lack of comprehension. The latter group, the feigners, may not be willing to admit that they care about these things. They may not be willing to divulge a connoisseur's knowledge about skin care products or a craftsman's wisdom regarding Restoration Hardware dining room tables. Or, on the contrary, they may in fact be extremely abreast of the different legumes and vegetables available at Whole Foods and, be willing to discuss it. They may even wish to discuss it with the same fervor that was once used for the Super Bowl. The point is, that they can, will, and often do. Not all men in North America, but a sizeable proportion have something to say about the subjects that not too long ago were the preserve of women. Go into a large department store and you will still see many women perusing the selection of underwear. But you will also see many men spending an inordinate amount of time at those displays, pondering Calvin Klein, Jockey, Nautica, and other offerings.[3]

Underwear and other commercial products are very much used as symbols of masculinity. No longer are they merely utilitarian or sanitary, functional or practical. Like cars, cologne, and coats, they have become signs that let both the wearer and the observer know what a man is thinking about when it comes to an image of masculinity that he is defining. Fashion and consumption are increasingly tied to identity definitions. This has been the case for women for quite a bit longer than it has for men. The fact that men today define themselves so often by what they purchase suggests that fashion, shopping, and identity are not only linked, but are essential barometers. There are numerous sartorial templates from which to choose. No longer are suits the dominant form of hegemonic masculinity, but a variety of clothing options are present, which reflect the multiplicity of masculinities defined by the media. As one writer has observed, "When a unified male identity was replaced by a manifold identity, wardrobes multiplied to match each of the possible new identities."[4]

It is now possible, probable, and often laudable for men to display an awareness of products, services, and concepts that were previously taboo or at least heavily confined to a very specific subset of cultures.[5] Men today are contradictions and anomalies, characterized by extreme disparities of masculinity. They are comfortable and uncomfortable with all that is available to them, to try and peruse, to sample and sort. They can be fit and active, traditional and conservative and yet, it is okay for them to be boorish and chauvinistic, concerned about their hair, and worried about their weight. It is a staple of Hollywood comedy to have the masculine guy comment on some aspect of fashion or reveal that he himself uses a moisturizer. They can and do cry publicly with much more frequency than ever before, at least as far as televised inductions into various Halls-of-Fame suggest. They can still be rugged, martial, and stoic while at the same time, they can exhibit emotion, feelings, and caring. This is also particularly pronounced at the end of a movie or a sitcom. It is still looked down upon to gush vociferously, and to be too open, but it can be done. It is not always easy and for boys in particular, it can have dire consequences, but the possibilities exist. They are most often defined for men in the media; through movies, televisions shows, and magazines. Newspapers and online journals and sites also showcase the contradictions and the variety. And this gives credence to both the effervescence of the masculine situation and its dependency on the media. The writer Ian Brown in his introduction to a collection of essays on men, sums it up nicely by stating: "Instead of an unwritten and largely unspoken and often unquestioned code of manhood, there are now many codes. The definition of what a man is changes from one *New York Times* Sunday Styles section to the next."[6]

Much of this latent variety comes from the plethora of books and material available in the aftermath of 9/11.[7] This must be qualified with the fact that there was an emphasis on archetypal masculinity, which served as a reconstituted model, and one that allowed for a cascade of other forms of ideal masculinity to come out. In the post-9/11 period there was an outpouring of manly models. The ability to be a real man and to fight, save, and act heroic was etched with precision on the faces of men who were often at the forefront of the effort to rescue survivors of the World Trade Center towers. The stoic determination captured by numerous photographers gave way to a variety of images that quickly found their way onto various television shows. It was possible for them to be manly and to be traditional, but as well, to care. It has taken a while for this inconsistent duality to receive public acceptance but it has occurred. And it has been tempered over the past decade, ebbing and flowing, morphing and reconstituting itself. Although tempered, the rise of traditional masculine behavior is once again applauded—one sees variations from *Rescue Me* to *Mad Men*—and this must now coexist with other forms of masculine experience.

Enormous pressure still resonates within society for men and boys to exhibit what are often termed traditional masculine qualities.[8] Men are often put in compromising positions as far as striving to attain a proper masculine form. They are fighting what was traditionally a prescribed script. They no longer have the financial power to wield over women, yet in many cases they are still expected to pick up the check. Boys are told to play gentle and to share; yet they quickly learn it does not work in most situations, be it games or sports. Men are often praised for being fit and tailored and thus, must succumb to the same fashion and image pressures that have been affecting women for years. As a consumer base and an important series of demographics, men have become enormously important to companies that are in the appearance business. The body, in its real and implied signals, is still oriented around the traditional ideas of strength and dependability, power and masculinity.[9] Even in these so-called liberated times, if a man does not act manly, his sexuality is held in question. For young men, nothing is worse than an inquiry on his masculinity—despite the fact that gay liberation is forty years old. As well, over the past few decades, the notion of the ideal man comes complete with large doses of empathy and emotion, something that just does not fit with many media images, not to mention many social realms.

Television channels have increased dramatically in quantity and in the different shows they offer. No longer is this a "big three" world but rather from cable to satellite to local to international, a vast array of channels needs enormous amounts of product to show. This same evolution has also occurred in film. Where once there was dominance in the form of major studios, a host of independents and non-aligned films reach audiences with subject matter that before would have been dismissed as not profitable enough. Magazines and especially online magazines can speak to a niche audience and still be profitable. In essence, the media needs material and is willing to portray, feature, and promote a wide selection of masculine images that appeal to different audiences in a strategic manner. Thus it is possible to now show more than one version of masculinity. As Robert Connell noted in *Gender and Power*, "when looking at masculinity it is essential to be aware of the many masculinities in circulation."[10] The varieties of masculinity as presented by the mass media open themselves to contradictions.

Can all of the varied tropes and contradictions of masculinity and "being a man" survive? Or rather, can they survive through media images and in turn, influence men? The short answer is yes—they will and currently, they do. Men can have it all and many attempt to do just that. What this work suggests is that there are many variations of masculine experience as recommended by an assortment of mass media. Not all are achievable and as well, many men select deviations and different levels out of the myriad offerings. For example, they will stay at home with the kids and while they are napping, watch NFL or NASCAR. What this book suggests is that there is no longer one dominant form of masculinity according to what is offered through the media. Many competing versions exist. Most owe some great form of origin to historically charged versions and mythical creations such as the cowboy or the businessman. And, it is possible to see more and more modern versions arising.

This book is concerned with American and Canadian men, heterosexual, mostly white males and the templates they follow by consuming media images and influences. It begins with an analysis of some of the key theoretical concepts, which are used to both frame and explain contemporary masculinity, its plural nature and the importance of the media in illustrating these images. The richness of historical ideas and models is an especially robust arena as far as masculine templates are concerned and in particular, the mass media's use of them. Thus, there is a focus on bringing in historical and contemporary analysis, especially with regard to the (role) models and exemplars of masculine ideals. The second chapter deals specifically with the mass media and its impact and influence. Magazines, films, radio, and television offer the most tangible and powerful look into the cultural manifestations of masculinity. These range from talk radio to cooking shows.

The fact that men are extraordinarily preoccupied with how they look and what they wear is the topic of the following chapter. Never before have so many men been so concerned with their appearance. And, never in history has there been such an array of looks and style to chose from. Even the periods of the Renaissance and the heyday of the dandy pale in comparison to what is offered through magazines, movies, and television. If George Clooney gets a new haircut or David Beckam adopts a new style, many men will attempt to mimic that look. The impact of fashion and male grooming products is indicative of one of the central concerns of this book: that men can and do pay close attention to the formerly mundane world of personal appearance. If Tiger Woods or some other athlete is promoting a particular shaving product, chances are that a number of men will buy it.

Chapter 4 focuses on books and the culture of reading. It uses the printed text to show the stability in the varieties of masculine experience as well as grand deviations. A number of the many books on superficial masculinity are discussed in order to demonstrate how popular these texts have become. One only had to do a quick search on Amazon.com to get a sense of the quantities available. As well, a host of literary offerings are examined to chart the different versions of masculinity in a consumer culture.

The historical tropes and concepts, which have so influenced contemporary masculine aspirations, are the subject of chapter 5. It is my contention throughout this book that certain seminal historical periods, especially in recent history, continue to impart a variety of messages about style, deportment, carriage, and identity. This plays out in a discussion of "doing it yourself." Men and boys constantly seek the visceral satisfaction of all-male pursuits and in building things they find a satisfying outlet. Through various media, one is taught that it is a high mark of masculinity to be able to fix and repair, to build and construct. These were once abilities that were lauded and now, because of technology and automation, do not hold the same level of appeal. The surrogate element of hobbies and even tinkering is all that is left. Perhaps this explains the popularity of "fix-it" shows that dominate certain channels. Hobby culture and collecting came of age in the 1950s. Although around since the 1920s in their modern form, the culture of the Cold War was intimately related to a redefined masculine domesticity which made workshops and home repair quite popular. On the other side of that sphere was a deepseated rebellious nature that began to percolate. Chapter 6 discusses the influence of rebel culture and attempts to portray "domesticated" men. Owing much to Barbara Ehrenreich, it deals with the rise of key male archetypes, resuscitations of older avatars, and the burgeoning array of nontraditional expressions of mediated masculinity. These include the Brando- and Dean-influenced rebel as well as the playboy.

The subject of men and violence is discussed next. Violence takes on many different forms as portrayed in the media. It is one of the great contradictions that most of the dominant, archetypal masculine constructs involve, in some degree or form, a level of violence. Whether soldier or explorer, cowboy or adventurer, either a small or great element of violence is involved in the forging of this typology. And there is no doubt that it permeates even the most sanitized versions of contemporary culture. Some have suggested that this has always been the case and no matter what, men are hard-wired for this type of approach. The plethora of books that have been published over the last few years on raising nonviolent boys indicates that this has touched a great nerve. The focus on raising boys who are not prone to violence shadows the juvenilization of men thesis that both Gary Cross and Michael Kimmel have discussed.[11]

Technology is a masculine enterprise. Men gravitate toward all forms of technology—both modern, as in computers, and traditional, such as with architecture—in numbers that make the equation of technology with masculinity almost synonymous. Men who are not always exemplars of physical masculinity will often utilize masculine tropes in the technological realm. For over sixty years, one prosaic version of technology, the car, has been a significant crutch for men from a variety of cultural spectrums. The car and its resonant culture have shaped North American masculinity, as defined by the media, in very specific ways. Chapter 8 concentrates on this interesting conflation.

If one is to look carefully at masculine space, one only has a few options. Beyond the garage and the "man cave," the office or home office is a significant treasure trove of revelation as far as exemplifying a man's character. Chapter 9 begins by looking at "the objects on men's desks" in order to assess what messages are being conveyed from this arena. What do these items say? What do they signify? If male space is expanded, there are a few other rooms that delineate how men define their material masculinity. The den, the media room, and other such male preserves also shed light on this multifariousness of perception.

In chapter 10, the discussion turns to sports. Sport is perhaps the dominant realm where masculinities are portrayed, tested, and defined. Participating in sports is almost a "must" for boys. Whether team sports such as soccer, football, baseball, or hockey, or individual sports such as canoeing, hiking, golf, or skiing, it is an essential aspect of growing up and becoming a man according to most media. Boys who don't show an interest are quickly defined as not being part of a larger male subgroup. Many challenges and changes have occurred in this area, most notably the massive growth of girls' participation in all sports. Through spectatorship and fandom, sport reaches out to the non-athlete. The rise or rabid fandom and sports talk culture is especially important in satisfying many men's interests. It offers a form of vicarious attachment and at the same time, allows them to bond with other men (and boys) in an accepted and safe manner.

The chosen topics for examination here all focus on some facet of male culture and in particular how various mass media portray and embody a wide array of models and paradigms. One uniform theme throughout the book is that there are a variety of competing masculinities, all jockeying for legitimacy in the pantheon of masculine templates often offered up by the media. Many of these can and do coexist with variations on hegemonic masculinity, which gives them both a sense of legitimacy as well as a form of substance. Men can and do embody many of these "avatars" which fluctuate depending on the dictates of media, culture, and society. They select portions or whole chunks within the vast spectrums of masculinity and sort and choose what they want, what they aspire toward and how they wish to be thought. There are many contradictions and numerous inconsistencies, but rather than posing obstacles, they seem to serve as markers. To some extent, this makes the selection offered up by the media rife with dissonance. Yet, it also provides safety and cohesive platforms on which to stand.

The desire to comport oneself as supremely masculine is a common ingredient in many media portrayals. Whether it is the influence of the James Bond Syndrome from the 1950s and 1960s or a more modern reworking of this tableau, it is evasive and ephemeral as a guide to many men and boys. If difficult to articulate, the templates that often were forged in the 1950s are still easily mimicked and very accessible.

NOTES

1. Peter Hyman, *The Reluctant Metrosexual: Dispatches from an Almost Hip Life* (New York: Villard, 2004), p. xv.

2. Edisol Wayne Dotson, *Behold the Man: The Hype and Selling of Male Beauty in Media and Culture* (New York: Harrington Park Press, 1999), p. 39.

3. For one version of the emerging sense of awareness about fashion and masculinity and the concerns that this generated, see Eric J. Segal, "Norman Rockwell and the Fashioning of American Masculinity,"*Art Bulletin* 78, no. 4 (December 1996). On page 641, Segal writes: "A distinction was also to be made between a legitimate masculine interest in sartorial matters and the effeminate implications of an overly narcissistic investment in one's clothing. This distinction was expressed in retail clothing trade handbooks and self-teaching manuals circulated to train sales staff (it would not be until 1933 that male clothing consumers would have their own publication in the form of *Esquire*)."

4. Giannino Malossi, "Material Man: Decoding Fashion, Redefining Masculinity," in *Material Man: Masculinity, Sexuality, Style*, ed. Giannino Malossi (New York: Abrams, 2000), p. 30.

5. See Jean M. Twenge, *Generation Me* (New York: Free Press, 2006), p. 197. Dr. Twenge writes: "It does seem that young men are now more comfortable with the more appearance-based 'feminine' things—witness the recent emergence of the manicure-loving, fashionable-shoe-wearing metrosexual. Suddenly, just because you know how to dress well doesn't necessarily mean you're gay."

6. Ian Brown, "Introduction," in *What I Meant to Say: The Private Lives of Men*, ed. Ian Brown (Toronto: Thomas Allen, 2005), p. xvii.

7. See Patricia Leigh Brown, "The Return of Manly Men," *New York Times*, October 28, 2001, p. 4.

8. On this point, Robert Connell writes: "School Studies show patterns of hegemony vividly. In certain schools the masculinity exalted through competitive sport is hegemonic; this means that sporting prowess is a test of masculinity even for boys who detest the locker room. Those who reject the hegemonic pattern have to fight or negotiate their way out."*Masculinities*, 2nd ed. (Berkeley: University of California Press, 2005), p. 37.

9. Brenda R. Weber, "What Makes the Man? Television Makeovers, Made-Over Masculinity, and Male Body Image,"*International Journal of Men's Health* 5, no. 3 (Fall 2006), p. 291.

10. Robert W. Connell, *Gender and Power* (Palo Alto, CA: Stanford University Press, 1987).

11. See Gary Cross, *Men to Boys: The Making of Modern Immaturity* (New York: Columbia University Press, 2008) and Michael Kimmel, *Guyland: The Perilous World Where Boys Become Men* (New York: HarperCollins, 2008).

ONE
History and Theory

Ideas of what constitute the cultural offerings of masculinity or the physical parameters of maleness are those that often evolve on a continuum.[1] What was supremely definitive as an icon or emblem of masculinity forty years ago may seem dated and embarrassing today.[2] What was dismissed as girlish or feminine in comparison to masculine twenty years ago may be considered hyper-masculine in the not too distant future. Masculinity is evolving and changing; what gives it such elasticity are the varieties of masculine experience.[3]

Masculinity refers to socially fabricated patterns or positions embodied by men. In essence, masculinity is a "social construct" which can stand alone from male biology. This is why forces and cultural trends can have such an enormous impact on masculine interpretations, both personal and public.[4] Research suggests, "masculinities are multiple":

> Historians and anthropologists have shown that there is no one pattern of masculinity that is found everywhere. Different cultures, and different periods of history, construct masculinity differently.[5]

Robert Connell, the dean of academic writing on theoretical masculinity offers up the theory that different cultures have different notions of definitive masculine interpretations. In some cultures, violence is "the ultimate test of masculinity" while in others it is looked down upon. Consequently, two things can be inferred: notions of heroes and heroic endeavor, important to all cultures will vary widely, and are dependent on masculine archetypes. In western societies where the population is diverse and multicultural, assorted and variegated ideals of masculinity compete and exist in relation to each other. Further, diverging interpretations of masculinity can occur as a consequence of class. What is considered supremely masculine in working class or "blue collar culture" does not hold sway in upper class environments, despite the fact that the boundaries are more porous than ever. As Connell suggests, these varied forms of masculinity can exist—compete and jostle—within one "cultural setting." This could be a workplace, an academic arena, or within a social grouping.[6]

It is important, as Connell notes, that the jostling for position or the privileging of some form of masculinity over another is constantly occurring. Some forms of masculinity are disparaged, while others are lauded. The type that is privileged or "culturally dominant," Connell terms "hegemonic masculinity." This is more about guidance as opposed to ascendance in a full manner. In turn, this allows for competing or alternate versions of masculinity to exist or even coexist with hegemonic forms. Importantly, hegemonic masculinity is often seen as the ideal; the one that boys and men strive for as a definitive standard.[7]

A significant determinant to defining socially constructed masculinity is the fact that male role models are often either manufactured from versions of reality or, they as exist as total fictional creations. Whether composed of archetypes from the past or revitalized media fabrications, these representations are key in defining how males think of themselves and importantly; they suggest specific ideals to follow.[8] The models that are depicted are fused together by popular or mass culture. It is significant, if not vital, to understand masculinity and the polarities of masculinity in these terms. Although they exude an enormous influence, the role models to whom many men aspire are often totally and completely unattainable.[9] All of these combine to form both the central aspects of character definition and in many cases, notions of the self. As Kath Woodward notes in her examination of boxing heroics, whether real or fictionalized, it almost does not seem to matter,

> fantasy and reality are inextricably combined. Public stories, symbolic representations, unconscious desires and anxieties and embodied experience and iterative practices are all constructions of identity.[10]

The fact that this is something that is often unrealistic doesn't deter men and boys from modeling their behavior and aspirations on an unreachable set of assumptions. An often-cited example of this is Ian Fleming's James Bond who was born in books and lives on through movies. While in charge of his school's library, Francis Spufford, age thirteen, learned rather quickly that it was the James Bond books that disappeared. "Every copy," he writes,

> vanished to become somebody's private primer. The thing that made them so attractive to us at that particular age was that they led you seamlessly from the boys' stuff you had coveted last year—sports cars equipped with machine guns—on to the enticements that were just starting to figure in your fantasies, and would dominate them next year—naked odalisques painted gold, and female pilots who unzipped their flying suits from neck to crotch in one sinuous southward motion.

> Unlike the films, the original Ian Fleming novels fit all the diverse
> attractions of Bond's world together as component pieces of one sexed-
> up, Gentlemanly poise.[11]

In certain cases, a mélange of styles is mixed together for the role model, distilling only the most masculine. The result is a form of hypermasculinity, a definitive form of masculine modeling that gravitates toward extreme or super-pronounced postures. The growth of bodybuilding and the emphasis placed on size and definition is also derived from the images and examples filtered through the media and advertizing. Whether it is the body-building hulks featured on the covers of weightlifting magazines or the extremely sculpted look of elite athletes and movie stars, the unrealistic images and their subsequent impact on boys and men are intensely motivating, all the while being impossible to achieve for most men.[12]

In contemporary culture the few defined roles within the complex rubric of masculinity have fragmented to the point there is a multiplicity of expectations, all competing for supremacy.[13] Another way of locating this is to suggest that whereas templates exist and numerous possibilities are allowed, a significant amount of latitude is granted. As Mark Gallagher writes,

> The sheer multitude of possible representational modes and strategies
> means the perspectives on men's activities, men's expected roles, and
> men's actual relation to some culturally determined notion of masculinity are always contested or in flux.[14]

This has a tendency to create dissonance for men. Whereas during and after World War II the templates for masculinity were relatively robust, in the following half-century, that proved to no longer be the case. One observation about this is that men today, and in particular, young men, have no set of masculine identity constructs on which to model themselves. Michael Kimmel writes that "today's young men are coming of age in an era with no road maps, no blueprints, and no primers to tell them what a man is or how to become one."[15] This can be and often is liberating in that it provides a break in the hegemonic masculine calendar, but can also give rise to a form of template ignorance. To explain both the popularity of so many "new" men's magazines as well as so many books on masculine/male/manly culture, it is suggested that their reason d'etre as well as their role as pedagogic indicator has to do with the fact that "contemporary young men have forgotten how to act 'natural.'"[16] One tendency among young men in particular is to revert to an exhibition of "rough manners." This means that "in order to show that they are real men," they must make their masculinity visible. As Franco La Cecia puts it, "They must produce rowdy noise and make scenes—the roar of a Harley-Davidson, popping wheelies on a Vespa, a certain tone of voice."[17] This variant also finds its way into emerging "guy culture" or "heavy masculinity." The hallmark here is usually oriented around social or leisure gatherings that deliberately and specifically exclude women.[18]

Another very prominent masculine archetype, one that has emerged in the past thirty years, has been the rise of the geek as a cool icon. The computer nerd, the pasty entrepreneur, and the Woody Allen–like neurotic have also edged their way into the pantheon of masculine experience. The media celebrates various versions of this especially on television. From *The Big Bang Theory* to one of the characters on *Two and a Half Men*, this is an extraordinarily popular variation of masculinity. This was not something that would have occurred in the post–World War II period and one can surmise that the rise of feminism and "touchy-feely" culture, prominent in the 1970s, has allowed this variant to survive and mature.

Throughout history but in particular, throughout the last 150 years, much discussion has been devoted to ideal forms of masculinity. In the period immediately following World War II, the notion of an ideal male archetype—as an extension of the warrior—became a staple of masculine mass culture. This was, in the words of Abigail Solomon-Godeau, an "elastic" version of ideal masculinity; one that could be applied to any number of arenas and that would not necessarily undermine the "patriarchal order."[19] Commenting on Solomon-Godeau's observations, Patricia Vettel-Becker buttresses the ideas raised above, in her assertion that "gender constructions are never stable; nor do they ever fully explain or match the actual lived experiences of individuals, who must navigate their way through these shifting ideologies."[20] Another way of putting this is to suggest that there are "paradigms of socialization" that jockey for supremacy at different times and in different eras. Like Thomas Kuhn's "dialectic theses" or at least according to Chris Blazina's interpretation of it as it applies to this topic, there is a "waxing and waning" of "competing models" which leads to newer versions jostling with older ones.[21]

Despite the varied, multiple nature of masculinity, specific elements of masculinity that are historical, meaning, they have existed before, continue to linger on and exert an influence on perceptions and the possibilities in defining masculine culture. This can also be considered a variation of Connell's hegemonic masculinity. It is fundamental to recognize as well, that masculine identity often latches on to established and proven male archetypes in some form or another. Men, both consciously and unconsciously model and mimic the dress, behavior, and mannerisms of key archetypes such as the cowboy, the adventurer, and the big game hunter, even though these are long past their veracity. Modeling occurs despite the fact that many of the conventions that contribute to these iconic presentations, no longer exist, with the exception of their mediated presentations. Why they are employed by marketers and by men themselves, speaks to the staying power of their influence, but also of and to their embeddedness as supremely well-drawn-out masculine illustrations. To some extent the impact of these models has been fueled and mythologized by mass culture and in turn, has been coopted by marketing and consumption.

Douglas B. Holt and Craig J. Thompson advance the notion that many men define and prove their manhood by utilizing props and products in the form of "compensatory consumption."[22] The symbolism and semiotic suggestions that these purchases give off define how a man thinks of himself and infer to others what he wished to be thought of. The "compensatory consumption thesis" indicates that in order for men to "prove their manhood," they grasp at and utilized a wide array of consumer products that symbolically define or buttress individual and collective notions of masculinity. The Harley Davidson motorcycle for example, is a significant and expensive extension or prosthetic accouterment in specifying one's masculine character. The legitimacy of this thesis is based on the notion that routine jobs and the potential of societal emasculation forces men to compensate through the purchasing of these products.[23] At the same time, the resiliency of classic or early modern archetypes, often employed in advertising imagery, speaks to the insecurities facing contemporary men. Beyond Harley Davidson, another product that evokes masculine attributes is Jack Daniel's bourbon. This product has evolved into a brand with a robust association with rebel manhood, frontier individuality, and connotations with the gunfighter mystique. By focusing on strong drink and in particular, libations such as bourbon and whiskey in movies and television and through novels, men have learned how and what to drink. In the saloons, which apparently dotted the West as in *Deadwood* and other westerns, all the real men drank it. Thus Jack Daniel's has an almost historic access to the hearts and gullets of men who desire and are please by this association.[24]

Two related archetypes, the warrior/soldier and the explorer/adventurer continue to exist via the media in the contemporary masculine imagination as touchstones of inspiration. Both serve as templates to be refined and have spawned a variety of variations. Whether it is the outdoorsy, rugged man, or the athletic doer, the essence of these remains the same: either as conformist or as rebel poser. Linking the two are a variety of subgroups and defining models that often have two factors in common—especially in advertisements for SUVs; there is the focus on the outdoors or a simulated version of nature, and often, a conscious desire to be away from women.

It is worth mentioning that, regardless of the changes affecting contemporary society, and one may even suggest, in spite of the changes, there is a constant and consistent attraction to both the warrior/soldier and explorer/adventurer templates. To even surmise that these have been eradicated as archetypes that still hold a lot of weight is to ignore the evidence from film and television, advertising, leisure, and video games to name just some of the media that continuously utilize these tropes.

Historically in the United States, there have been various epochs that have set the tone for the above and that have allowed for the fermentation of these models. Michael Kimmel suggests that American history if filled with periodic outbursts of "homosocial preserves," in particular during the nineteenth century. The "Go West Young Man" focus was a particularly potent manifestation of this and its resonance echoes on today. The California Gold Rush of 1849 was unprecedented and the men who flocked to seek their fortune embraced or degenerated into unabashed natural masculinity. They cast off their eastern affectations and the trappings of civilization, adopting names that were "manly and rough" and engaged in hypermasculine behavior. This included bare-knuckle fighting as well as excessive gambling, swearing, and drinking.[25] This set the tone for a specific model of male comportment where there was a glorification of a wild and untamed type of demeanor.

The action-adventure hero of the period from 1870 to 1940 lives on in a variety of incarnations. He exists as a potent model for men, media representations, and marketing. The popularity of the *Indiana Jones* films and the repute of the adventure wardrobe testify to the staying power of this dated symbol. In various cities, men can be seen walking on the street dressed in hiking boots, multi-pocket cargo pants, worn leather jackets, and a version of the hat that Harrison Ford has worn in the films. It is a look one sees at universities and at cafes. It is an intelligent version of the masculine experience—at least sartorially speaking and exudes both confidence and seriousness. In essence it speaks to one variation of the contemporary masculine experience, which has resurfaced as a celebration of masculine culture.

From the late 1970s on into the 1990s, men vacillated in a period of cultural stasis. By this grand generalization, what is meant is that there were perhaps a few extremes—hardhats, hippies, Peter Pans, *Magnum P.I.* clones—yet everything seemed tinged with a sepia-tinted patina that now appropriately resembles an old photograph. There was not a full-fledged awareness of the varieties of masculine experience—at least not reflected through the visual media—and one can't help wonder if at the beginning of the period this was due to the impact of third wave feminism.

A standard for recent masculinity and all of its contradictions is found in Bill Clinton. Clinton exuded the macho confidence of a variety of traditional masculine archetypes but at the same time was also vulnerable and compassionate. He was portrayed as intellectual and highbrow in some respects, all the while continuing to be a "good ole boy." In essence, according to Brenton J. Malin,

> Clinton's masculinity was thoroughly conflicted—embracing a kind of new, sensitive, nontraditional masculinity at the same time that it

sought to demonstrate a powerful, thoroughly established sense of 'real' American manhood.[26]

The portrayal of Clinton as a contradictory sort of masculine figure highlights both the negative and the positive forms of masculine character and at the same time, gives evidence of a resurgent form of masculinity. This is especially interesting in the context of the steady diet of soul-searching that men and the media undertake, most notably under the term of a crisis.

In two distinct periods over the last 150 years, there have been times when men have consciously reasserted their masculinity due to a perceived "crisis of masculinity." Balancing both of these eras was the fear of feminization. The first period preceded World War I, while the second one was most pronounced during the 1950s. The attempt by men to compensate or overcompensate during these periods still lingers in the twenty-first century. One indicator of the efficacy of these concerns is the language used by journalists and writers. Another gauge is advertising from the periods. The distillation of strategies, both real and imagined, to prompt men to be assertive and supremely macho can be seen in the trend toward historical masculinity and retro-masculinity. In both these periods there is the constant exhortation of men to be strong and to reassert their traditional and historical rights as men.

Commentators, politicians, speechwriters, and journalists pick up on these fears and translate them into potent epithets and sayings. When men are weak, the thinking goes, so too is the country, its foreign policy, and by default, its culture. "We must be strong and we must show our strength" is a time-tested way of thinking. This was pronounced in the decades before World War I and was once again a feature of society during the late 1950s and early 1960s. The touchstone that often sets off these fears is the worry over decadence, and importantly, the subsuming of hardiness in favor of luxury. Chuck Palahniuk's quote from his novel *Fight Club* is not too different from JFK's Cold War/nuclear threat remarks: "We have gone soft—physically, mentally, spiritually soft. We are in danger of losing our will to fight, to sacrifice, to endure. The slow corrosion of luxury is already beginning to show."[27]

A distinctive aspect in viewing contemporary masculinities has to do with the distance and the appropriation that many varieties seek in dealing with what Kevin Boon calls "congenial masculinity." Boon suggests that feminist theory and anti-aggression rhetoric focused men away from vigorous manliness and dominating hegemonic masculinity, and literally unmoored, for a time, its ties to tradition and proven models. Dealing with the attempt to distance themselves from the uglier notions of conservative masculinities, Boon implies that ambivalence with and attraction to strong codes characterize many contemporary variations.[28] One of the reasons why so many versions of masculinity can coexist may be traced to this assumption.

It is important to bear in mind that the appeal of retro-masculinity still lingers in a very pronounced and potent way. It surfaces in a wide array of cultural practices, media messages, and marketing programs. It can manifest itself in individual terms but often seeks to find expression and fulfillment in group settings. It borrows freely from stereotypes and archetypes that were dominant in the late Victorian period as well as from the 1950s.

On a Thursday night in early winter, a group of men are gathered in a bar. They are drinking vodka martinis, single malt scotch, and some are clustered in a secluded area smoking large cigars from Cuba and the Dominican Republic. Just down the street there is a steak house, packed with men, aggressively cutting into filet minion and New York sirloin. For briefly a decade—from the late 1980s to the 1990s, these kinds of indulgences were seen as taboo; unhealthy and too hearty to be politically correct. Now it is a common component on numerous TV shows and in magazine features. In pre–*Mad Men* culture, for at least a decade, this masculine indulgence was absent from depictions in popular culture. In his novel, *Brightness Falls*, Jay McInerny details the horrors of smoking and drinking in pristine, health-conscious L.A. The main character is made to feel like a pariah for wanting to sip a martini and eat a big steak. Now, this is back with a vengeance. Men are often encouraged to return to this world to indulge and consume in a way that was once thought to be supremely brawny. Guy's night out is becoming a must in the weekly schedule or monthly calendar of most men. In some instances this is a routine endeavor, while in others, such as Gillette's "It's a guy thing," or Coors promotions, it is manufactured.

These gatherings are celebrated as macho meetings; masculine attempts to redefine what male culture is currently thought to be. This renewed sense of embracement of all things male and of all activities thought to be thoroughly masculine, comes with a post-modern twist. These activities are done with a keen sense of variation. For example, the culture of marketing that is dedicated to males, offers a vast array of products. On one hand, these range from purely traditional "things" such as sports, beer and women, to the more uncommon; male hair care products, fashion, and entertainment.

In the movie *Sideways*, there is an interesting focus on the various forms of masculinity now featured and accepted. Thomas Hayden Church plays a character that exhibits what one could call the traditional forms of masculinity; he's good looking in a rugged way, athletic and very self-absorbed. At the other end of the spectrum is Paul Giamotti's character, still reeling from a divorce, totally incapable of having fun, worried, neurotic, and intensely morose. They bond in a very bizarre way, on a wine tour of the vineyards of northern California. This film is a study of diverse forms of masculinity but it also subverts the buddy movie genre and becomes a touchstone for contemporary masculinity. What is significant here is the fact that no matter what, men must keep to their bonds of loyalty. A best friend must lie, risk his life, and do whatever he has to not to break the bond. Another striking aspect about the movie is the fact that there is diversity across the spectrum of what constitutes masculinity. There is a pronounced sense of elasticity regarding masculine attributes. There is the insecure, emotional male and the narcissistic god-like man who has had it pretty easy. Although the customary depiction of the male as a hyper-masculine person is present, other varieties peek out.

A version of this is similar to the "double bind." According to Susan Bordo, who depends on Gregory Bateson, what this means is that there are often "mutually incompatible instructions" directed toward people, with the expectation that both have to be fulfilled.[29] Building on Bateson's ideas, Bordo suggests that, especially for boys, there is an expectation to be masculine and to celebrate traditional masculine skills and accomplishments. At the same time, boys have to pull back and respect what society now deems inappropriate. There is a cyclical attempt to be manly and emotionally respectful at the same time — which causes young boys contradictions in interpretation. Bordo cites the example of Mike Tyson who was paid to be violent and aggressive yet when that behavior occured outside the boxing ring, he became a thug.[30]

Whatever the manifestation of the masculine experience and its varieties, there has often been an emphasis placed on aggressiveness. This trait or its reflection via the media is admired on the playing field, the arena, the schoolyard, and in the boardroom. Whether it surfaces as belligerence or competitiveness, it is a seminal and significant consideration of what many expect of a man. To a large extent, not only is aggressiveness and aggression expected to be a significant part of a man's makeup, but also it is increasingly viewed as normal.[31]

The above concern is the subject of William Pollack's book, *Real Boys' Voices*. Pollack interviews young boys in a variety of settings and one of the clearest ideas to emerge from the book is that boys are troubled by the fact that they are often conditioned not to show pain and in order to deal with problems, they have to act out, most often by fighting. Boys can't cry, can't show emotion, can't display feelings, and can rarely even talk about what is troubling them. Even the ability to confide and to simply discuss issues becomes suspect:

> I have discovered a glaring truth: America's boys are absolutely desperate to talk about their lives. They long to talk about things that are hurting them — their harassment from other boys, their troubled relationships with their fathers, their embarrassment around girls and confusion about sex, their disconnection from parents, the violence that

haunts them at school and on the street and their constant fear that they might not be as masculine as other boys.[32]

At the heart of this barrier is what Pollack deems "the mask of masculinity," which he defines as a "stance of male bravado and stoicism that many boys develop to cover their inner feelings of sadness, loneliness, and vulnerability." Solutions to this "crisis" included the creation of avenues to comfortably allow boys, and men, to talk, and importantly, a rejuvenation of comfort zones.[33]

What Pollack highlights has been an issue that has been part of the masculine code or makeup since the classical Greek period. In an article on the origins of this stoic masculine mask, Hans Van Wees suggests that this has been in place—and has ebbed and flowed—since Homer. Yes, Van Wees argues, in the first versions of the *Iliad* and the *Odyssey* to be written down, there was a fair amount of crying by the dominant characters, Agamemnon, Achilles, and Ulysses. Van Wees writes, "There is, however, no getting away from the fact that all Homer's heroes display sadness and despair far more extrovertly and frequently than classical and modern audiences have regarded as normal and appropriate for men." As time marched forward, newer versions of the poems were presented without the crying and wailing by men, which had been excised from the text. Crying became increasingly associated with women. Van Wees feels that it was Plato who suggested that it was improper for men to cry, especially heroic men. It was Plato, in the *Republic*, according to Van Wees, who takes out the episodes of weeping and tearing by men and who puts forth a standard of masculine emotional control that has come to be seen as definitive.[34]

A strain within Men's Studies suggests that the authoritative masculine traits have been around for a long time and have not varied much in centuries. There is the penultimate trait: to be masculine or not to be deemed effeminate—synonymous with Connell's hegemonic masculinity—and this is followed by the competition ethic, then the coolness factor, which means being extremely detached, and lastly, there is a daring ethos which suggests that a man must be willing to get involved and take risks.[35] These four groupings or rules are constantly featured in the mass media and remain staples of masculine imagery and barometers to be measured against. Rightly or wrongly, positively or negatively, they are very much in play but without the ironclad expectations that used to be inherent within them.

The era that defined masculine media behavior in modern terms has to be the 1950s.[36] This period was enormously influential in defining and surveying the poles to play and the models to imitate. It was the decade that still carried the influence of the war, but that also gave birth to a myriad of masculine manifestation. In the United States, Eisenhower was in the White House but Kennedy was just around the corner. It was the period of Cold War conformity and stoicism, the invisible enemy as well as the rise of suburbia and shopping malls. It was the era of change as well as consolidation. The 1950s gave birth to the Beats and to jazz, to television and juvenile delinquency, to Hugh Hefner's *Playboy* and to rebellion. Some of these movements and cultural variations did not mature until the 1960s or even the 1970s, but their influence was pronounced. The period also saw the publication of Ian Fleming's James Bond series of novels, Mickey Spillane's Mike Hammer, *The Catcher in the Rye*, and the rise of stars such as James Dean and Elvis.[37]

Historian Lynn Luciano feels that after World War II, things began to change in unique and specific ways as far as men were concerned. Prior to that time, what a man did, his activities in all their manifestations, defined his masculinity. Throughout the 1950s, this was still a significant feature of American masculine interpretation. The focus was often outward with a slight seasoning of inner approaches. Any male who showed too much interest in his personal appearance was suspect. Luciano makes the point that as men competed for economic accessibility in the workplace with women, and as social mores evolved in the later part of the decade and early part of the 1960s, men had to do something more to compete, to stay employed, and to get noticed. With no guarantees in the workforce and with a factor of competition unheard of in previous decades, something had to be done. "To maintain an edge," writes Luciano, "it became important not just to be qualified for a job but to look as if one were; and that mean looking dynamic, successful, and above all, young."[38] The focus on youth and youthful appearance begins at this point in time to take on an enormous array of consequences and ramifications. It begins to permeate mass culture through the media and inevitably suffuses society, politics, and culture.

Whereas the immediate post–World War II period may be characterized by an attempt to reassert the values of traditional American society, the Great Depression and the war were so significant as forces of change that the reserved nature of the early post-war period could not be continued. As people became more enamored with leisure and consumer culture and as society saw that there were counterpoints to the nuclear family model, there was an unleashing of possibilities. The emphasis on youth was one, but this was often combined with a new series of masculine templates.[39]

A significant impetus in this orientation comes with the constantly photographed JFK. While he was a senator and after he became president, he was deemed a "golden boy," a handsome example of robust masculinity. Unlike Teddy Roosevelt, another example of an adventurous masculine character, Kennedy actually looked great—fit and tanned, handsome, and in his writing and broadcasts, articulate. His appearances were as close to star worship as a politician had then come. He was the embodiment of healthy vigor (although the truth said otherwise), and exuded a natural masculinity complete with hearty fitness. His trim figure, aided by chemicals, custom-fit suits, and exercise, was there for everyone to see.[40]

The move toward the embracement of consumer and lifestyle preoccupations during the 1960s was intensely hedonistic. It manifested itself in the Beach Boys and rockers as much as the bachelor culture of the time. Pleasure, indulgence, and a turn inward, toward the self—all, often through consumption—were significant hallmarks.[41] It would take another thirty years for this to fully bloom into metrosexuality, which, despite the emphasis at times on the traditional expressions of activities and products oriented around masculine culture, owes its birth to the consumption and youth-obsessed marketing foundations of the 1960s.

In his amusing collection of essays, *The Reluctant Metrosexual*, Peter Hyman writes that it is an explosion of "male vanity" that is behind the massive array of products and services which had hitherto been the preserve of women or gay men. "Men," he writes, "apparently care more today about the way they look than ever before."[42] Key here is the issue that it is now possible to indulge in what was once the arena of gay manhood and that is no longer a suspect preoccupation. As Hyman relates,

> Metrosexuality, in its highest form, is supposed to represent the freedom for the straight male to tap his creative and sensitive well springs, without fear of reprisal. As the rigidly constructed roles regarding masculinity are loosened, these gray-area "feminine" behaviors become more acceptable . . . [43]

This is one of the varieties of masculine experience as defined and suggested by the media. It is at the far end of the spectrum and is balanced by the resurgence of what has been defined as typical male fare, in the form of events and offerings that appeal to the middle of the road set, or the four barometers of masculinity mentioned previously. It is part of a larger trend which allows for men to indulge in plastic surgery and get Botox injections. These men, according to one plastic surgeon, are very much pressured to care about how they look and how attractive they are.[44]

Since its acceptance into contemporary parlance, the idea and the definition of metrosexuality has evolved. One of the essential concepts is no longer the association with pure male vanity; the narcissism so inherent in the original appellation has progressed to the point that it has taken on other virtues. As the writers of a study on the "future of men" postulate in this context, metrosexuality is about adapting to the "modern world." They write: "Rather than adhere to the strictures of their fathers' generation, they are willing to move beyond rigid gender roles and pursue their interests and fancies regardless of societal pressures against them."[45] What the authors suggest is that metrosexual propensities are no longer confined to shopping and fashion. They have expanded the repertoire to define it as a much more holistic idea that includes emphasis on feeling and emotion, commitment and comfort.

Despite attempts to recalibrate the terminology, some of the antecedents till linger. In a series of advertisements that ran throughout 2007 and 2008, Canadian Club whiskey made a statement that their ideal customers were traditional men who did not indulge in the effete and goofy endeavors of the metrosexual. "Your Dad Was Not A Metrosexual" went the title of one ad, with a large picture of a 1960s or 1970s brush-cut he-man. "He didn't do pilates, moisturize, or drink pink cocktails. Your dad drank whiskey cocktails . . . damn right your dad drank it."[46] The brush-back approach has its fans.

It is important to concede that the metrosexual category has antecedents that predate marketing categories. The two intertwined ancestors of the metrosexual are the dandy and the *flaneur*. The *flaneur* is the quintessential man about town; the individual who walks the city streets at a leisurely pace; he is usually well dressed, well accessorized, confident, curious, and thoughtful. The *flaneur* takes his time; he examines and stops, wanders and ponders. He is often a student or a scholar, a passionate collector, and most probably a connoisseur. Historically, Baudelaire and Benjamin were both the templates and journalists of the *flaneur*. The *flaneur* was and "urban voyeur, an individual who lived life on, and inspired by, the streets."[47] The dandy is extremely concerned with his appearance, perhaps too much so. The defining feature of the dandy is both the clothes worn and the theatricality of his appearance.[48]

The progenitor dandy was George Beau Brummell, who lived from 1778 until 1840. His humble origins were rendered inconsequential by his choice of clothes and the way he looked. As Rhonda K. Garelick writes, "Brummell was known for his impeccable grooming, his exquisitely simple and elegant clothes, and his androgynous appeal."[49] He was entertaining and his circle of admirers never knew what he would wear. Yet, there was something refined in his ritualistic attachment to clothes and to all the trappings of his person. Men would gather in his dressing room to watch him attire, to listen, and to look. On their way to another event, they would stop by his bachelor house and pick up pointers.[50] The point with Brummell was the clothes—not the overblown peacock garments, but the sophisticated and tasteful choices. This attention to detail and care in choosing what he wore and how he appeared allowed Brummell to move into the upper echelons of society in late-eighteenth-century England. His focus was on the attire, the clothing, and the overall "look."

Brummell is a key link between clothes and the body and especially between masculine appearance and metrosexual assurance.[51] Brummell has been described as possessing a "fine figure" in the age in which he lived, which was one the witnessed the rise in appreciation for the male body. Physical culture had begun, by the end of the eighteenth century, to take on a more prominent role. This in turn serves as a key marker for masculine experience. As Ian Kelly observes,

> Brummell's early celebrity rested on the role he assumed as poster-boy for a new version of metropolitan masculinity: restrained, muscular, unfoppish, anything but the "dandy" of folklore. His rapidly established status as a leader of fashion, quite separate from his reputation as a wit, was built on a "look" that perfectly mirrored the age.[52]

While the dandy and its variations exemplified a specific masculine type, there were the complete antitheses that came to the fore in the late nineteenth century and early twentieth century. Unlike Brummell, who was more concerned with clothes and material finery, later nineteenth century men began to adopt more emphasis on body improvement. Men like Eugene Sandow and Bernard Mcfadden illustrated a perfection of the physical body, later to be taken up by Charles Atlas and the Weider brothers. The apotheosis of this was the mainstreaming of bodybuilding culture. In essence it was no longer what a man wore to conceal and display, but the inverse, the physical body itself.

The alpha male posturing, so familiar to young men out in public space, has been a staple of masculine behavior for decades. Although touched on in the films and culture of the 1940s, where a rougher template was featured, it did not mature until the next decade with a more polished series of variants. Given its first taste of visual glamour by the films of the 1950s, this preening and posturing has evolved into a dominant male archetype. Its most extreme manifestation is the oversized, exaggerated, muscle-laden man. The popularity of Arnold Schwarzenegger s *Pumping Iron* and the rapid acceptance of the sport of bodybuilding have made this individual the unequivocal recipient of the hyper-masculine male. Sam Fussell, Oxford graduate, son of Paul Fussell, the distinguished professor, embarked on an intense bodybuilding program after graduating. He chronicled his rise—perhaps his obsession—in a memoir, aptly titled *Muscle: Confessions of an Unlikely Bodybuilder.* The opening paragraph of the book zeroes in on this unique subculture:

> You spot them on the streets of the city and, increasingly, in the malls and parks of the suburbs. Sometimes they band together. Mostly, they walk alone. Bodybuilders. You know the kind. They strut like no others, hold their elbows wider than their shoulders, legs far apart. I know, I was one of them.[53]

Fussell's depiction of large men and their subculture set the tone for a variety of recalibrated celebrations of the male body. The hyper-masculine male form could be compact and tight just as often as huge and strapping. In the early 1990s, the singer and model Marky Mark was displayed as a veritable poster boy for the extreme depiction of the *über-*masculine male. Posing for Calvin Klein ads and seeming to appear virtually naked in almost every photograph, Mark Wahlberg was seen and depicted as having the ultimate male physique. Commentators suggest that this can backfire in the sense that instead of relieving anxiety about manliness and body image this form of hyper-masculinity brings it to the surface. His body now becomes his main attribute.[54] For Wahlberg, acting in a variety of serious movies over the next decade, producing and in general reducing his cut body image from the public, allowed for a recompensatory quality to emerge.

This obsession has also given rise to what the authors of one book call "The Adonis Complex." No amount of convincing men—who are actually in very good shape and are extremely defined—can get them to understand this disorder. There is the association that being preoccupied with one's body is deemed effeminate or gay, yet there is the equally problematic dissatisfaction with how one looks. [55]

The male body appeared in a variety of versions from the 1980s onward. From posters and pinups to advertisements and commercials, near-naked men seemed to rival women in the number of images. On the screen there was the hyper-masculine, muscled version as well as the slim-downed, toned, and chiseled variation. There was a transition period where a variety of body types could compete for popularity.[56] What is interesting is the fact that in contrast to women, these images seemed devoid of sexual appeal. A calculated intention is present here. With regard to film, Philippa Gates offers the following commentary:

> The exposure of the bodies of action stars like Schwarzenegger, Stallone, Gibson, and Willis offers a multiplicity of pleasures to different members of the audience—an appeal that can be an erotic one to desire or an ideal to imitate. These images of "muscularity" are geared toward action cinema's dominant heterosexual male audience not necessarily for the purpose of sexual titillation of the ego ideal. The display of the male body can be consciously offered by mainstream cinema to attract a male heterosexual spectator but can also offer that spectator pleasure in looking without eroticism necessarily being the primary effect.[57]

Gates suggests two reasons for this focus. The emphasis on the body as a form of display is designed to compensate and perhaps address anxieties over both "masculinity and nationalism" while another focus, which is related, centers on the fact that muscularity, in any guise, is a defined biological advantage for men over women. It is the tangible evidence of male domination.[58] By the 1990s the more boyish version of cinematic muscularity had come into being. As Gates argues, by the end of the decade, a variety of different and extreme versions of masculinity were being presented.

The premium in most cultures placed on hugeness and large size, has in turn, reinforced the attraction to these hyper-masculine males. Defined and pumped, the bodybuilder is but one manifestation of this exaggeration. In basketball, Shaquille O'Neal raised the bar as far as hugeness. Zdeno Charra, now of the Boston Bruins is recognized not so much for his skill but for the fact that he is 6'9". Linemen in the NFL routinely tip the scales at over 300 pounds, while not too long ago the 300-pound player was an anomaly. According to NFL statistics cited by Michael Oriard, "in 1988 there were 17 300-pounders in the league; by 2002 there would be 331; in 2005, over 500."[59]

The return of brawn and girth, mass and largesse to the spectrum of society is reflected in so many aspects of contemporary masculine culture. This manifests itself in the cars and SUVs that are being purchased in significant numbers—despite the rising cost of gas and the impact on the environment—as well as in more mundane ways. The large-headed driver, first designed by Callaway, has become a staple on the golf course. Each year, larger and larger drivers are produced; the Nike Sumo is the latest example. All of these are enormous in comparison to what was used and available twenty years ago. In fact, some are so grand that even a miss-hit can propel the ball two hundred yards. The significance and symbolism of this giant is quite obvious and goes much farther than the ability of the average duffer to hit longer on a more consistent basis.

At the same time as this emphasis on hugeness and largeness exists, so too does a streamlined version, a tight and compact robustness. This sleekness is embodied in the small-scale electronic components, miniature phones, and nearly microscopic gadgets that permeate the world today and which go by names such as micro and nano. It is also part of a new health and body regime; the toning and tightness of the physique that contrasts with the exaggerations stated above. The ideal body can take a number of forms and be appealing to many people. Men can be coiled and taut, not just large and hyper-muscled.

Marketers are often the first to spot the new variants of masculinity and to name them with clever monikers. The director of strategic content for JWT Worldwide, Marian Salzman, whose book *The Future of Men* profiles this mixture of the metrosexual with the exaggerated masculine model, terms this strain the ubersexual. The ubersexual differs from the metrosexual in that he is less concerned or obsessed with grooming and fashion, is more cultivated and highly principled, and most significantly, is intellectually focused. In a piece profiling Salzman's book, Jon Stewart, Pierce Brosnan, Barack Obama, George Clooney, and Bill Clinton are typified ubersexuals.[60]

The media provides an enormous outlet for showcasing such diversity and this can occur in a variety of formats that are online, on-screen, and in person. Although sporting events, gun shows, car shows, and monster truck rallies have been around for decades, a noteworthy new trend that captures the new male ethos has been the creation of events that merge all of the above offerings into one grand event. For three days recently in Toronto, the *UGS*, or *Ultimate Guy's Show*, was designed to appeal to a wide variety of men or "guys" in the same way that craft shows and antique gatherings appeal to women. The organizers of the show appeal to men in the same manner that the new men's magazines attract interest. Everything from golf to boating to home theater is available to be seen and touched. And of course, there are cars and trucks, beer and women.[61] Events such as these mark both a return to the trappings and hobbies of men and at the same time, they jump-start and awaken men to worlds that haven't been seen in a while or that haven't been seen at all. All of this serves to reaffirm certain masculine ideals and restructure masculine behavior.

A significant measure of how things have evolved, yet again, is the fact that language that ten years ago would not have been tolerated, is allowed once again to surface. What was thought banished from the linguistic terrain of the late 1980s and early 1990s has been allowed to reappear. As Walter Newell has observed:

> Suddenly you can use the forbidden words again, the everyday casual talk by which men and women relate to each other, often in the guise of jokes, as they search for a common ground for understanding one another's differences. Guys and chicks. Guy talk. Chick flick. Be a man. Be a guy . . . [62]

Like much of what has been deemed taboo by mainstream culture, the acceptable boundaries of being a man have expanded. No longer is it inappropriate to eat steak, drink hard spirits, or go away on a golf weekend. Swaggering masculinity, infantile masculinity, and preening masculinity are all possible to exist and can all be combined at the same time.

Since September 11, 2001, it has been suggested that "manhood" is once again being held in "high esteem."[63] With the return of the traditional male heroes—firemen, policemen, soldiers—a renewed emphasis on "going back" has been in vogue. The return of the honest hero as a character and type resonates throughout culture and media. The appeal of the policeman may be that with notable exceptions, it is a working-class heroic archetype that can mirror the purity of customary masculinity. The policeman and the fireman seem anachronistic as templates, because of the fact that they hearken back to a simpler time, when masculine brawn and toughness were stand-alone characteristics, unaffected by the influences of feminism.[64] This has been celebrated by some and criticized by others.[65] This is also why there is less of a willingness to mature and grow up. Young men are quite happy prolonging the aspects of youth culture and avoiding the complexities and inroads that mature masculinity dictates. This "guyland" way-station allows for no commitments and as much fun as possible.[66]

Some suggest that perhaps this return to the staples of being a man has a lot to do with the insecurities that men feel and experience in the world of work and the pressures of being an emotionally "in touch" spouse and a father who is engaged in every aspect of his children's life. To debate whether there is another crisis is perhaps to miss the point. A robust and diverse array of examples exists in the media.

NOTES

1. Kenneth Mackinnon, *Representing Men: Maleness and Masculinity in the Media* (London: Arnold, 2003), p. 11, and Chris Blazina, *The Cultural Myth of Masculinity* (Westport, CT: Praeger, 2003), pp. xi–xiii.

2. Brenton J. Malin, *American Masculinity under Clinton: Popular Media and the Nineties "Crisis of Masculinity"* (New York: Peter Lang, 2005), p. 2.

3. Chris Blazina, *The Cultural Myth of Masculinity*, pp. xi–xiii.

4. The general starting point for this discussion begins with Robert Connell. See his summary article "Studying Men and Masculinity," *Resources for Feminist Research*, Fall/Winter 2001, pp. 43–47. Also see his *Masculinities*, 2nd ed. (Berkeley: University of California Press, 2005).

5. Andrea Cornwall and Nancy Lindisfarane, eds., *Dislocating Masculinity: Comparative Ethnographies* (London: Routledge, 1994), cited in Robert Connell, "Studying Men and Masculinity," p. 46.

6. Robert Connell, "Studying Men and Masculinity," p. 46.

7. Robert Connell, "Studying Men and Masculinity," p. 47.

8. See S. Craig, *Men, Masculinity, and the Media* (London: Sage, 1992), p. xii.

9. James Gilbert, *Men in the Middle: Searching for Masculinity in the 1950s* (Chicago: University of Chicago Press, 2005), p. 16.

10. Kath Woodward, *Boxing, Masculinity, and Identity* (New York: Routledge, 2007), pp. 1, 2.

11. Francis Spufford, *The Child That Books Built: A Life in Reading* (New York: Metropolitan/Henry Holt, 2002), p. 160.

12. Harrison G. Pope Jr., Katharine A. Phillips, and Roberto Olivardia, *The Adonis Complex: The Secret Crisis of Male Body Obsession* (New York: Free Press, 2000), p. xv: "This problem, we believe, is created by biological and psychological forces that combine with modern society's and the media's powerful and unrealistic messages emphasizing an ever-more muscular, ever-more-fit, and often-unattainable male body ideal."

13. See George L. Mosse, *The Image of Man: The Creation of Modern Masculinity* (New York: Oxford University Press, 1996), p. 184.

14. Mark Gallagher, *Action Figures: Men, Action Films, and Contemporary Adventure Narratives* (London/New York: Palgrave Macmillan, 2006), p. 3.

15. Michael Kimmel, *Guyland: The Perilous World Where Boys Become Men* (New York: HarperCollins, 2008), p. 42.

16. Greg Lindsay, "Man vs. Man," *Advertising Age* 76, no. 24 (June 13, 2005), pp. 1–2.

17. Franco La Cecia, "Rough Manners: How Men Are Made," in *Material Man: Masculinity, Sexuality, Style*, ed. Giannino Malossi (New York: Abrams, 2000), p. 39.

18. Michael Kimmel, *Guyland*, p. 4.

19. Abigail Solomon-Godeau, "Male Trouble," in *Constructing Masculinity*, ed. Maurice Berger, Brian Wallis, and Simon Watson (London: Routledge, 1995), p. 73, cited in Patricia Vettel-Becker, *Shooting from the Hip: Photography, Masculinity, and Postwar America* (Minneapolis: University of Minnesota Press, 2005), pp. xi, xii.

20. Patricia Vettel-Becker, *Shooting from the Hip*, p. xii.

21. Chris Blazina, *The Cultural Myth of Masculinity*, pp. xiv, xv.

22. Douglas B. Holt and Craig J. Thompson, "Man-of-Action Heroes: The Pursuit of Heroic Masculinity in Everyday Consumption," *Journal of Consumer Research* 31 (September 2004), p. 425.

23. Douglas B. Holt and Craig J. Thompson, "Man-of-Action Heroes," p. 425. Also see Marian Salzman, Ira Matathia, and Ann O'Reilly, *The Future of Men* (New York: Palgrave MacMillan, 2006), pp. 53–55, and Frank Mort, "Boy's Own? Masculinity, Style, and Popular Culture," in *Male Order: Unwrapping Masculinity*, ed. R. Chapman and J. Rutherford (London: Lawrence and Wishart, 1988), p. 202. In his fascinating examination of men's spaces, James Twitchell consistently utilizes both individual advertisements and marketing campaigns to bolster his central focus that men need to go to certain realms in order to indulge their masculine tendencies. James B. Twitchell, *Where Men Hide* (New York: Columbia University Press, 2006).

24. Douglas B. Holt, "Jack Daniel's America," *Journal of Consumer Culture* 6, no. 2 (2006), p. 360.

25. Michael Kimmel, *The History of Men: Essays on the History of American and British Masculinities* (Albany: SUNY Press, 2005), pp. 22, 23.

26. Brenton J. Malin, *American Masculinity under Clinton*, pp. 7, 8.

27. Cited in Sharon Ghamari-Tabrizi, *The Worlds of Herman Kahn* (Cambridge, MA: Harvard University Press, 2005), p. 28.

28. Kevin Alexander Boon, "Men and Nostalgia for Violence: Culture and Culpability in Chuck Palahniuk's *Fight Club*," *Journal of Men's Studies* 11, no. 3 (Spring 2003), pp. 267, 268.

29. Susan Bordo, *The Male Body: A New Look at Men in Public and Private* (New York: Farrar, Straus & Giroux, 1999), p. 242.

30. Bordo is referencing Joyce Carol Oates' ideas. Susan Bordo, *The Male Body*, pp. 242, 243. Tyson announced his retirement with the coda that he did not have the killer instinct within him anymore. David Remnick, "D.C. Postcard: Tyson's Corner," *New Yorker*, June 27, 2005, p. 35. Also see the 2008 film by James Tobak, *Tyson*.

31. Kenneth Mackinnon, *Representing Men*, p. 11. Mackinnon suggests that to counter-balance the fear of homoeroticism so prevalent in Hollywood action movies, fighting, torture, and graphic violence are employed to cover up any focus on the male body being too appealing to the heterosexual audience (p. 12).

32. William S. Pollack, with Todd Shuster, *Real Boys' Voices* (New York: Random House, 2000), p. xix.

33. William S. Pollack, with Todd Shuster, *Real Boys' Voices*, p. xxv.

34. Hans Van Wees, "A Brief History of Tears: Gender Differentiation in Archaic Greece," in *When Men Were Men: Masculinity, Power, and Identity in Classical Antiquity*, ed. Lin Foxhall and John Salmon (London: Routledge, 1998), pp. 10–18.

35. Elisabeth Badinter, *XY: On Masculine Identity* (New York: Columbia University Press, 1995), p. 130.

36. See K. A. Cuordileone, *Manhood and American Political Culture in the Cold War* (London: Routledge, 2005); James Gilbert, *Men in the Middle*; and Bill Osgerby, *Playboys in Paradise: Masculinity, Youth and Leisure-Style in Modern America* (Oxford, UK: Berg, 2001).

37. See David Halberstam, *The Fifties* (New York: Villard Books, 1993) and Fred Kaplan, *1959: The Year Everything Changed* (Hoboken, NJ: Wiley, 2009).

38. Lynne Luciano, *Looking Good: Male Body Image in Modern America* (New York: Hill & Wang, 2001), pp. 4–6.

39. Bill Osgerby, *Playboys in Paradise*, p. 3.

40. David M. Lubin, *Shooting Kennedy: JFK and the Culture of Images* (Berkeley: University of California Press, 2003), p. 130.

41. Bill Osgerby, *Playboys in Paradise*, p. 3.

42. Peter Hyman, *The Reluctant Metrosexual: Dispatches from an Almost Hip Life* (New York: Villard, 2004), p. 36. The first use of the term "metrosexual" dates from 1994 and Mark Simpson's "Here Come the Mirror Men" article in *Independent*, November 15, 1994.

43. Peter Hyman, *The Reluctant Metrosexual*, p. 37.

44. Cited in Susan Palmquist, "Handsome Ambitions," *Psychology Today* 37, no. 4 (July–August 2004), p. 33.

45. Mariam Salzman, Ira Matathia, and Ann O'Reilly, *The Future of Men*, p. 56.

46. See *Sports Illustrated* 107, no. 21 (November 26, 2007).

47. Alice Cicolini, *The New English Dandy* (New York: Assouline, 2005), p. 66.

48. See Susan Fillin-Yeh, "Introduction: New Strategies for a Theory of Dandies," in *Dandies: Fashion and Finesse in Art and Culture*, ed. Susan Fillin-Yeh (New York: New York University Press, 2001), pp. 1–3.

49. Rhonda K. Garelick, "The Layered Look," in *Dandies: Fashion and Finesse in Art and Culture*, ed. Susan Fillin-Yeh (New York: New York University Press, 2001), p. 36.

50. Ian Kelly, *Beau Brummell: The Ultimate Dandy* (London: Hodder & Stoughton, 2005), pp. 157–162.

51. Ian Kelly, *Beau Brummell*, p. 94.

52. Ian Kelly, *Beau Brummell*, p. 169.

53. Samuel Wilson Fussell, *Muscle: Confessions of an Unlikely Bodybuilder* (New York: Poseidon Press, 1991), p. 15.

54. Murray Healey, "The Mark of a Man: Masculine Identities and the Art of Macho Drag," *Critical Quarterly* 36, no. 1, p. 88, cited in Kenneth Mackinnon, *Representing Men*, pp. 5, 6.

55. Harrison G. Pope Jr., Katharine A. Phillips, and Roberto Olivardia, *The Adonis Complex*, pp. xiv–xv.

56. See Susan Jeffords, *Hard Bodies: Hollywood Masculinity in the Reagan Era* (New Brunswick, NJ: Rutgers University Press, 1993) and Latham Hunter, "The Celluloid Cubicle: Regressive Constructions of Masculinity in 1990s Office Movies," *Journal of American Culture* 26, no. 1 (March 2003).

57. Philippa Gates, *Detecting Men: Masculinity and the Hollywood Detective Film* (Albany: SUNY Press, 2006), p. 40.

58. Philippa Gates, *Detecting Men*, pp. 40, 41. Gates adds a codicil to this. She suggests that during the 1990s, women increasingly appeared as muscled and physically buff, which further eliminated or eroded the biological difference. Linda Hamilton as Sarah Connor in *Terminator 2* is one example. Another variation occurs with the young, slim "boy" taking on a role that replaces the hulking versions of masculinity (p. 41). In *The Adonis Complex*, the authors confirm Gates's assertion. They suggest that a "threatened masculinity" derived from the fact that women can now do anything that men can do, leads to only one arena where men can exert their "superiority" or difference: that is in muscle size and complexity. As they write, " . . . muscles are one of the few areas in which men can still clearly distinguish themselves from women or feel more powerful than other men. But muscles are a tenuous foundation on which to base all of one's masculinity and self-esteem." Harrison G. Pope Jr., Katharine A. Phillips, and Roberto Olivardia, *The Adonis Complex*, pp. 23, 24.

59. Michael Oriard, *Brand NFL: Making and Selling America's Favorite Sport* (Chapel Hill: University of North Carolina Press, 2007), p. 122.

60. Becky Ebenkamp, "The Uber-Measure of Man," "Out of the Box," *Brandweek* 46, no. 38 (October 24, 2005), p. 16.

61. Samantha Grice, "Boys Will Be Boys," *National Post*, April 10, 2004, p. 7.

62. Walter R. Newell, *The Code of Man* (New York: HarperCollins, 2003), p. 234.

63. Jamie Glazov, "Men on Men: Intellectual Locker Room Talk," *American Enterprise* 14, no. 6 (September 2003), p. 24.

64. Philippa Gates, *Detecting Men*, pp. 135, 136.

65. Richard Goldstein, "Neo-Macho Man: Pop Culture and Post-9/11 Politics," *The Nation* 276, no. 11 (March 24, 2003), pp. 16–19.

66. See Michael Kimmel, *Guyland*, p. 4, and Kay S. Hymowitz, "Child-Man in the Promised Land," *City Journal*, Winter 2008.

TWO

The Media and Men

More so than interacting with other men, images from the media provide examples and models for men to follow. Whether it is in films, on television, or from magazines, the media provide surrogate examples of the many variations of masculine experiences through templates that straddle numerous tropes. To underestimate the power and pervasiveness of the many media offerings is to ignore the single most authoritative forces in conveying opinion.

There are a plethora of magazines devoted to selected activities that cross this spectrum. There are traditional guns-and-ammo-type products and subtle offering such as in house magazines and Websites. There are the mainstays such as *GQ* and *Esquire,* and then there are the newer hybrids such as *Maxim* and *Stuff.* The explosion of British-based magazines for men signaled something new and dynamic. A group of these magazines came out in the mid-1990s and attempted to reach a younger, more energetic audience. There was an extremely wide array of offerings—*FHM, Arena, Loaded*—but what they all had in common was a cutting-edge hipness that spoke to a young urban market. These magazines were grittier than the more established ones; more versatile, responsive, and definitively appealing in ways that *GQ* and other were not. They were also created with a marketing sophistication that was so well calibrated that even their publishers were shocked by the circulation numbers.[1]

What occurred was that the market was opened up to a variety of new offerings that were not thought about previously. These magazines were specifically tailored to young men and the contents honed in on their tastes and disposable income as well as their obsession with things and style.

In keeping with the diversity of masculine archetypes and male models available, print media responded to the selection of types. *MH-18* was a teen magazine that specifically targeted young men and was image focused. It contained an abundance of articles and advertisements that fixated on grooming and fashion. *Men's Journal* focuses on a robust, outdoor type and its pages have a propensity of advertisements and articles focusing on active adventures, thrilling escapes, and comparisons of different kinds of outdoor equipment ranging from hiking boots to GPS devices. One of the most remarkable of the men's magazines, at least as far as popularity, is *Men's Health*. This is noteworthy not just because of the supposed concern with wellness, but rather, because of the enormous focus on fitness and looking good. *Men's Health* went from a small but popular magazine selling 250,000 copies per month in the early 1990s, to a circulation of 1.5 million near the end of the decade.[2]

The rise of *Playboy*'s progeny, at least as far as men's magazines are concerned, received a boost in the early 1990s with the rise of a variety of heavy-handed publications which were designed to challenge the market that *Esquire* and *GQ* controlled. There was also an attempt to move the men's magazine market a couple of notches forward as far as celebrating the life of the male. To some extent, this capitalized on the men's movements of the 1980s but it also focused on both the unabashed celebration of men's consumption habits and the awkward but pronounced return to chauvinistic male culture. This was led in Britain by the "Lad's" movement and its glossy result was *Loaded*, which one journalist called an "irreverent publication [that] was billed as an antidote to the snooty fashion magazines of the time," such as *GQ* and *Esquire*.[3]

Esquire became a leader in the men's magazine industry during the 1930s because it performed a key function for men. It offered them a place to go, on a monthly basis, where they could find out how to dress and what was in "good taste." This was supplemented with lavish illustrations as well as accents to clothing such as quality writing, advice on where to travel and what foods to eat. In one monthly package a man could learn and could be informed on an extensive assortment of issues.[4] *Playboy* further refined this formula, expanded on it, and certainly accented the flavor with pictures of naked women in the 1950s. The magazines of today, with their hyper-visual style, still deal with the same kind of offerings and have outpaced the more genteel *GQ* and *Esquire*.

The launch of *Vogue-Man* in 2006 was designed to answer the often-thought but unasked question, "Why don't men have a magazine like this?"—meaning *Vogue*. While European editions of *Vogue* for men have existed for years, their focus was purely on fashion. The fact that *Vogue-Man* folded in print as of 2009 speaks to economic conditions more than content ones. In the 2006 inaugural issue, George Clooney was on the cover. The choice of Clooney was appropriate because he was, and still is, the embodiment of perfect masculinity. Handsome, funny, masculine, and intelligent, he holds appeal to both men and women. Other than the fictional James Bond, no other star has his appeal. He is a guy's guy and is known to hang out with his buddies, yet he is always impeccably dressed. His recent choice of films suggests an intelligence that is above average and the fact that he resides in Como, Italy, reinforces his good taste. For many, he has credibility in the way that David Beckham lacks, and he comports himself like a modern-day Cary Grant. His deep voice, heavy beard, and expressive eyes make him highly attractive in a supremely masculine way.

The media, in conjunction with marketing, offer a barometer of what is going on—in fact, it is the media that often define the varieties of masculine experience. There has been an explosion in the diversity of offerings, almost a renaissance in presenting different cultural forms that range from the high brow to the mid-range to the low. The latter is often quirky and weird but either way there is a robustness of masculine styles and manly icons.

The media of television, film, and magazines may be said to follow trends in advertising and marketing that seek to define and capture certain assemblages of people. Advertising agencies and marketing research firms employ a host of sophisticated tools to project and delineate different categories of people—in this case, men—who may be targeted to purchase specific products and services. This is a far more complex approach than was historically utilized.

During the late-Victorian and Edwardian period, advertisers and media outlets sought to move consumption from its association with women and to place it in a more masculine mindset. Advertising copy was tight and terse, attempting to create and convey "an attractive image of manly vigor and productivity."[5] Drawings of forceful, manly males were employed to give visual evidence of the ability to shop and still be masculine. Importantly, definitive icons of the potency of the masculine archetype were employed to buttress these ideas. Sportsmen and soldiers were utilized to give added weight. Advertisers, according to Brent Shannon,

> strove to masculinize goods and to make the consumption of those goods appear safe and attractive by directly associating them with strong, robust male figures whose masculinity was seemingly self-evident.[6]

The sophistication with which men have been segmented and targeted has grown in detail and accuracy. Beginning in the 1950s with Ernest Dichter, polished and refined in the 1970s with the Values and Lifestyles Programs, and reaching a high point of verity with demographic segmenting today, research into male categories can be extremely nuanced. A recent study by eMap, owned by *American Demographics*, divided men into two main categories, "inner-directed" and "outer-directed" and further, into five key categories: Traditionalists, Searchers, Achievers, Fast-

Trackers, and Young Urban Techies. What these men want and how they think of themselves are key in allowing companies, from magazine and publishing corporations to the advertisers who support most of these journals, to have a clearer idea of whom to pitch. [7]

What is learned in advertising and marketing is applied to cultural products and cultural marketing. Beyond products and magazines, certain books, movies, television shows, and other creative endeavors pick up on trends and seek to give them life in a more polished and sustained conception.

Numerous films that have been released by Hollywood can be said to have influenced a number of definitive masculine models. A cluster of films from the 1950s, starring Marlon Brando, James Dean, and Montgomery Cliff all had enormous influence on the style and look of masculinity. In the 1960s, films that featured Paul Newman, Clint Eastwood, and Steve McQueen took this influence in other directions. By the 1970s, a veritable cornucopia of templates were available. There are the action adventure staples, which promote a certain kind of masculine toughness; these can range from the silent taciturn hero to the explosive, borderline psychotic guy who is troubled to the point of cracking up. One of the trends over the past few years has been the evolution of the "action hero." In the 1960s there were the vestiges of the old John Wayne type, giving way to Steve McQueen, and finally in the 1970s and 1980s, the full-blown hyper-masculine stare embodied by Sylvester Stallone and Arnold Schwarzenegger.

It was during the late-1960s and into the 1970s and 1980s, that masculinity was worked once again on the screen. This was especially the case with regard to American masculinity and its association, or lack there-of, with the war in South-east Asia. As James William Gibson details, "The bitter controversies surrounding the Vietnam War have discredited the old American ideal of the masculine warrior for much of the public." [8] Gibson suggests that both Clint Eastwood as Harry Callahan and later Charles Bronson in *Death Wish* take a "new" war to the streets. It is not until Stallone's Rambo films and their clones that a full-fledged attempt to reposition filmic masculinity is undertaken. Gibson makes the point that while critics panned these gung-ho, glorious war epics, for many people they were not dismissed but actually meant something important. For men watching these films, the content and the hero's actions were vital in recapturing something essential. As he writes,

> behind the Indian bandana, necklace, and bulging muscles, a new culture hero affirmed such traditional American values as self-reliance, honesty, courage and concern for fellow citizens. [9]

The heroes and the content of the film spoke deeply to many people and provided a focus for masculinity's place in society. Many felt that the qualities exhibited on the screen were missing in society and had to become a part of the ingredients of masculinity. No matter what lengths society goes to make the archetypical template of the warrior hero less threatening, it still resonates with many men, especially in North America.

Variations of the above have included the less-buff Bruce Willis and Kevin Costner. Russell Crowe stands in as the heir apparent of the embodiment of all things male—but there are many interesting variations. Perhaps the most unique is the choice of Tobey Maguire as *Spiderman*. As trend spotters Marian Salzman, Ira Matathia, and Ann O'Reilly observe, "As Peter Parker in *Spider-Man 2*, Tobey Maguire not only looks like a schoolboy, he positively oozes sweetness, good manners, and the ability to save old ladies from certain death."[10]

Similar to the likes of Vin Diesel and The Rock is this slight but very emotional super/action hero. According to journalist Sharon Waxman, "Some say the evolving style of the Hollywood leading man may reflect a more feminized American society, the rise of the metrosexual male and the absence, until recently, of war and true hardship in the last two decades of American life."[11] This last point is particularly important and very relevant to this work. As in the period before World War I, when there are vacuums in traditional ways to define and illustrate masculinity, suitable alternatives have to be found, as do interesting variations.

As detailed earlier, the unequivocal poster boy for the hyper-masculine star is currently George Clooney. Clooney has been voted the "world's sexiest man" by *People* magazine and his appeal transcends gender—men are equally attracted to him. He is sophisticated and cool, athletic and pretty, but is often deemed a "man's man." He is not overblown or super-muscular, yet still exudes a total masculine package. This has been evident since his time on *ER* but came to the fore in two of his early movies—*One Fine Day* and *The Peacemaker*. In both of these films, Clooney exhibits a controlled and exacting sense of masculinity. It was to peak in *Ocean's Eleven*. Clooney is often juxtaposed with Brad Pitt, but despite Pitt's popularity he is not in the same masculine league as Clooney. He is too artistic, too weird, and too pretty. Clooney most resembles Cary Grant. In Grant's Hitchcock films and elsewhere, he pulled off an enormous role reversal. Grant moved from very simple and even low culture origins to an artistic high point in masculine style. Like Clooney, he was as appealing to men as to women and he always stood out. He was visible because of his classic good looks, his distinctive voice, his sense of humor, and his exceptional wardrobe choices.

Following Clooney there is soccer phenom and metrosexual supreme, David Beckham. What makes Beckham such a fascinating case study is that he is one of the best athletes playing soccer today. Yet he is equally well known for his wife and specifically, the attention he plays to his appearance. His hairstyle changes every few months and when it does, photographs quickly appear and often there is a magazine cover illustrating his new look. His clothes and his overall sense of style are commented on more than his scoring prowess. According to marketing gurus, Irving Reign, Phillip Kotler, and Ben Shields, his attention to personal appearance is key in making him more than an athlete. In fact, he is now a brand. Beckham is watched to see what he will wear or do, stylistically, next. Whether sporting a mohawk, ponytail, or cornrows, everyone takes note. When he wore a sarong, people discussed it for days. The attention to his personal appearance is enthralling to many and what he does can effect changes in fashion and appearance, almost over-night. [12]

There is a supreme anomaly in the characterization of masculine imagery through the media. This anomaly has to do with the fact that no matter what Clooney or Beckham do for masculinity they still have to compete with a series of fictional characters and the actors who play those characters. Sometimes this throws the various visual equations out of whack.

Tony Soprano has become one of the most unlikely masculine role models. He is heavy, bald, and loudly dressed. As played by James Gandolfini, he exudes both raw power and sensitivity. *The Sopranos* in general opened up a window on vulnerable masculinity and the troubles that men experienced. [13] Yet Tony Soprano kills with impunity and is a profligate womanizer. Soprano straddles the old-world creation of mafia loyalty with the new-world pressures to conform and remake oneself. [14] He is distressed and burdened by the pressures of what he does and seeks help in getting over the mental and physical afflictions. This desire to seek help, to open up, to talk to a psychiatrist, adds to the complexity of his appeal. [15] As well, Tony Soprano, while being a big man, is not fit and is not glamorous in any traditional way. His image is a far cry from standard masculine templates.

The pre-1914 period and the interwar years resulted in a number of mutations in body presentation but it is the post–World War II period that is especially unique. One manifestation of this is male body image. To look at Steve Reeves, Charles Atlas, John Derrick, and other body beautiful males is to see a defined and compact physical masculinity. By the 1970s, to see Arnold Schwarzenegger and Lou Ferrigno, not to mention the men on the cover of bodybuilding magazines, is to see something grossly aided and abetted by biotechnology. The hefty weightlifters from the Soviet Union were more like Tony Soprano in their raw and sloppy masculinity. The bodybuilders of the 1970s and onward seemed to parody the cars that Detroit was producing: while impressive for a while, they simply could not retain their appeal, let alone stay at the top of their game. In a very compressed period of time, these goliaths seemed too awkward and too cumbersome. Like their rust belt counterparts, they appeared both wasteful and inefficient. When looked at today, the images of these hulks take on the appearance of nineteenth-century factories.

The sleek, almost "trim" body favored by today's role model has its counterpoints in the form of World Wrestling Federation hulks and UFC goons in the heavier classes, but by and large, the understated fitness of many male actors and performers seems to dominate. One can also see a parallel of the overmuscled monster in the plastic action figures that are specifically designed for boys. Those produced forty years ago were slim and compact, whereas the versions produced in the last ten years are hypertrophied—muscles upon muscles. If the recent GI Joe Extreme was life size, he would have thirty-two inch biceps as compared to the original, whose life-size equivalent would display only twelve-inch biceps. [16]

The two "bookends," cinematically speaking, that have been used as examples of masculine extremes, as least in the last ten years, have been *Fight Club* and *Gladiator*. References, parodies, and touchstones from these two films have literally saturated both society in general and mass media in particular. The cultural capital and authority in influencing interpretations of masculinity through the media are enormous. According to one interpretation, *Fight Club* gives us a duality that is very defined. In terms of the supremely masculine or macho, if a man is not a fighter, he is a "wimp." There is no middle ground; the violent and sexual male reigns supreme.

In *Gladiator*, Russell Crowe's character, Maximus, is stoic and secure and seemingly above it all. Not only is he the ultimate leader of men, but he is also lethal as a fighting man. Not a bully, mind you, but a skilled general and commander who excels in individual combat. He is also devoted to his family and to The Emperor, and importantly, is "dignified" in his sneering deportment. These characteristics are virtually the same as Gibson listed in discussing the post-Vietnam era. According to one authority, Maximus is the missing link in the recipe of manliness and a key and influential model of late. [17]

Chuck Palahniuk's 1996 novel was the basis for the movie *Fight Club* starring Edward Norton and Brad Pitt. In the book there was a conscious attempt to move away from the softness of contemporary masculine culture embodied in the metrosexual's awareness of home furnishings and fashion and to strip away this material cloak. [18] As well, Palahniuk references the fact that men were and are being raised by women and are thus supple—even feminized. [19] To counterbalance this and to rescue masculinity, one must return to the most primal male instincts; not only must one be able to fight but one also has to be able to take a punch, to literally get beaten up!

Critic Nick Rombes feels that the book and the film are nostalgic. They are so in the sense that they hearken back to a time when men were essential to society and were key participants and actors in seminal events. These include the wars and the economic upheavals of the past century. The anti-history feature of both the book and the film casts men adrift and leaves them aimless in their goals and objectives. That is why rules and organization are so vital to both.[20] That is also why *Gladiator* resonated so strongly. It answered *Fight Club's* key questions.

Gladiator resuscitates a supremely defined male protagonist; a ripe Hollywood heroic figure that is admirable and dependable. Maximus is the congealed essence of perfection in the cinematic hero. He is everything the stereotypical male hero is supposed to be. He is unwavering, loyal, committed, and above all, conforms to ideals and morals thought to be lost in contemporary society. This is why he was so appealing and popular as a character and one of the reasons why the movie resounded so positively with audiences and critics.

Gladiator, besides resuscitating so many key male archetypical qualities, simplifies masculinity. By simplification, complexities and problematic definitions are made accessible; it does not trivialize the essence of masculine behavior, but rather, glamorizes and glorifies it in ways that contemporary men can understand. Maximus does not have the hang-ups of Jack or the mania of Tyler Durden in *Fight Club*. He is secure in a man's world. Maximus is the consummate hyper-masculine creation.

Although Crowe is Australian and the movie is set in ancient Rome and directed by an Englishman, *Gladiator* speaks to the quintessence of a certain form of masculinity that is highly touted in the United States. As Mark Allister has noted, "American masculinity is notable for its emphasis on a certain conservative outward demeanor, on physical prowess, personal restraint, doing rather than thinking."[21] Allister suggests that this typology of masculinity can be traced back to America's frontier focus in taming the land and in conquering nature.[22] The attraction for Canadians is virtually the same and one could argue that the dominance of American popular culture has disseminated this idea so widely that it is nearly universal in its appeal. The archetypes of this multifaceted idea of masculinity are at one and the same time, historical and contemporary. Although they originated with the pioneer, the hunter, and the cowboy, these models resonate today in their historical associations and within contemporary versions of those spirits.

The attempt to recapture the essence of traditional maleness, those signature qualities that are universal among men and their admirer has become an industry in itself. Whether it is the BowFlex commercials, featuring sinewy brawn and the ultimate in high technology casting or the next generation of power tools, both efficient and beautiful in design, versions of traditional maleness are back. One observer has suggested that when we think of masculinity we think of the "outside," we think of the appearance and of actions, not of the mind. To some extent the return to select versions of traditional masculine portrayals has a great deal to do with the trappings of outward appearance and outside accomplishment. Accordingly, Mark Allister remarks,

When we generalize, in our culture, about "man," we usually attribute to masculinity characteristics such as reason or intellect, elevating the mind over the body. I would argue, that when we are asked to name particular American men we associate with the term "masculinity," we don't usually name men who use their minds, but men who exhibit prowess in "nature," outdoors, in sports arenas, or "through" nature, by being rugged and handsome.[23]

The utilization of the outdoors and of nature as a template and demonstration vehicle for masculine action provides a foundation for mediated varieties of exploration into other realms. Although a substantial amount of what is on television can appeal to a gender-specific audience, men have lacked a full-fledged guys television station. *Spike TV* came on the air in August of 2003. Its mix of reality programs, sports, and bizarre comedy all appeal to a wide cross-section of male viewers. As well as more serious fare, a plethora of fighting shows, James Bond movies, and wrestling all seem to dominate the network's offerings. Perennially popular movies in the action adventure genre are also featured with a grand emphasis on motor sports. Reruns of proven male-oriented shows such as *CSI*, *MacGyver* and *Star Trek*—as well as *The Three Stooges* occupy a substantial amount of program time, or at least did, during the network's early years.[24] But *Spike TV* was not all-encompassing and other networks picked up the slack, offering niche programs and strategically placed shows that appealed to men in various demographics and to couples who could watch together. Important shows for men specifically began to appear on other networks. Thanks to the proliferation of channels, strong market segmentation occurred, allowing the Discovery Channel to air *Monster Garage* and *American Chopper*. These shows on mainstream networks allowed men to delve into "a nostalgic desire for traditional masculine identities."[25]

One authentication of modern culture has been the bifurcation of the western world into public and private spheres. Males, as this division goes, were supposed to be outside, working, and the home was where women ruled. As far as cooking, unless one was a French chef or a short-order cook, the kitchen was generally perceived to be off limits. As the idea of the suburban home, complete with backyard, possibly a deck, and maybe even a pool, came into being, men ventured first to the backyard barbeque and could indulge in cooking in a manner that was acceptable to other men.[26] Flipping burgers and grilling steaks quickly became the preserve of the man of the house and was the only way that males could cook without arousing the suspicion of their insecure and possibly homophobic pals. Barbequing as a male endeavor has now become a major industry. There are dozens of shows on various networks, accessories galore and of course, billions of dollars in equipment for sale.

The move to make the barbeque a male-oriented application came complete with cookbooks, recipes, uniforms, and tools that were designed specifically for the man. In essence, barbequing in its modern manifestation was specific and defined in its appeal to men. Meat was at the center of this focus, in particular steaks and ribs, but also chicken and chops. Advertisements and recipes dating from the 1950s strongly suggested that cooking over an outdoor charcoal grill was a man's job. The funny aprons, comical hats, and the rest of the accoutrements that have become staples of the man's barbeque also came into being during the 1950s. What is most interesting is the range of tools and cooking implements that were created solely for the man. Outdoor cooking required large, heavy implements, tongs, and forks that were geared toward men.[27]

During the post–World War II building boom, the creation of the suburban mentality came into being within the confines of North America. It took a further thirty years to permeate Western Europe. Men were not supposed to be too occupied with domestic chores, especially anything that was traditionally the preserve of a woman. A combination of factors led to the refocusing of the male into the role of the domestic cook. One such idea stemmed from the fact that throughout history, men had been chefs, and in a more recent format, the army had virtually all male cooks. The rise in the image of the male as a barbeque master built upon this but was also intertwined with the marketing of outdoor grill products, the creation of the domestic barbeque industry, and the reorientation of a man's obligation toward domestic life.[28]

Cooking outside, even if adjacent to the house, on an open grill, under the sky, had some resemblance to the rough-and-tumble atmosphere of a campfire. Hunting and camping, fishing and hiking, came with a certain series of codes. The attempt to harness this and to retool it as a supremely masculine activity led to the full-scale creation of the backyard barbeque. Allowing men to construct their own pits, to handle their own forged utensils, to sample sauces and to marinate and spice meat, created a subculture that was quite unique. Steaks, chops, burgers, and the like took on a masculine linguistic force that merged with the increasingly heavy use of adjectives to describe all aspects of barbeque culture.[29]

Inside the house, and in particular, within the kitchen, an array of gadgets and tools were marketed to men, as if to assuage their reservations about being in the kitchen. From juicers to coffee grinders to carving knives, both electrical and manual, men were enticed to play in the kitchen. Sets of high-quality steel were especially appealing as far as knives were concerned and with the influx of electric knives, the same do-it-yourself ideas that were applied to power tools now extended to men in the kitchen. Ellen Lupton has remarked that the

> electric carving knife is a rare instance of domestic appliance addressed to male users. A transitional object that mediates between the interior, service space of the kitchen and the public, ceremonial space of the

dining room, the electric knife belongs to a population of machines that play an ancillary role in the larger architecture of the domestic environment, mechanizing the labors of modern life.[30]

The success of the knife with men quickly led to a host of other consumer items that were produced or remarketed with men in mind—especially those that stayed home and were increasingly comfortable in the kitchen. By the mid-1960s, electric shavers and electric or mechanical fire starters as well as electric knives were being marketed to men.[31] Lupton cites Margaret Visser on the importance of the ceremony of cutting meat. In *The Rituals of Dinner*, Visser, according to Lupton, suggests that meat, because of its "perishable nature" and the arduousness of obtaining it, takes on a seminal role and one that is almost religious in its implications. The "hunt" was a male endeavor and the danger associated with killing the animal could be replicated by cutting it up in a public fashion.[32] This ceremonial aspect of dining and consuming became a part of every mediated holiday ritual, from Thanksgiving to Christmas. It was a staple of television shows, a core part of many films, and a constant feature in magazines.

In the 1970s, Chef Graham Kerr paraded onto TV as a chef in a manner that was novel, even outrageous, and significant. He concocted dishes with flair and élan, and always, at the end of the show, allowed someone from the audience to sit down and join him. Since the advent of cable and then satellite, the demand for programming content has increased to satisfy the rise of 24/7 viewings.[33] There are now numerous shows that feature a male chef and networks such as the Food Network have made these a staple of their schedule. For those who have come of age in the last generation, this is a far cry from Julia Child, Graham Kerr, and the numerous local variations that often featured some eccentric culinary amateur. Now, there are dozens of superstar chefs, famous for their restaurants, who can be found all over the screen.

There is Emeril with his aggressive, street edge, the polished Bobby Flay with his urban, cool sophistication. Explosive and belligerent Gordon Ramsay is a prime-time media darling who brings in enormous ratings. Jamie Oliver is a near boy-man whose carefree enthusiasm and passion for food crosses boundaries and borders. Oliver is very appealing to both men and women. In essence, most of the popular TV chefs are guys. To the TV kitchen, they bring an accessible level of polish and erudition in their cooking, which is a far cry from the way it used to be. According to journalist Anne Kingston, "no longer does guy food mean going out to kill something, marinating it in a garbage bag for a week, then throwing it on a to a fire pit."[34] There are shows that feature strictly drive-in style, and others that travel the country for the best of a certain type of food that in general will appeal to men. Three buff guys comfortably dish out food in *Man-Made Food*.

The success of Bill Buford's *Heat* has captured the evolution of cook-ing, making connoisseurship with regard to olive oil and basting sauces as important as knowing about socket sizes. According to a review by Craig Macinnis,

> Men are all about the gustatory excellence lately, have you noticed? I have male friends—urban-dwelling, well-paid, middle-aged guys; def-initely not gay—who would just as soon talk about their experiences making "black cod with miso" or pronounce on the intricacies of flash-grilling a piece of marinated flank steak, as yak about the Jay's chances in the AL East.[35]

What Macinnis is alluding to is that through two processes, once can utilize cooking as a masculine endeavor. The first is the encyclopedic knowledge and insight that crosses all lines from the intricate to the macro. As with their perceptiveness toward different fishing lures or stereo components, the levels of awareness and the systems are very important. This means that in order for one to be considered a proper male/guy chef, you have to know the temperatures, viscosity levels, and importantly, you must possess the right tools for cooking properly. The other result is the sense of bravado that comes from creating the best, doing it well, and ensuring that everything is in its proper place. Cooking for men has much in common with the various sports that they watch and follow, as well be being seen within hobby culture.

If one has been watching movies, TV shows, or perusing men's maga-zines, it has become a significant component through these media, that defining and strutting one's masculinity has a firm tie to cooking. Being a man today, according to many media, means knowing your way around a kitchen and knowing how to cook well. As if an inversion from the domesticity of the 1950s, it is essential know as part of one's masculine repertoire, to understand the process of food preparation. In many cul-tures, this is important and even on the fringes it is a requisite. T. C. Boyle's novel, *Talk, Talk*, has the main character, a fraud artist, with a black belt in karate, engaged in cooking and obsessed with the right ingredients, the proper knives, and the best stoves and ranges. Boyle describes his preparation of a meal,

> For dinner, he was going to make sea scallops braised with scallions and garlic, with a sauce he'd learned years ago while fooling around at the restaurant (a white wine reduction flavored with shallots and a splash of sherry, dollop of butter, fold in the cream at a galloping boil and reduce the whole thing again till it was a fifth of what you started with). He was thinking of rice with it, flavored with bouillon, sherry and sesame oil, and maybe a salad and some sautéed broccolini on the side.[36]

The main character steals other people's identities. He has a family but it is a lonely life. If he bumps into someone who knows him by another name and profession, there is a problem. He thus must act alone and often; eat alone or with his family. Unlike the group of guys that Craig Macinnis describes, the guy is a solitary creature. There is no social or communal element to his meals, just strict preparation. In essence, he has no friends, no buddies. But, eating and drinking should be done with others.[37]

According to popular culture and the media if a man is not a pure lone wolf then he must be a social creature. For the purposes of story telling, men are often more entertaining in the company of other men. A significant aspect of contemporary popular culture is the concept of the "buddy film." To some extent this came out of Women's Liberation and the Civil Rights movements of the 1960s, when the bonds of masculine culture were loosened. Through this vehicle, men could talk to each other and have "relationships," joke, and open up in ways that were not often featured in films prior to the late 1980s. The "buddy" films of that period and into the 1990s, such as the Lethal Weapon series were especially relevant in that the conventions of male bonding could often be stretched through violence.[38] Cynthia J. Fuchs suggests that throughout the 1980s the Reagan administration's legacy resulted in more extreme versions. "Significantly," she writes, "the transition from Reagan to Bush has yielded ever more formulaic buddy films, featuring higher body counts, larger numbers of interracial and cross-class buddy teams, and increasingly homophobic comedy."[39]

The safety and security found in the homo-social grouping, whether sports teams, work colleagues, or in a fictional portrayal, is a key marker in contemporary culture and masculine imagery. It is found in a variety of formats and media and transcends different cultures. What is significant about this is both its popularity as a safe zone as well as its problematic implications. The unleashing of in-your-face immature masculinity came in increments but permeated all media. From *Maxim* to the content of certain video games to a series of films running from *American Pie* to *The 40-Year-Old-Virgin*, there seems to be a pattern surrounding the making and the popularity of all these throwback offerings. This is a form of male backlash and insecurity at defining and being a man. Unlike the relative sophistication and tameness of *Playboy*, this is quite different.[40] Radio provides an interesting illustration.

Radio shows offer traditional male fare such as shock jocks elaborating on women, deep-voiced or manic sports DJs commentating on all variety of sports, and authoritative-sounding classic rock know-it-alls. Beginning about ten years ago, there seemed to be a marked return to formats and content that had been pushed aside as being politically correct and Neanderthal-like. It did not take long for these kinds of shows to spread from radio to television. Like the changes wrought by *Playboy* and other new trends in the 1950s, this version unleashed a significant amount of pent-up frustration.

One interpretation of this trend is that what had been put on the back burner a while ago—a form of suppressed chauvinism—began "making a comeback." For a while, TV's *The Man Show* set the standard for this type of formula. David Brooks wrote that this show, which ushered in a new variety of dated masculine preoccupations, allowed men to gape at "women in teddies jumping on trampolines" and had "men getting spanked by bikini-clad 'juggies'—the shows term for its female cast members." Brooks felt that this was simply one indicator that the restraints of "polite opinion" have been cast off and there was a full-fledged return to "piggery." Accordingly, he wrote, "It is as if millions of American men—many of them well educated—took a look at the lifestyle prescribed by modern feminism and decided, no thanks, we'd rather be pigs." [41]

Howard Stern's popularity seems to waver every year. Now confined to Sirius Satellite radio rather than the mainstream bandwidth, he still retains a core audience of admirers and devotees who will do anything to ingratiate themselves with their idol. Stern spews out a steady invective of inappropriateness, all the while commanding strong demographic numbers in spite of his run-ins with the FCC. He remains the epitome of the "pig," a holdover to sexist, almost racist, buffoonery as embodied by a cross between Richard Pryor and Archie Bunker. His popularity, which waxes and wanes, has influenced a generation of boys and men, further perpetuating a specific masculine stereotype.

Stern, like other mainstream radio personalities, has a significant audience that is overwhelmingly male. He indulges his fans with throwback, sexist, and patriarchal references and jokes and is almost an anachronistic figure with his antics. Yet his popularity speaks to a sizeable population. To some extent, and before he went to satellite, his program reinvigorated radio, much as talk radio has. Both his shock jock and talk radio in general feature dominant males who perpetuate stereotypes and pander to their predominantly male audience. The rise of sports talk shows on radio has been especially pronounced as a surrogate male space.

With changes in leisure habits, deregulation, and the fragmenting of the market, sports talk radio channels have blossomed over the dials of North America. Virtually every market has a series of local and national offerings that mix opinion and fact on practically every facet of sport. This has become a safe haven for males, allowing them to glean information, to laugh, and to discuss what is perhaps the last area of male sanctity. Often dismissed as trivial and irrelevant, talking about sports and listening to talk about sports is an important mental and social outlet for men. As Don Sabo and S. C. Jansen write,

> Sports talk, which today usually means talk about mediated sports, is one of the only remaining discursive spaces where men of all social

classes and ethnic groups directly discuss such values as discipline, skill, courage, competition, loyalty, fairness, teamwork, hierarchy, and achievement. Sports and sports fandom are also sites of male bonding.[42]

The rise of sports talk radio stations is another attempt by men to either reclaim or recapture some form of homosocial preserve in a world that is increasingly ambivalent about male-only pursuits. According to a dissertation on the subject, sports talk radio contains elements of traditional male bonding culture mixed with "frat boy" elements to create a forum for male sports addicts.[43] There is also aggressiveness to the tone of the commentary; a tough and taunting element in much of sports talk radio that moves from bombast to macho posturing.[44]

This demeanor and its flavor also comes out in a number of ways in other media. One manifestation is in the rise of situation comedies and other television fare that feature a "good ole boy" as the main character. This is not the redneck typically defined in these realms, but a guy who is apolitical and simply likes his beer and his sports. James Belushi plays such a character in *According to Jim* as does Charlie in *Two and a Half Men*. This is completely in the opposite direction of *Will and Grace* and other more progressive shows, and is also a touch more sophisticated from Norm on *Cheers*, but all involve a goofy guy who indulges in his own tastes. In commercials, there is Bud Lite and a host of scenarios where there is an average guy, a pal, who plays a specific role. These guys are paired up with someone else and they often become a surrogate for the average viewer. He may wish to be like the cooler guy, but the reality is that he is a sidekick. This works to great impact in sports play-by-play. According to Ava Rose and James Friedman, the commentator bridges a gap and ingratiates with the viewer as "one of the guys." This in turn, "establishes a collective male identity through television sports." "This is achieved," write Rose and Friedman,

> through the form as well as the content of the commentator's discourse. In providing knowledge, gossip, and narrative information, the commentators give the viewer the tools he needs to perform a dominant reading of the sports text. These tools enable the sports fan to engage in a range of discourses and practices that connote "maleness" in our culture.[45]

A variation on the above is the ubiquitous Three Stooges, which seems to be the definitive thing that women hate and men love. The staying power of this trio and their bizarre appeal to so many men creates a cleavage that is very hard to explain. The slapstick physicality of their humor seems to be the main reason why so many women find the ménage grotesque. It may also help explain the appeal of violent highlight footage. Using the Stooges as a point of reference coupled with the foolish buddy, it is not a large leap to portray the prototypical male—the dad—as buffoon.

The work of Paul Nathanson and Katherine K. Young take this buffoonery to another level, an academic one. In the first volume of a proposed trilogy, *Spreading Misandry*, the scholars dissect the consistent and often accepted portrayal of men in popular culture as idiots and incompetents. Their study suggests that this "teaching of contempt for men" ranges broadly across all facets of the mass culture universe. It is found in Hallmark greeting cards, situation comedies, and feature films. Their argument is that not only is it pervasive, it is accepted in a way that a similar portrayal of women or any ethnic group, would not be tolerated.[46] Situation comedies in particular, they observe, "have probably done more than any other genre to turn men into objects of derision."[47] The stupidity of men is especially pronounced in such 1990s offerings as *Men Behaving Badly*, *The Simpsons*, and in particular, *Home Improvement*.[48]

The popularity of *Home Improvement* was astounding—both during its run on television and in its current life as a rerun. The show was based on Tim Allen's comedy routines, which focused on the traditional association of men as "pigs." Loud and obnoxious, obsessed with their needs, and always trying to deceive, Tim did not exactly exemplify the high points of male behavior, but the show consistently landed in the top five in the ratings. By utilizing especially artless stamps of male behavior, Allen somehow reached a huge male audience who could not get enough of his antics and fixation with power tools, cars, boats, and banality.[49]

Popular culture, from television situation comedy to Hollywood film, to Hallmark cards to commercials of all sorts have singled out the father as a figure to be poked fun of. Father's Day cards alone can be singled out. "The dominant view," according to one authority, "is of fathers as lazy shirkers, whose interests revolve primarily around watching television, golfing, and fix-it projects."[50] Not a very esteemed portrait, but one that is eminently familiar to most people. Whether it is Peter Griffin from *Family Guy* or Al Bundy from *Married with Children*, there is a remarkable degree of consistency in their constructed juvenile antics and their emotional retardation. Other males on TV from *The King of Queens* to *Everybody Loves Raymond* to characters on dramas also exhibited arrested development.

Often they lack a certain physical presence in comparison with the many iconic heroes of the TV universe. The man, who is not physically fit, or even slim, is often the subject of abuse. Most of the "comic" personas on television and within popular culture have a tendency to be less attractive than the men who embody stereotypical features of heroic masculinity. They are not as slim and they can be bald or balding and are less likely to be taken seriously than the fit and nonbalding man. Being short as well as overweight is also significant, as embodied by the character of George from *Seinfeld*.

To some extent, men are culpable in this construction. A variant on this theme has been detected in the content of a series of beer and alcohol advertisements that ran a number of years ago. The authors of the study found that the primary "construct" in their analysis is that of a "white male 'loser.'" The political and social ramifications are detailed in the following passage:

> He hangs out with his male buddies, is self-mocking and ironic about his loser status, and is always at the ready to engage in voyeurism with sexy fantasy women but holds committed relationships and emotional honesty with real women in disdain. To the extent that these themes find resonance with young men of today, it is likely because they speak to basic insecurities that are grounded in a combination of historic shifts . . . [51]

Some of these "shifts" include the decline in the importance of heavy industry, the suspect role of the male breadwinner, deindustrialization, and the challenges to hegemonic masculinity brought on by feminism and identity politics.[52] Watching numerous television commercials and reruns of old shows generally confirms this picture. To some extent the danger of these portrayals is that they set up not just a very unattractive picture, but for young men, they don't exactly provide the most stimulating role models.

During the late 1980s and into the 1990s a plethora of television shows attempted to recalibrate masculinity by imposing a form of masculinity that was influenced by both feminism and the rise of "touchy feely" men's movements. This resonates today with contemporary teen dramas and vampire shows that all feature an enormously in-touch, emotionally vulnerable series of males. The emotionally sensitive man and the caring boy who always does the right thing—and who are capable of "talking"—were noticed as characters and popular, especially with female viewers. On *Party of Five*, the main male character Charlie, who becomes the head of the household after his parents died a tragic death, exuded an emotional level of sensitivity that was off the charts comparatively to anything ever seen. Even Dylan and Brandon on the original *Beverly Hills 90210* were obsessed with sharing their emotions and making nice. To some extent, this drove Dylan crazy, which in turn, brings up a further complication: many of the main male characters from these shows were completely dysfunctional. In essence, trying to be a 'new man' had dire consequences. One panacea to it all may have been the attempt to imprint purely masculine role modes that had staying power.

The conception of heroic role models and reconception of them highlights both their connectivity and their durability. When danger is real and evident, societies grasp onto heroic figures. Heroes and role models are needed in times of crisis. A crisis can be public and global but it can also occupy a smaller space. Another explanation for the durability of the hero in times of crises has to do with the defined and specific set of characteristics associated with being heroic. The ideal and revered individual who is classified as a hero defines traditional forms of masculine character and these in turn serve to counterbalance the inroads and variations that have impacted established male norms.[53]

It is important to distinguish between the hero and the role model or celebrity. The hero embodies the essence of a glorious past and contains within him or is invested with all the makings of a near mythological god. He straddles the mortal world, resting at the upper echelons. The role model or the celebrity is someone to whom we can much more easily relate. Heroes seem to stand high above celebrities and are less likely to be toppled by the capriciousness of fame. Role models also have a built in whimsical nature and can rise and fall as scandals become public and past misdeeds are revealed. From Mark McGuire to Tiger Woods, indiscretions can have an enormous impact, especially given the access of technology to reproduce or spread rumor almost instantaneously. The idea of role models is quite problematic today. Overpaid athletes who make multi-million dollar paychecks are not the stellar emblems that most wish to emulate. This is especially problematic when scandals such as banned substance use or substance abuse in general reaches the tabloids. Manufactured media darlings such as those who pop up during reality TV shows are not long lasting and the shows that bring them to prominence are themselves quick to fade away.

Kevin Alexander Boon remarks that the hero can revitalize and rally a culture, but at the same time can have a series of negative effects on individual masculine identity. The bar is simply too high for the mere mortal to reach: the average male cannot possess the definitive supremely heroic characteristics. Importantly, it serves as something to which one should aspire but can't reach.[54]

During the 1950s, the polarities of stoic, reticent John Wayne were played off the emotional and sexual Elvis Presley.[55] John Wayne personified a peculiar kind of masculinity that did not lend itself to displays of emotion. Presley let it all hang out. John Wayne walked a very defined line, never letting it out and always reigning in his feelings. He did not care about his hair or his appearance for that matter. His persona defined to many young men, a very specific male type. Presley went in a completely opposite direction that was at once liberating but at the same time terrifying to many. Wayne did not speak that much in his films, and this "nonverbal" trait was hugely influential. It went with the idea that the true male was silent, stoic, and one who would not get gregarious or open his mouth at the wrong time. This was indicative of the control that men were supposed to exhibit in life and on the battlefield—or its screen surrogate. Like the ubiquitous Marlboro Man, John Wayne posed in a knowing fashion, rather than moved. Elvis literally gyrated and jiggled, twisted and turned, unleashing something sexual, yet still masculine. The two went their separate trajectories—Wayne influencing Eastwood and McQueen, Stallone, and Seagal, while Presley opened up a wriggling can of worms that was not seen until decades later. Emotions were something that could finally be revealed, and longing and desire, thanks to Presley, could now be exhibited. The model was broken after Presley took vulnerability and detachment to new, dangerous places.[56]

With the publication of Alfred Kinsey's studies on male and female sexuality in 1949 and 1953, there was a shocking candor that was finally allowed to come to the fore regarding sexual matters. For the first time, sexual activity reached a mass audience that made the books best sellers. No doubt, Kinsey's research had much to suggest to young people and would pave the way for frankness in these matters, never seen.[57] They were controversial when they came out, as shocking as anything that had been published. As much as they attempted to liberate sexuality, the two volumes caused enormous controversy. For some, the publications were synonymous with the end of civilization and the breakdown of traditional morality. To a large extent, this was not a far off conclusion. As K. A. Cuordileone has written, "The Kinsey reports were perhaps the most important catalysts in the rising perception of a breakdown in sexual order in American life." The suggestion that homosexual behavior was more common than assumed and the revelations that adultery and pre-marital sex was much more common came as quite a stunning series of revelations to some.[58]

It has been suggested that once upon a time, men who showed too much interest in fashion and design were either dandies or men who lacked traditional male interests. Fashion was a realm that homosexual men were thought to inhabit. But today, men seem to want to look good, to wear the latest fashions, to participate in spheres that were once barred to them. Shows like *Queer Eye for the Straight Guy* attempted to redress the wrongs in heterosexual fashion, style, and grooming sense and hearken back to the days when it was acceptable, even normal, for the average heterosexual male to be a complete dolt when it came to fashion and grooming.[59] Today one would be hard-pressed to see a man in or on virtually any media who does not look well-groomed.

Traditional building shows and outdoor life broadcasts such as fishing programs buttress the established and "nostalgic" sense of masculinity but can alienate female viewers. Home design and décor shows bring both males and females together. But thanks to the multiplicity of channels, the Internet, and numerous magazines, there is an enormous array of choices for men and increasingly a sense of polish and style on most men's shows. Even on the chopper and home reno shows, guys are impeccable in their jeans and their grooming.

One of the reasons why "looking good" and being fit has grown beyond the confines of weightlifting culture and health fanatics has to be the outing of homosexual culture. The muscular homosexual came out of the closet and onto the streets in the 1970s. It traversed a range of male archetypes yet had at its core a tough-looking exterior. This was accentuated with specific clothes and tattoos, a number of defined hair styles, and a visual look that moved beyond the gay fringe to many places in society.[60] This in turn paved the way for the appropriation of a number of styles into mainstream culture that had originated from gay male communities in New York and San Francisco.

Heterosexual male culture owes a surprising amount—stylistically and culturally—to homosexual influences in dress and design. This "mainstreaming of gay culture" implies that heterosexual males can pick and choose from the diversity of gay fashion and style culture.[61] From the models embodied by the Village People to cross-gender dressing as defined by numerous pop stars, significant elements of gay "visual" culture have impacted heterosexual notions of appearance. Importantly, the stereotype of the effeminate gay male has given way to a hyper-masculine pattern that has become an important staple of straight masculine culture and appearance. Gay culture has become a dominant style influence in all its variations and consistently influences fashion and design trends. As far as the body is concerned, gay culture has also had colossal authority in defining and dictating the right physical looks. While the physical fitness boom of the 1970s surely imparted a considerable investment of inspiration, the rebirth of weightlifting and the orientation around muscularity owed much of its impact on the physicality inherent in resurgent gay culture.[62]

At the core of many of these changes and what allows for the varied nature of the mediated masculine experience is the consumption ethos. What men buy and how they learn what goods to purchase has often dictated the trends, the role models, and the images they seek to emulate. Almost any category of masculine identity or definition has a counterpart in the world of marketing. In the late Victorian period, specifically in England, there was a deliberate attempt to target male consumers by using hyper-masculine role models. During the 1950s, the pervasiveness of certain male figures was employed to harness an array of masculine archetypes. Just perusing through the pages of magazines from this period is illustrative of a wealth of images. The late 1990s had created a massive male-industrial-complex designed to offer specific products and lifestyle items which were geared to a variety of different groups within the masculine experience. If one symbolic male were to be chosen as the lightening rod for all of this, it would be the character of James Bond. The potency of this mediated creation is nothing short of a phenomenon.

First appearing in print in the 1950s and then a feature of film from the 1960s onward, James Bond has become a definitive icon of male style. Even as this book goes to print, the images of the latest incarnation, Daniel Craig in his Tom Ford suits, speak to the staying power and influence of the character. The James Bond character has become the quintessential repository of all things male and masculine. He has appeal that evolves and transcends generations, just as appealing to men in the 1950s as he is in the second decade of the twenty-first century. Put simply, he is positively cool as a masculine character and can be endlessly repackaged to reflect changes in society.

Ian Fleming wrote fourteen James Bond books.[63] There have been over two dozen movies to date, making the film series the most consistent and popular in the history of film. As well, the billions of dollars that the films have generated in box office, DVD sales, and numerous product tie-ins—the Omega watch for example, demonstrate the bottomless financial potential. The staying power of the character and the popularity of this creation—which holds many anachronistic elements, are truly amazing. What the popularity of the James Bond franchise suggests is that whether comically constructed or played tongue-in-cheek, Bond has become a definitive touchstone of masculinity. This fictional creation and the actors who portray him supercedes virtually every other archetypical creation. The character holds within it the seeds of popular masculine mythology and contains specific and consistent characteristics that men never seem to tire of. Bond has military experience, he is sophisticated with regard to dress and drink, and he is very specific and knowledge-able when it comes to possessions such as watches, cars, and guns.[64] His attitude toward women has changed, and in keeping with the times, so too has his outlook on life. Bond keeps himself fit and unlike the rest of us, never gets a paunch. He has an automatic know-how of recall so that regardless of the situation, he always knows what to do. He is also very adept at using all the latest technology and all the cutting-edge gadgets—a source of enormous appeal and marketing excitement in every film. When given a bulky manual on a product, like a true digital native, he just ignores it and plays around, mastering its purpose.[65] His charm for many is threefold: he knows who he is, gets the job done, and knows what he wants. Naturally this is highly outlandish and unrealistic. But it does not matter that it does not carry over for viewers into their real lives. What is appealing to male viewers is the consistency and calmness of the character.

Created after World War II, during the poverty-stricken gray days of the decline of the British Empire, Ian Fleming's creation held enormous appeal because of its associations with luxury and rarity. Bond got to do things that were in counterpoint to the everyday; exotic travel, exotic food, exotic wine, and exotic women were all part of the point. This held special appeal to those living in Britain and who were deprived of all of the above in the post-war depression.[66]

A significant secondary facet to the Bond appeal is the whole idea of style.[67] The character as created by Fleming, was not a member of the aristocracy, but he understood and learned what to do in all situations—physical, sexual, intellectual, and aesthetic. Beyond his ability to kill, to seduce, to make a clever comment, Bond exuded an enormous stylistic appeal that transcended class and fused together various forms of masculinity. He dressed well and owned nice things; he knew about wine and food—all the while having a robust masculine essence. He provided the perfect fusion of a stylistic trend, which was to emerge, once the excess and silliness of 1970s style had run its course. Bond was a modern, updated, and less problematic version of George Beau Brummell. The focus on his clothes alone would make the comparison apt, yet like Brummell, there is both the coolness and the completeness to his sense of overall style.

Bond's—and Fleming's—influence crops up in so many ways, in so many memoirs, and in so many childhood reminiscences that it is truly amazing to ponder his masculine cultural charm and his manly legacy. In an informal survey of men no younger then forty, the James Bond archetype resounds with approval as to the quintessence of style and the coolness factor. The trappings of what make this so special deserve further contemplation.

NOTES

1. See Ben Crewe, *Representing Men: Cultural Production and Producers in the Men's Magazine Market* (Oxford, UK: Berg, 2003).

2. Cited in Harrison G. Pope Jr., Katharine A. Phillips, and Roberto Olivardia, *The Adonis Complex: The Secret Crisis of Male Body Obsession* (New York: Free Press, 2000), p. 31.

3. Scott Deveau, "Lad Mags' Last Stand," *National Post*, February 24, 2007, p. FP5.

4. Bill Osgerby, *Playboys in Paradise: Masculinity, Youth, and Leisure-Style in Modern America* (Oxford, UK: Berg, 2001), p. 43.

5. Brent Shannon, "Refashioning Men: Fashion, Masculinity, and the Cultivation of the Male Consumer in Britain, 1860–1914," *Victorian Studies* 46, no. 4 (Summer 2004), p. 602.

6. Brent Shannon, "Refashioning Men," p. 602.

7. David Whelan, "Men, Their Motives, and Their Magazines," *American Demographics* 23, no. 10 (October 2001), p. 18.

8. James William Gibson, *Warrior Dreams: Paramilitary Culture in Post-Vietnam America* (New York: Hill & Wang, 1994), p. 5.

9. James William Gibson, *Warrior Dreams*, p. 10.

10. Marian Salzman, Ira Matathia, and Ann O'Reilly, *The Future of Men* (New York: Palgrave Macmillan, 2006), p. 32. The authors also make another important point on the connections between masculinity and the media: "In other words, the media not only reflect but also help create popular ideas about what it is to be masculine. Once upon a time, leading men in American movies came with an imposing physique and a square jaw: John Wayne, Humphrey Bogart, Robert Mitchum, Lee Marvin, and William Holden, among them. As soon as they passed their sell-by dates, they were replaced by a new batch of masculine role models, including Marlon Brando, Steve McQueen, Clint Eastwood, and Robert De Niro. The characterization of the male hero became a little murkier in the 1970s, with the birth of such Hollywood anti-heroes as Dirty Harry. How times have changed. Nowadays, for every Russell Crowe there is a baby-faced, effeminate Tobey Maguire, Orlando Bloom, Keanu Reeves, or Ben Affleck. Our role models have changed, it seems, and so has modern man" (p. 47).

11. Sharon Waxman, "The Next Action Heroes," *National Post*, July 2, 2004, p. PM4.

12. Irving Rein, Phillip Kotler, and Ben Shields, *The Elusive Fan: Reinventing Sports in a Crowded Marketplace* (New York: McGraw-Hill, 2006), p. 177.

13. Alessandra Stanley, "Men with a Message: Help Wanted," *New York Times*, January 3, 2010, p. 22.

14. See Fred L. Gardaphe, *From Wiseguys to Wise Men* (London: Routledge, 2006).

15. Alessandra Stanley, "Men with a Message," p. 22.

16. Lynne Luciano, *Looking Good: Male Body Image in Modern America* (New York: Hill & Wang, 2001), p. 175.

17. Walter R. Newell, *The Code of Man* (New York: HarperCollins, 2003), p. xxx.

18. Lynn M. Ta, "Hurt So Good: *Fight Club*, Masculine Violence, and the Crisis of Capitalism," *Journal of American Culture* 29, no. 3 (September 2006), p. 265.

19. See Michael J. Clark, "Faludi, *Fight Club*, and Phallic Masculinity: Exploring the Emasculating Economics of Patriarchy," *Journal of Men's Studies* 11, no. 1 (Fall 2002), pp. 65–76.

20. Nick Rombes, "Restoration, American Style," *C Theory* 23, no. 1 (May 31, 2000), p. 1.

21. Mark Allister, "Introduction," in *Eco-Man: New Perspectives on Masculinity and Nature*, ed. Mark Allister (Charlottesville: University of Virginia Press, 2004), pp. 1–2.

22. Mark Allister, "Introduction," p. 2.

23. Mark Allister, "Introduction," p. 1.

24. See www.spiketv.com for a listing and a brief overview.

25. Peter Tragos, "Monster Masculinity: Honey, I'll Be in the Garage Reasserting My Manhood," *Journal of Popular Culture* 42, no. 3 (2009), p. 542.

26. See Harvey Levenstein, *Paradox of Plenty: A Social History of Eating in Modern America* (New York: Oxford University Press, 1993), p. 132.

27. Jessamyn Neuhaus, *Manly Meals and Mom's Home Cooking: Cookbooks and Gender in Modern America* (Baltimore: Johns Hopkins University Press, 2003), pp. 191–195.

28. Chris Dummitt, "Finding a Place for Father: Selling the Barbecue in Post-War Canada," in *Home, Work, and Play: Situating Canadian Social History, 1840–1980*, ed. James Opp and John C. Walsh (Don Mills, ON: Oxford University Press, 2006), p. 93.

29. Chris Dummitt, "Finding a Place for Father," pp. 94–96.

30. Ellen Lupton, "The Electric Carving Knife," in *Stud: Architectures of Masculinity*, ed. Joel Sanders (New York: Princeton Architectural Press, 1996), p. 41.

31. Ellen Lupton, "The Electric Carving Knife," p. 44.

32. Ellen Lupton, "The Electric Carving Knife," p. 45.

33. Neil Postman, *The Disappearance of Childhood* (New York: Vintage Books, 1994), p. 82.

34. Anne Kingston, "Too Many Cooking Shows . . ." *National Post*, December 16, 2004, p. AL1.

35. Craig Macinnis, "Macho, Macho Chef: I Want to Be a Macho Chef," *Toronto Star*, August 20, 2006, p. A6.

36. T. C. Boyle, *Talk, Talk* (New York: Viking, 2006), p. 94.

37. See Douglas Brownlie and Paul Hewer, "Prime Beef Cuts: Culinary Images for Thinking 'Men,'" *Consumption, Markets, and Culture* 10, no. 3 (September 2007), pp. 239, 240.

38. Cynthia J. Fuchs, "The Buddy Politic," in *Screening the Male: Exploring Masculinities in Hollywood Cinema*, ed. Steven Cohan and Ina Rae Hark (London: Routledge, 1996), pp. 195–196.

39. Cynthia J. Fuchs, "The Buddy Politic," p. 196.

40. See Kay S. Hymowitz, "Child-Man in the Promised Land," *City Journal*, Winter 2008.

41. David Brooks, "The Return of the Pig," *Atlantic Monthly*, April 2003, p. 22.

42. Don Sabo and S. C. Jansen, "Prometheus Unbound: Constructions of Masculinity in the Sports Media," in *MediaSport*, ed. Lawrence W. Wenner (London: Routledge, 2000), p. 205.

43. David Keith Nylund, "Have a Take: Masculinity and Sports Talk Radio," PhD diss., University of California, Davis, 2004, pp. 12–16.

44. David Keith Nylund, "Have a Take," p. 35.

45. Ava Rose and James Friedman, "Television Sports as Mas(s)culine Cult of Distraction," in *Out of Bounds: Sports, Media, and the Politics of Identity*, ed. Aaron Baker and Todd Boyd (Bloomington: Indiana University Press, 1997), p. 6.

46. Paul Nathanson and Katherine K. Young, *Spreading Misandry: The Teaching of Contempt for Men in Popular Culture* (Montreal, QC, and Kingston, ON: McGill-Queen's University Press, 2001/2006), pp. ix–xv.

47. Paul Nathanson and Katherine K. Young, *Spreading Misandry*, p. 35.

48. Paul Nathanson and Katherine K. Young, *Spreading Misandry*, pp. 35–39.

49. Paul Nathanson and Katherine K. Young, *Spreading Misandry*, pp. 39–41.

50. Cited in Anne Marie Owens, "Dads Are Always Good for a Laugh," *National Post*, June 19, 2004, p. A1.

51. Michael A. Messner and Jeffrey Montez de Oca, "The Male Consumer as Loser: Beer and Liquor Ads in Mega Sports Media Events," *Signs* 30, no. 3 (Spring 2005), p. 1882.

52. Michael A. Messner and Jeffrey Montez de Oca, "The Male Consumer as Loser," p. 1882.

53. Kevin Alexander Boon, "Heroes, Metanarratives, and the Paradox of Masculinity in Contemporary Western Culture," *Journal of Men's Studies* 13, no. 3 (Spring 2005), pp. 301–312.

54. Kevin Alexander Boon, "Heroes, Metanarratives, and the Paradox of Masculinity in Contemporary Western Culture," p. 304.

55. See Gary Willis, *John Wayne's America: The Politics of Celebrity* (New York: Simon & Schuster, 1997). On Wayne's longevity as a popular hero, Willis writes: "He has to fill some need in his audience. He was the conduit they used to communicate with their own desired selves or their own imagined past. When he was called *the* American, it was a statement of what his fans wanted America to be. For them, Wayne always struck an elegiac note. He stood for an America people felt was disappearing or had disappeared, for a time 'when men were men'" (p. 14, italics in the original).

56. Tim Riley, *Fever: How Rock 'N' Roll Transformed Gender in America* (New York: St. Martin's Press, 2004), pp. 3–26.

57. See David Halberstam, *The Fifties* (New York: Villard Books, 1993).

58. K. A. Cuordileone, *Manhood and American Political Culture in the Cold War* (London: Routledge, 2005), p. 83.

59. Diane Barthel, "A Gentleman and a Consumer," in *Signs of Life in the USA: Readings on Popular Culture for Writers*, ed. Sonia Maasik and Jack Solomon (New York: Bedford/St. Martin's, 2003), p. 171.

60. Lynne Luciano, *Looking Good*, pp. 153–154.

61. Claire Atkinson, "He's Tough, He's Soft—He's Complex," *Advertising Age* 75, no. 19 (May 10, 2004), p. s4.

62. Garry Whannel, *Media Sports Stars: Masculinities and Moralities* (London: Routledge, 2002), p. 70.

63. Simon Winder, *The Man Who Saved Britain: A Personal Journey into the Disturbing World of James Bond* (London: Picador, 2006), p. 7.

64. See Thomas Fink, *The Man's Book* (London: Wiedenfeld & Nicolson, 2006), pp. 144–145. Anyone reading this probably can name the type of gun that Sean Connery's Bond used—and perhaps tell you the "why" behind the choice. Interesting as well is the consistent popularity of encyclopedias and books on Bond, which are always available in various formats from bookstores. Amazon.com has a virtual industry devoted to Bond culture.

65. See Tricia Jenkins, "James Bond's 'Pussy' and Anglo-American Cold War Sexuality," *Journal of Popular Culture* 28, no. 3 (September 2005), p. 315.

66. Simon Winder, *The Man Who Saved Britain*, p. 84.

67. See Mark Gallagher, *Action Figures: Men, Action Films, and Contemporary Adventure Narratives* (London/New York: Palgrave Macmillan, 2006), pp. 8–9.

THREE

Masculine Adornment

Men have always been the primary collectors of "things." Throughout most of recorded history, it was men who commissioned art and sculpture, collected and minted the coins, and men who made the fine jewelry given as gifts to women. For men who were serious collectors, the content of the collection was meant to be possessed and to be held—in private. It was shown, like the Medici treasures, but only to a privileged few. Although certain trappings were worn and periodically lent out, for the most part it was a personal compilation and not meant for public display.

Throughout the last one hundred years some elements of male finery and acquisition were acceptable, often dependent upon class, while others were best left at home. Too much glitz or too many objects could cause problems in perception. Only certain things were deemed acceptable for men to display. As far as personal jewelry, cuff links and a tie bar were it when I was growing up, but these disappeared during the 1980s and were confined to a very few menswear stores.

The Tiffany advertisements that run in the Sunday *New York Times* suggest that it is okay to wear cuff links. The products that are offered to men are new in the sense that they were absent from mass culture for a few decades. Not since the 1950s have the accoutrements of maleness been so visible and so acceptable. A variety of forms of jewelry are now more acceptable than in the past. For a while now men have worn bracelets, necklaces, dog tags, rings, and earrings.

Men can now take a serious interest in home décor as well, in rooms that go beyond the den, or the study. The products that they choose to display indicate that masculine material culture is alive and well. Men who thirty years ago would have balked—at least publicly—in the acceptance of this "metrosexual" category with their display and consumption of such things. The embracement of products, clothes, styles, and designs is now a full-blown industry where once men only showed peripheral interest. As Edisol Wayne Dotson writes, "A concern for male beauty, once regarded as a trait of questionable sexuality, has been introduced fully into heterosexual culture."[1] Another manifestation of this is the range of masculine products and items, objects and furniture that are now marketed to men. In a discourse on the "objects on men's desks," detailed in chapter nine, the objects range from sports memorabilia to playthings.

Watches, or timepieces, are one of the safest and most popular objects for men to own. Despite the penchant among the young to use their cell phones for time keeping, watches are enormously significant as far as masculine adornment. They still hold power and weight as far as a system of signals goes. "The wristwatch," writes Deyan Sudjic, "still retains its prestige."[2] In the past twenty years, watches have ballooned in popularity with men. Whether it is the Cartier, the Patek Phillipe, or the Rolex, it is a desirable object that compliments the Mercedes, BMW, or Audi. There are now over a half-dozen watch magazines at the neighborhood store, showing watches that range from the clunky to the gimmicky to the ultra-expensive. Pocket watches have always had a classic association, but in the past two decades, wristwatches have soared as a prestige item for men. They are more utilitarian than cuff links, less showy than tie bars, and much more practical than pocket watches. They carry weight, both figuratively and literally, and send out a complex series of messages. Virtually all major men's magazines have at least a half-dozen advertisements for watches, ranging from the makes listed above to Omega, Tudor, Longines, Swiss Army, Swatch, and Corum. Watches can serve as a form of jewelry but they also have "gadget" appeal, especially with alarms, timing and depth functions.

In the *New York Times Men's Style* magazine, journalist Lynn Hirschberg suggests that watches are the male corollary to jewelry, but they also take on other features for men. They are, she writes,

> Baubles camouflaged as gadgets: they have function, they convey status and, like cars, you can have several that fit different moods and uses. Unlike most toys, watches have emotional weight: they convey personal history, real or imagined.[3]

As the Patek Phillipe advertisements make quite clear, the watch is more than just a mechanical object to mark time. They are potential heirlooms, meant to be passed down to the next generation. They are also subtler than cars in their meaning. They can suggest control and success, but also and importantly, taste. Watches are marketed as the definitive tools of good taste and success.

The acceptance by the heterosexual male community of luxury and objects of refinement and sophistication was once the preserve of the elite and the very wealthy. This group has always collected and surrounded themselves with the trappings of luxury and the average male either could not afford these indulgences or simply did not know about this world. As well, having the qualities of taste and refinement and paying too much attention to one's appearance was often associated with homosexuality. Men who embraced items of sumptuousness were suspect. From Oscar Wilde down through the fictional Joel Cairo, there was a strong association of luxury with homosexuality.[4]

There have always been dandies, Beau Brummells, clothes horses, and men in general who were sharp dressers and very concerned about their appearance. It should be mentioned that in literature the examples are bountiful, from Diderot's rumination on his dressing gown to Jay Gatsby's massive selection of shirts. There have been positively pathological examples such as Bret Easton Ellis's *American Psycho*, which gives obsession of this kind a bad name. In film, two interesting cases stand out: one is Richard Gere's character, Julian, in Paul Schrader's *American Gigolo*. From a 1980s vantage point it was a truly remarkable sight to witness the focus on clothing and appearance in this film. There was a fair amount of screen time devoted to the selection of clothing and to the display of it, in almost fetishistic terms. Michael Douglas's Gordon Gekko, in his Allan Flusser–tailored suits, comes across as symbolic of the high-flying 1980s in *Wall Street*. Rather than serving to critique the excesses of the period, they glorify both wealth and luxury. To say that these two iconic characters are dandies is a bit extreme, for they fall into a different set of categories.

When we discuss the concept of the dandy, we are generally talking about an early nineteenth-century English stereotype that became popular in both England and France. This is or was a man who was quite concerned about appearance but who had a tendency to over extension and a propensity for excessive indulgence. Colin Campbell makes the important point that Brummell's "contribution to male fashion was not flamboyancy but quality, refinement, and attention to detail." Brummell's lasting influence was in "his obsessive concern with excellence in both the material and the fit of his clothes." As well, Brummell was exceedingly concerned about cleanliness and hygiene. Refinement, quality, and elegance seem to sum up the legacy of this influential style icon.[5]

The sense of deportment and fastidiousness has always found an audience among men. One reason for the Ralph Lauren Polo phenomenon being so successful is that it is a tailor-made—pun intended—shortcut to this form of appearance. There are clear and defined patterns, rules and coordinating conventions. Further to this, the popularity of bespoke tailoring and sharply cut suits in elegant fabrics is directly traceable back to the Brummell fascination with this kind of approach.

Men today who take their cues from the Brummell sharpness and cleanliness have it easier if they wear a form of uniform. Whether it is khaki pants and a button-down shirt with tasseled loafers, there is neatness in this form of uniformity. Adding a v-neck sweater or a navy blazer accentuates this look while varying it from its traditional focus. Like military uniforms, this civilian version carries authority and the impression of control and possibly power. It is simple and regimented but has its semiotic power.

The obverse of this is the man who is concerned with his appearance but goes to great lengths to hide how much thought has gone into how he looks. Some focus on certain things can be acceptable, but too much emphasis can be problematic. Susan Cheever's memoir of her father, the short-story writer John Cheever, remarks on the importance of appearance to him. She strikes it as a way of validating style while at the same time minimizing vanity:

> Clothes were important to him, and by the end of his life he had developed an aristocratic casual style that reflected his personal horror of vanity in men. This collided with his sharp sense of the importance of appearances. He didn't like to be caught looking in mirror, and he felt that men shouldn't think too much about their hair or their clothes. They should, nevertheless, always look terrific. It was an eccentric double standard that reflected his rigid and confused ideas about correct masculine behavior. Sometimes his shirts were frayed, or his sweaters worn out at the elbow, or his shoes down at the heel, because men didn't bother about such things. But he never would have worn a soiled shirt or gone a day without shaving—*that* would have been sloppy.[6]

John Cheever was casual about his appearance and elegance. But that in itself is a style and a look. One could even suggest that much more was at work than simple covering. This forced nonchalance and impeccable neatness counted as much for Cheever as it did to Brummell.

Beginning with J. C. Flugel's *The Psychology of Clothes*, published in 1930, many commentators have recognized a supreme correlation between sartorial appearance and identity. At certain periods of time there was an extreme connection between the two, when men spent an inordinate amount of time preparing their dress. This emphasis, especially among the upper classes lasted until the French Revolution. With the decline of aristocratic privilege came the commensurate waning on the focus of excessiveness in dress. Flugel, according to Ted Polhemus, suggests that the impact of the French Revolution on fashion in France in turn impacted men's attire in England. There was a move away from extravagance and a focus on more pedestrian clothes that "signaled sobriety, responsibility and hard work, rather than frivolity, privilege and leisure."[7] Polhemus implies that this focus on the mundane fluctuated in popularity for two hundred years but has been revitalized by periodic infusions by different subcultures. He lists working-class influence, homosexual culture, African-American and Latino culture, as well as other variations that have risen up to restate or recalibrate a unique and possibly new version of masculine identity. As he intimates, "distinct social groups and cultural institutions" have served to retain "a positive vision of the male body" which in turn has "thrived within the context of twentieth-century popular culture."[8]

Much of the research on shopping and consumption used to focus on women as the primary consumers. Increasingly, men and even young boys have demonstrated a willingness not only to go shopping but also to be seen in places beyond the stereo shop, the sporting goods emporiums, and of course, car lots. And we are not just talking about garage sales and auctions. Men, simply put, increasingly own up to the fact that they derive as much pleasure and satisfaction as women in the shopping experience.[9]

An interesting trend of late has been the purchasing of small, luxury items—not tools, knives, and the like—artifacts that were once the sole preserve of the female consumer. Although studies indicate that men like to go in and buy what they need and then exit immediately, the practice of lingering and looking is increasing among men. Younger men in particular seem to enjoy shopping and seem to be comfortable moving in new directions, as anyone in a Banana Republic or Abercrombie store can attest. They are not as self-conscious in areas that were once the preserve of women and are also quite willing to ask for help.[10]

It is not uncommon for men to covet something extraneous or indulgent—beyond a car or a big-screen TV. Small luxury items such as a fountain pen or a letter opener can be of great appeal. Items that suggest a wide array of characteristics, from taste to sophistication to utility can be as entrancing for men as they are for women. Essayist Joseph Epstein ponders the fact that when he was a "professional smoker" he was "enamored of a cigarette lighter, a gold, pebbly-grained Dunhill that sold for $45, at a time when $45 represented close to half a week's salary." He made a number of visits to Dunhill's to look at it, to hold it, flick it, to caress it. The lighter occupied a great deal of his thinking time and he eventually purchased it. "The lighter," he writes, "gave great pleasure. Every time I reached into my pocket to light a cigarette, I felt a minuscule but real jolt at the thought of my owning such a lighter, a small thing but the best and most elegant of its kind."[11]

The proliferation of products and things, the expansion of the ephemera of life, has had an impact on the way things are carried. As the three-piece suit declines in popularity and has given way to items such as cargo pants, men could still have pockets to carry the bits and pieces they needed. But to a point: it was not convenient or sufficient to stuff everything into one's pants. Even as vests from Tilley and coats from Swiss Army provided ingenious features for one's accoutrements, it still was not enough. What men have begun using are bags. The ubiquitous laptop computer bag has taken over from the briefcase and morphed into a variety of satchels and mesh carryalls. Men now utilize canvas duffle bags from Gurka and lush leather weekend bags from dozens of companies and designers, innovative sacks with pockets and Velcro that take on a multiplicity of shapes. These are supremely masculine and contrast quite severely with the men's purses of the 1970s. Watching men—especially young men—walk the city streets, what one sees is a veritable array of sleek luggage and body pouches that are designed to carry everything from iPods to phones and moleskin notebooks.[12] These are not the fanny packs of the 1990s but often, ergonomically sophisticated masculine containers constructed out of leather, rubber, or some new-age hybrid. They have replaced the briefcase as a dominant masculine signifier and exude a whole series of meanings. Every large menswear section of every department store now stocks a selection of these bags.

Pulitzer Prize–winning novelist Michael Chabon has thought about the bag quite a bit. Beginning with his utilization of a baby bag, his adoption of a "murse" came complete with an analysis of everything necessary to carry and the hows and whys one does so. A knapsack would not do and neither would a briefcase. As he tells it,

> Saggy-bottomed and stained from sitting around in puddles of beer, the knapsack is—along with its sober older brother the briefcase—one of a limited number of stealth purse strategies by which men routinely attempt to circumvent, elude, or transcend the cruel code of the pocket. The advent of the laptop computer has led to a kind of renaissance in the category of luggage formerly occupied by the satchel, an all but forgotten item just a few years ago, now more commonly designated a messenger bag and hybridized in leather, nylon, and plastic, leading to all kinds of knapsack-cum-attaches and tote-cum-briefcases.[13]

The mass consumption of specific luxury items by men has only been possible in the past thirty or so years. Prior to that time, only the super-rich could afford these very specific trappings of wealth. With the democratization of luxury, more and more men could purchase what was once too dear or too rare.[14] Originally, companies such as Dunhill, Burberry, and Turnbull & Asser never pandered to the hoi polloi. The offerings of Saville Row were beyond the capacity of most, and even their watered-down American counterparts, such as those retailed by Brooks Brothers, were still quite expensive. A mass reorientation of image and style was needed and this occurred on both sides of the Atlantic. It took an American marketing and design genius to retool the concept of luxury and finery and make it appealing to many men. At the same time, it took an Italian marketing and design genius to create high-end sartorial splendor in the clothing equivalent of a Ferrari.

Ralph Lauren was and is at the forefront of mass luxury and the marketing of the accoutrements of elegance. Lauren and his empire brought a dignified appreciation for quality clothing to the masses. If a man was not sure what was appropriate, fashionable, or even acceptable, the world of Ralph Lauren could provide the answers. In some of his advertisements and stores, in his boutiques and shops, he provides a return to the luxurious finery and elegance of the men's club. Leather and antiques, chrome and brass art deco, luscious wood and muted colors in the stores, paisleys and pinstripes, spread collars and cashmere in his clothes, all combine to permeate his creations with a weighty form of substance. His clothes, especially the Purple Label, evoke a timeless elegance.[15]

Lauren has made it easy for men to shop by a form of sartorial shorthand. If one sees his name, his labels, his polo player, then one is aware that this connotes a certain level of sophistication and suggests a certain level of luxury. The ubiquitous button-down or the snappy polo, the chinos or one of the iconic seasonal outerwear pieces made the staidness of Brooks Brothers look dated and tired. Here now was a fresh approach to a classic style, one that would change but that exhibited to the wearer and his audience a classic and cool elegance.

Where Lauren followed a classic series of lines, Giorgio Armani went postmodern. If Lauren stayed anchored to various lineages of Americana tinged with a British flare, the clothing that came from Milan was positively explosive in its use of fabric, color, and fit. The Armani brand, in all its manifestations, spoke to those who wanted something different from what their father wore. It was totally new and to some men, shocking. Unconstructed and loose in the 1970s, Armani constantly reinvented how men dressed and how they should look even in the most casual of occasions. For the man uncomfortable with the similarity of every item in his wardrobe, Armani offered and delivered change, and with it, substance.

It is important to note that "masculine consumerism" was born during the late 1950s and early 1960s but truly did not mature until the 1970s. What Don Johnson wore on *Miami Vice* in the early 1980s could not have happened without the enthusiasm for "vivacious youth" and "hedonistic masculinity" that originated in the 1950s.[16] The restraints of the post War period came off and unleashed a brand new kind of man. As Bill Osgerby notes, "Prosperous and independent, virile and irrepressible, the suave and smooth-talking playboy arose during the 1950s and early 1960s as one of the defining icons of American vitality and modernity."[17]

Osgerby suggests that it was Hugh Hefner's *Playboy* magazine, launched in 1953, that set this in motion. The content of *Playboy* was hugely influential in obvious and subtle ways, especially in allowing men to embrace a wide array of fashion, products, and ideas. More than just a sexual diversion or a radical change in sexual fashions, Hefner's magazine was arguably a vital catalyst in provoking male consumers to buy, and importantly, to enjoy what they bought. Just as significant as pictures of naked women and penetrating articles and journalism were the advertisements for consumer products. According to historian Steven Watts,

It became both a catalog for sophisticated purchasing and a guidebook for negotiating a daunting new landscape of material plenty. The pages of *Playboy*, along with Hefner's numerous public statements, articulated a credo urging unabashed enjoyment of the material goods that were flooding out to a middle-and working-class market. Addressing a simmering male identity crisis in modern society in which growing numbers of men no longer functioned as producers, the pages of *Playboy* offered the reassuring model of stylish consumer. [18]

Playboy, and by extension Hugh Hefner, promoted a lifestyle that dispensed with the cares that the previous generation of men had grown up with. Living for the here and now, but living suavely, was what it was about. Hefner promoted lifestyle changes in every direction, including the architectonic. *Playboy* pushed the idea that it was okay to pay attention to your dress, your home, specific rooms, and things as well as to be up-to-date on literature, politics, and most importantly, style. In the first issue there was an emphasis on celebrating what Steven Watts calls "material plenty." Watts relates that "a section titled 'The Men's Shop' offered a calfskin-covered ice bucket 'rimmed in high polished aluminum,' a mahogany 'Silent Valet' for hanging suits, a portable bar with 'black Formica top trimmed in red, green, ivory, or chartreuse Duran plastic,' and a stylish brass coat and hat rack." [19] Although looking through the early decades of the magazine reveals a dated tackiness by today's standards, it was in its time a definitive guide to masculine identity.

Playboy allowed men to have a legitimate interest in home décor and products, which were traditionally within the realm of the feminine. One could even argue that Hefner's magazine liberated men from the suspicion attached to paying too much attention to one's personal appearance and surroundings. "*Playboy*," as indicated byone of the editors of a book on post-war culture, "endlessly presented hyper-designed domestic interiors and ideal scenarios for bachelors, making it acceptable for men to be interested in architecture and interior decoration." [20] All the while, this template abutted the domesticized male in the suburbs, coexisting as a fantasy aspiration that often found common ground in the specific products that a married man could purchase.

Hefner's *Playboy* made it okay, even desirable, for men to want things that transcended the traditional masculine assortment of paraphernalia. It is interesting to contemplate that besides the shock value of naked women, *Playboy*'s lasting influence could be the orientation around the consumption of masculine possessions and the attempt to recapture the domestic sphere. For suburban males of the 1950s and 1960s in particular, *Playboy* was more than just a girlie magazine. It served as a bible to hip, masculine culture, guiding men on the "reappropriation" of domestic space, country houses, dens, and cars. [21]

Where *Playboy* may have been at the cutting edge for promoting many new masculine consumer ideals it did not necessarily cover every facet of that culture. One staple of advertising in the pages of *Playboy* that was anomalous falls into the personal grooming category. Until quite recently, *Playboy* and other male-oriented consumer publications, did not offer much in the way of advice or advertising in the realm of male products. One was forced to settle with Hi-Karate, English Leather, Old Spice, Brute, and of course, Aqua Velva as late as the 1980s, before the pervasiveness of Aramis and Polo made an olfactory impact. Until the early 1980s, standard male offerings could not yet be called grooming products and usually came from corporations such as Johnson, Mennen, and Gillette. Brill-cream and a few similar hair slickers, the shaving brush, and a simple razor were all that rested in the medicine cabinet beyond Bayer aspirin and milk of magnesia. There were no seventy-dollar eye creams for men, no skin toners with tea-tree oil, and no selection of Kiehl's. Now, the selection is endless for men's grooming products. Glancing at the toiletries available for men, one is struck by their quantity and diversity, to the point of amazement. From Neutrogena to Clarins to Nivea for Men to C. O. Bigelow, the selection is staggering. These are just medium-range offerings. At the higher, more exclusive end, the availability of products from the Art of Shaving to Biotherm to Clinique, is just the tip of the iceberg. All major European companies, which used to pander to women, now have a men's offering. These range from L'Occitane to Loreal to Aveda. In the realm of scent, the choices in certain stores number sixty different colognes and aftershaves. There are balms, moisturizers, lotions, and razor-burn emulsions. Facial scrubs, washes, and body sprays also complement the assortment. Perhaps all this began with Aramis, from the Estee Lauder Corporation, the same people who brought Clinique for Men to the market. Once Polo and Calvin Klein got into the act, the avalanche of products was unstoppable. The advertisements for these products fill the pages of men's and women's fashion and lifestyle magazines. They flash on Websites and popup on men's pages. The fact that there are so many speaks volumes about what has occurred around masculine hygiene in the past few decades.

In some department stores the selection of men's products and the space devoted to their display has gone from a minor little kiosk situated in a corner to a huge "set" that in some stores, rivals what is available for women at the cosmetics counter. Men's facial, hair, grooming, and scent lines are outpacing sales of women's products.[22] According to an article in the *Wall Street Journal*, "sales in some segments of the men's grooming market are growing at twice the rate of women's." Besides the traditional players, many of whom have created new lines or reconfigured and relaunched old ones, a host of new products "are looking to cash in on men's newfound desire to cleanse, pamper, exfoliate and hydrate."[23] Men's fragrances and other grooming products are now a multi-billion dollar business.[24]

If one were to peer into the shaving kit of a man from forty years ago, there would be the following items: soap, razor, deodorant, clippers, and not much more. Today there would be at least six more items, ranging from lotions and sprays to cleansers and bronzers. Most men were unaware that a different soap should be used on the face—not the same one for the body. They were content to shower as quickly as possible, to get in and out, without the bother of using different products. Most men now use a variety of cleansers for different parts of the body. Stores that once had a small selection of offerings now provide whole aisles for men's grooming products.[25]

Major consumer product corporations are now launching high-end and medium-priced lines—Estee Lauder, Gillette, Neutrogena, and Nivea—to name a few, and more are in the works.[26] Some observers feel that this is simply the beginning of a trend and it will only grow.[27] Once a month it seems like a new product line is launched. Men who traditionally would have been horrified or mildly embarrassed about discussing exfoliants and shower gels are now considered part of the pack.[28]

Glancing at the March/April 2007 issue of *Men's Vogue*, the content of the advertisements and the mini-features is quite revealing regarding men's grooming products. Interspersed between pages and pages of ads for clothing, watches, cars, and electronic devices, there are advertisements for a new Calvin Klein perfume, "euphoria," Loreal's Vive Pro, thickening shampoo, and a feature on different aspects of shave oils. The March 2007 issue of *Men's Journal* contains advertisements for Gillette Fusion power razor, Loreal shampoo for men, Zest body wash, and a feature on "chop shops" were men can get a shave, a haircut, and other offerings in personal grooming.

Men have always shown some interest in their grooming rituals. Often it was middle-class men mimicking the upper-class inclinations. Men who worked in factories or on farms did not have the time, proclivity, or money to spend grooming themselves other than for special occasions. For miners and men engaged in other working-class labors, this was obvious. It took both the urbanization and the commodification of culture to change this. Beau Brummell was not solely concerned about his clothes; he cared deeply about every facet of his appearance and spent hours preparing himself. He bathed daily in a time when this was rare, using hot water and milk. He also took a great deal of interest in the art of shaving, its hygienic aspects, and the accoutrements necessary for a good shave. As Ian Kelly details, a significant amount of money and selection was involved:

> The Dandiacal Body [Brummell] bought cakes of shaving soap (1s, 6d.), badger brushes (5s, 6d.) and razors (sixpence a sharpening) from Renard's of St. Jame's, along with toothbrushes, nail brushes, combs and soap. Brummell used a series cut-throat razors, then applied himself to

"stray hairs" with the aid of tweezers and a dentist's magnifying mirror.[29]

The evolution of shaving and the issues surrounding the beard have an interesting history. In the middle of the nineteenth century, beards began to appear in Victorian Britain. Some commentators felt that this was a direct result of the vogue for facial hair sported by returning soldiers from the Crimea.[30] Whatever the reason, there was a full-fledged "beard movement" in Victorian Britain. According to Christopher Oldstone-Moore, the movement was initiated to elevate the importance of the change in a man's appearance and at the same time, to "promote a new masculine image" in which beards played a seminal role. Beards became "integral" features of visible masculinity; they served as evidence of male characteristics in a time when society, thanks to industrialization, was changing. They became signifiers of "masculine identity." From Medieval influences to military fashions, beards had become popular trappings in the repertoire of masculine appearance. With hunting and the outdoors movement becoming all the rage, the mania for beards appealed to the rough and natural associations inherent with nature.[31] The beard came to be seen as the definitive masculine "body" statement, an emblem of manliness. It was contrasted with the feminine qualities associated with the clean-shaven face and the desire to evoke the spirit of manly independence. By the early years of the twentieth century, with the invention of the safety razor and concerns over hygiene in large associations such as armies, the beard fell out of favor as a definitive masculine symbol.[32]

Through the early twentieth century and into the period of World War II, men's grooming remained relatively stable. Having a beard or a mustache involved keeping the hair trimmed and required a fair amount of work in grooming. Some men went to barbers daily while others spent time in front of their mirrors. With the invention of home-use trimmers, things got a little easier. But like so much involved with masculine appearance, there are the two general preferences: the traditionalists and the technophiles. Some men prefer the long-established shaving ritual while others are very committed to electric razors such as those produced by Braun and Phillips.

The recent plethora of products for men harkens back to the heady days of male grooming, especially the period from the 1930s to the 1950s. At certain points, fashion trends attempt to reaccess and activate styles that have long since passed. There is glamour in attempting to recapture certain stylistic icons and to reinvigorate them with a new twist. The recent mania for hats is one example, as is getting dressed up and donning a tie. Grooming in its essential sense is "back." Stylists and designers mine old magazines and photographs for hints and ideas. Many of the perusers of these media access memories of their fathers wearing a hat or a well-tailored three-piece suit.

In old films and photographs, men are wearing hats, ties are obligatory, and most have their hair neatly combed. Hats in particular were a staple. In his amusing history of JFK and the demise of the hat industry, Neil Steinberg relates the following,

> Everyone has seen those old photographs of crowds—at baseball games, typically, or parades, or pouring out of subway stations—an unbroken sea of straw boaters, black, beetle-backed derbies, or snap-brim fedora, depending on the mandatory fashion of the year. Wearing a hate while on business was a given, like wearing shoes.[33]

Hats were a definitive marker for men; like a beard, they were emblems of masculinity and signs of wealth, class, and achievement.[34] They were essential and regardless of occupation, you wore one. "The social pressure," suggests Steinberg, "was strong enough to make almost every man go through the bother and cost of wearing hats—the purchase, the maintenance, and the daily ransom from the hat checks in every hotel, club, and restaurant lobby."[35] With the demise of the hat came the subsequent demise of all the ancillary services associated with the hat. But unlike the hat, shaving paraphernalia and the shaving service has made a comeback in a much more substantial way.

The offerings from the 1930s to the 1950s as far as shaving products are actually quite varied and rich in comparison to other material artifacts of stylistic masculine culture. In a nostalgic look back at this period, Bob Sloan and Steven Guarnaccia have titled their book, *A Stiff Drink and A Close Shave: The Lost Arts of Manliness*. As stated earlier, many men forty and older can remember not only the products but watching their father shave at the bathroom sink, or take out bits and pieces from his pockets at the end of the day to put in a masculine dish or tray placed on a credenza or dresser. There were pocket knives, pillboxes, combs of tortoise shell, maybe a flask, a matchbook, a cigarette box, tiepins, wallets, and cuff links. In the medicine cabinet, a thick can of deodorant, blades wrapped in an interesting color paper, a shaver in stainless steel, bottles of smoky talc. The products that they have assembled represent a museum of masculine ritual that evoke the moments, smells, and habits of men from the middle of the twentieth century. "This was a time," they write,

> when men had a wide assortment of objects that they needed in the course of their day. Though they had no official designation, they were distinctly 'men's stuff'—what a man really used to groom, smoke, imbibe, to hold his tie in place . . . This stuff wasn't frivolous. It was pragmatic . . . And though most of these were common, everyday items, the men's stuff from this era infused a man's life with a sense of design and craftsmanship, of patience and sensual indulgence, of humor and whimsy.[36]

Shaving, according to the authors, was an experience to luxuriate in. You used a brush and mug, not a can. And you took your time; you were supposed to relish the experience.[37] This has returned to the fore, judging by the vast selection of shaving paraphernalia now available. One can purchase razors made from platinum and gold, silver, and high-quality steel. There are exotic shelled brushes composed of rare hairs, not to mention an impressive appointment of lotions and lathers.[38]

Something happened in the 1960s to temporarily "liberate" men (and women) from the dependence upon all these objects and products. There was a distancing from hair spray—thanks, perhaps, to Rachel Carson, and a return to simpler, more natural approaches to hygiene and grooming. "None the less," writes Arthur Marwick, "the sixties were marked by significant changes, most obvious in the grooming and fashion articles specifically aimed at men in a number of magazines, but also apparent in guides exclusively concerned with masculine appearance, and also in special sections in guides primarily aimed at women."[39] Marwick suggests that personal appearance and looking healthy and youthful were now front and center for men. Making the most of how one looked took on added importance and was important in success. From this point on men began a concern with fashion and style that was every bit as effervescent as what women were indulging in. Although there were low points in taste, after a few decades the stylistic component matured.

One could go so far as to argue that men today are obsessed with personal grooming in a way that rivals women. The growth of "grooming aides" and scents is just one indicator. In 1997, three billion dollars was spent on men's grooming products.[40] Today, the number ranges from ten to twenty billion, depending on what is included, and can go even higher if all men's products are considered. Even more money is being spent on men's cosmetic procedures such as hair transplants, liposuction, face-lifts and implants. Pedicures, manicures, masks, and mud packs are also increasingly popular with men.[41]

From manicure sets in exotic skins to the gold-plated shaving set to little, elegant traveling kits, men now have their own versions of luxurious travel accessories. The "kit" that was very utilitarian and functional is now an enhanced and elegant case. Much of the recent passion for the accoutrements of grooming may have originated with Gillette and Schick launching a selection of fancy razors and blades that were industrial design masterpieces. To complement these new, seminal artifacts came a host of supplemental products, lotions and oils, cleansers, and aftershaves, designed with sophisticated packaging and masculine uniformity. The combination of these items from the more basic to the very expensive propelled the sales of men's grooming products into the billions of dollars. It seemed that no matter what was produced, men were eager to purchase the latest conditioner or deodorant. Male body spray arose from nowhere to become a huge seller.[42] A significant part of the appeal of these products is not just their direction toward men, but their packaging and the hues that the boxes and containers come in. Complete with cool graphics, manly scripts, and interesting shapes, they have a unique charm for men.

Another fascinating evolution in men's fashion and style has been in the realm of color. Color has often been synonymous with gender. The most obvious manifestation of this has been the "blue for boys, pink for girls" dichotomy. On the one hand, this trend has continued. In the arena of marketing products to men, stately, masculine colors continue this theme—both in bottles and containers and in packaging. Various shades of blue, gray, and black continue to dominate. Clinique's men's line was packaged in these hues and became a very attractive offering for men. The traditional gray of the boxes was both comforting and nonthreatening. Varying wildly on the other extreme, there has been much experimentation with wild shades, bright and loud injections of color that jump out. This is now found not just in cologne and cream packaging but also in many elements of men's material culture. With the rise of a variety of new sports and new teams there was a quest to find something different to make the offering noticeable. Extreme shades for uniforms such as the "day-glo" look and tangerine and mauve, made their presence felt in everything from workout wear to sports drinks.

In their analysis of Clinique cosmetics for men, Pat Kirkham and Alex Weller write that the advertising campaign that accompanied the launch in the mid-1990s was polarized along the cultural constructs of traditional gender stereotyping. They observed that many men's products were depicted in black and white as if to deliberately underscore the seriousness of the purchase and its role as well as to ensure that these products were viewed as sensible and not in any way a threat to the consumer's masculinity. The color choices were designed to uphold and validate consumer masculinity, not to tarnish it. As well, they also found that many of the advertisements directed toward men contained much more printed text than had been the case in previous years. The use of this information strategy also suggested that this was a serious undertaking and would not in any way detract the potential purchasers' masculinity.[43]

Traditional preferences for men in the expanse of color have always focused on dark and sedate tones, shades that were harmonious with the focus of masculine identity. Black and browns, taupes and beiges, were the dominant tinctures. Whether in a man's room such as a library or a study or on his person in the form of a suit, these colors have been conventional staples of defining maleness or at least, acceptable public maleness. This explosion in color has also permeated to other male age groups.

One of the more fascinating trends over the past few years has been the marked attraction of young men and boys to personal care products, stylized clothing, and in general, their overall appearance. Journalist Sara Wilson profiled a thirteen-year-old boy named Nickolaus, who had been acclimatized to perfecting his appearance since age five. "Gradually," she writes, "he began to develop his own taste, favouring high-end designer kids labels . . . " Nickolaus became quite particular about his preferences:

> Now, at 13, his unofficial school uniform is a Dolce & Gabbana junior jersey and Lucky Brand jeans. He visits a stylist regularly for highlights and haircuts. His toilette consists of Nolita moisturizing shampoo and conditioner, Vagheggi face cream, Sebastian shaper massage texture gel mist, and Ice hair spiker blast.[44]

Wilson states that this grouping, "tween boys," is a major economic force affecting purchasing trends in ever-record numbers. They are buying clothing, jewelry, and skin and hair-care products at an ever-younger age.[45] Marketers and advertising executives are totally aware of this grouping of young people and attempted, through various media—especially on-line—to advertise directly to them. No longer monitored and focused around television, marketers bypass parents and crate whole product lines designed specifically to appeal to their tastes and their preferences. These "tweens" possess a ready-made desire to buy and are sophisticated in their choices. They are even more aware and consumer-oriented than previous generations. They constitute a multi-billion dollar segment of the market.[46] Whereas once upon a time this behavior and these preferences would have been deemed extravagant or suspect, now, thanks to the mainstreaming of fashion and the revealing of the beauty secrets of hyper-masculine Hollywood stars, it has gained acceptability.

Young boys now care much more about how they look and how they are perceived than those of a similar age a generation ago. They want to spend time and do spend money on their appearance even if they carefully construct an attitude that superficially says otherwise. Some can't wait until they can really indulge.

In most towns and cities, the simple barbershop still exits. It is Spartan in its décor, touched up with the odd "male" accoutrement, but generally is notable because of its sterile, ageless functionality. It survives simply as a place to get a haircut. It is the stuff of nostalgia and popular culture. The older barbers are still there and perhaps, a few younger-looking types. It is not an environment devoted to style and comprehensive grooming. Some of the more sophisticated of these venues may have a manicurist, *Playboy* magazine, and the ubiquitous blue containers of floating combs. It is almost purely functional though and Zen-like in its purpose. It is also disappearing. Yet the barbershop retains a comfort level that many men still seek. It is familiar and simple, evoking a past association of one's first haircut or the one time of the month you could do something with your father. The smells are familiar and so are the props: the chairs, the talcum powder, the zinc tops, and the maleness of the place. What is is of significance with regard to the old-style barbershop is the fact that not only did it not stand on ceremony, but it was also intensely egalitarian as a space and a place for men. In his survey of men's environments, James B. Twitchell singles out the "American Barbershop" for special consideration. Twitchell reminisces that the barbershop was the place where men were and still are "treated as equals."[47]

It is a place where one can make jokes, talk about sports, argue about politics, and in general, be accepted. It has been mythologized in countless movies and on television and occupies a central point in American collective memory. Yet it does not have the bells and whistles that the new grooming salons offer.

It is possible, and now, in some places, quite common, for men to receive the pampering beauty and health treatments that were once reserved for women. Spa treatments, massages, wraps, and pedicures are increasingly part of the personal grooming rituals for men. In the past there was a steam room in a steam bath or gym, with a male masseur giving the rubdowns. Most of these places have ceased to exist with the exception of Russian clubs, Jewish *shvitzes*, or gay male bathhouses. Chains have opened and closed in various cities that mix haircuts, massages, and other treatments for men in environments that closely resemble sports bars. In New York and other major centers, luxurious retrofitted barbering establishments have sprung up and offer a complete array of sophisticated grooming services.

High end, exclusive salons that are oriented specifically toward men are now in existence in most major metropolitan areas. There are more expensive hair salons and ones that deal with hair loss and hair treatment as much as cutting in most cities. And shops that feature a "shave" are proliferating, as if this is now the most sought-after luxury. On Madison Avenue in New York, it is possible to be groomed with the ultimate sense of care and cost at The Art of Shaving. Men can now have their moustaches trimmed for $15.00, have a haircut, and no doubt, have their nose hair clipped in a sanitary fashion. Shoeshines have also come back as a way for men to enjoy an almost anachronistic indulgence.

As with so much in the heterosexual world of image and fashion, it is gay culture, and in particular, certain aspects of gay fashion subculture that often starts the process rolling in the realm of trends and styles. The adoption of the traditional working-man's uniforms in the late 1970s, those of the "lumberjacks and construction workers,"[48] is one example of a trend that permeated the heterosexual world, in the same way that the moustache and close-cropped haircut did.

Leather, which vacillates from being emblematic of rebellious associations to a working person's garment to high end, also finds its way into stylized gay fashion, especially among certain designers, most notably the Claude Montana wear of the 1980s. The leather jacket that Brando wore or that Indiana Jones donned exemplified a robust and rugged masculinity and became for many both a statement and a code. It exuded toughness and a level of cool detachment that was obvious to the wearer and the watcher.[49]

One of the most consistent forms of male attire has been the suit. Whether in two-piece or three-piece formats, and with numerous variations, from the blazer and slacks to the tuxedo, the suit has endured as a prototypical male uniform. Although it has been modified and has evolved over the past four centuries, the suit retains its basic shape and structure as a definitive masculine garment. It has become synonymous with both a definitive form of masculinity as well as an emblem of the varieties of masculine experience. After the French Revolution, its template was firmly enshrined. As Anne Hollander observes in this important passage:

> The modern masculine image was thus virtually in place by 1820, and it has been only slightly modified since. The modern suit has provided so perfect a visualization of modern male pride that it has so far not needed a replacement, and it has gradually provided the standard costume of civil leadership for the whole world. The masculine suit now suggests probity and restraint, prudence and detachment; but under these enlightened virtues also seethe its hunting laboring, and revolutionary origins; and therefore the suit still remains sexually potent and more than a little menacing, its force by no means spent during all these many generations. Other ways for men to dress now share the scene with suits, so suits have shifted posture; but they remain one true mirror of modern male self-esteem.[50]

Hollander likens the suit to a form of armor, protecting and shielding, propping up and signifying for and to the male. It functions so accurately in that role that for some men, it is hard to take off. One is left vulnerable and casual, underdressed and exposed.

Although a number of major clothing concerns have gone under in the last few years, there is a robust market for made-to-measure or bespoke tailoring. Younger men are embracing a legacy of craftsmanship that their fathers may have skipped but their grandfathers patronized. High end, Saville Row–quality clothing has expanded beyond the confines of London and has attracted quite its share of customers, from all walks of life. Attempting to recapture the emphasis on style and fine fabrics, many other cities have seen a spike in the rise of cutting-edge tailors.[51]

Outside of major urban centers, generally, when one wears a suit, especially a well-made sharp suit, one is noticed. Characters on television stand out in suits.

In his memoir on teaching, Jay Parini singles out professors for their unique style of dress. Parini writes, "long after we've forgotten what our professors told us in college, we remember their clothes."[52] Parini recalls different professors at different colleges at different times. Each was cloaked in garb that was intended to make a statement and to convey both a personal and a political stance. He paid attention to what they wore, whether it was blue jeans and tweed jackets or three-piece suits, for a variety of reasons, but most probably, because he was looking for clues for what to wear when he himself became a professor. His message could be that men look at what other men are wearing and gauge the impression this gives.

Alan Flusser has written that men's clothing is now so popular because "of the cultural shift towards personal expression and individuality that took place in the latter third of the twentieth century." Clothing, over the past few decades, has come to be seen as legitimate "badges of communication."[53]

NOTES

1. Edisol Wayne Dotson, *Behold the Man: The Hype and Selling of Male Beauty in Media and Culture* (New York: Harrington Park Press, 1999), p. 4.

2. Deyan Sudjic, *The Language of Things: Design, Luxury, Fashion, Art* (London: Penguin Books, 2009), p. 95.

3. Lynn Hirschberg, "Face Time," *New York Times Style Magazine*, Men's Fashion, Spring 2005, p. 88.

4. John M. Clum, *"He's All Man": Learning Masculinity, Gayness, and Love from American Movies* (New York: Palgrave, 2002), p. 110.

5. Colin Campbell, *The Romantic Ethic and the Spirit of Modern Consumerism* (Oxford, UK: Basil Blackwell, 1987), pp. 167–168.

6. Susan Cheever, *Home before Dark* (New York: Bantam Books, 1991), p. 37.

7. Ted Polhemus, "The Invisible Man: Style and the Male Body," in *Material Man: Masculinity, Sexuality, Style*, ed. Giannino Malossi (New York: Abrams, 2000), p. 44.

8. Ted Polhemus, "The Invisible Man," pp. 47, 48.

9. See my *Shopping as an Entertainment Experience* (Lanham, MD: Lexington Books, 2007).

10. "Men Defy Stereotypes," *Global Cosmetic Industry* 170, no. 11 (November 2002), p. 14.

11. Joseph Epstein, *Snobbery: The American Version* (Boston: Houghton Mifflin, 2002), pp. 106–107. Although not quite an aesthete, Epstein's work is peppered with numerous descriptions of attractions to various products, from luggage to trench coats.

12. Annalisa Barbieri, "Bags of Masculinity," *New Statesman*, October 23, 2006, p. 53.

13. Michael Chabon, "I Feel Good about My Murse," in *Manhood for Amateurs* (New York: HarperCollins, 2009), p. 153.

14. On the democratization of luxury, see Richard Conniff, *The Natural History of the Rich* (New York: Norton, 2002) and Dana Thomas's excellent *Deluxe: How Luxury Lost Its Luster* (New York: Penguin Press, 2007).

15. See Michael Gross, *Genuine Authentic: The Real Life of Ralph Lauren* (New York: HarperCollins, 2002).

16. Bill Osgerby, *Playboys in Paradise: Masculinity, Youth, and Leisure-Style in Modern America* (Oxford, UK: Berg, 2001), p. 4.

17. Bill Osgerby, *Playboys in Paradise*, p. 4.

18. Steven Watts, *Mr. Playboy: Hugh Hefner and the American Dream* (Hoboken, NJ: Wiley, 2008), p. 4.

19. Steven Watts, *Mr. Playboy*, p. 124.

20. Beatriz Colomina, "Introduction," in *Cold War Hothouses: Inventing Postwar Culture from Cockpit to Playboy*, ed. Beatriz Colomina, Annmarie Brennan, and Jeannie Kim (Princeton, NJ: Princeton Architectural Press, 2004), p. 17.

21. Beatriz Preciado, "Pornotopia," in *Cold War Hothouses: Inventing Postwar Culture from Cockpit to Playboy*, ed. Beatriz Colomina, Annmarie Brennan, and Jeannie Kim (Princeton, NJ: Princeton Architectural Press, 2004), p. 222.

22. Hilary Howard, "For Men: Rub In, Say 'Ahh,'" *New York Times*, November 19, 2009, online edition.

23. Barmini Chakraborty, "Market for Men's Skin Care Grows," *Wall Street Journal*, April 20, 2005, p.1.

24. Edisol Wayne Dotson, *Behold the Man*, p. 5.

25. Naomi Aoki, "Real Men Exfoliate," *Boston Globe*, April 19, 2005, online edition.

26. Christine Bittar, "Men's Grooming: Past the Surface," *Brandweek*, December 13, 2004, p. 25.

27. Barmini Chakraborty, "Market for Men's Skin Care Grows," p. 1.

28. Christine Bittar, "Men's Grooming," p. 24.

29. Ian Kelly, *Beau Brummell: The Ultimate Dandy* (London: Hodder & Stoughton, 2005), p. 162.

30. Christopher Oldstone-Moore, "The Beard Movement in Victorian Britain," *Victorian Studies* 48, no. 1 (Autumn 2005), p. 7.

31. Christopher Oldstone-Moore, "The Beard Movement in Victorian Britain," pp. 8–18.

32. Christopher Oldstone-Moore, "The Beard Movement in Victorian Britain," pp. 19–29.

33. Neil Steinberg, *Hatless Jack: The President, the Fedora, and the History of an American Style* (New York: Plume, 2004), p. ix.

34. Neil Steinberg, *Hatless Jack*, p. xvii.

35. Neil Steinberg, *Hatless Jack*, p. xi.

36. Bob Sloan and Steven Guarnaccia, *A Stiff Drink and a Close Shave: The Lost Arts of Manliness* (San Francisco: Chronicle Books, 1995), p. vi.

37. Bob Sloan and Steven Guarnaccia, *A Stiff Drink and a Close Shave*, p. vi.

38. Barmini Chakraborty, "Market for Men's Skin Care Grows," p. 1.

39. Arthur Marwick, *The Sixties* (New York: Oxford University Press, 1998), p. 429.

40. Lyne Luciano, *Looking Good: Male Body Image in Modern America* (New York: Hill & Wang, 2001), p. 3.

41. Harrison G. Pope Jr., Katharine A. Phillips, and Roberto Olivardia, *The Adonis Complex: The Secret Crisis of Male Body Obsession* (New York: Free Press, 2000), p. 31.

42. Christine Bittar, "Men's Grooming," pp. 24–28.

43. Pat Kirkham and Alex Weller, "Cosmetics: A Clinique Case Study," in *The Gendered Object*, ed. Pat Kirkham (Manchester, UK: Manchester University Press, 1996), pp. 197–198.

44. Sara Wilson, "Oh Boy," *Globe and Mail*, August 28, 2004, p. L5.

45. Sara Wilson, "Oh Boy," p. L5.

46. See Juilte B. Schor, *Born to Buy: The Commercialized Child and the New Consumer Culture* (New York: Scribner, 2004) and Gary Cross, *The Cute and the Cool: Wondrous Innocence and Modern American Children's Culture* (New York: Oxford University Press, 2004).

47. James B. Twitchell, *Where Men Hide* (New York: Columbia University Press, 2006), p. 105.

48. James Sullivan, *Jeans: A Cultural History of an American Icon* (New York: Gotham Books, 2006), p. 174.

49. Mick Farren, *The Black Leather Jacket* (New York: Abbeville Press, 1985), pp. 6–8.

50. Anne Hollander, *Sex and Suits: The Evolution of Modern Dress* (New York: Random House, 1994), p. 54.

51. See Alice Cicolini, *The New English Dandy* (New York: Assouline, 2005).

52. Jay Parini, *The Art of Teaching* (New York: Oxford University Press, 2005), p. 69.

53. Alan Flusser, *Dressing the Man: Mastering the Art of Permanent Fashion* (New York: HarperCollins, 2002), p. 4.

FOUR

The Media and Men II

Throughout Western history, most of the literature that has become a staple of the canon features either a group of men or a lone protagonist on a quest for something: an ideal, safety, an object. From Homer onward, the development of the heroic male figure has taken on numerous variations yet retains certain specific features. The literature of war, of struggle, and of conflict—of men in groups and of the solitary hero, all have figured prominently in the West and many examples of these variations have become staples in the selection of popular and classic offerings.

Adventure stories and nonfiction accounts of harrowing tales, from Marco Polo and Columbus to the exploits of Byrd and Livingstone, all the way up to Edmund Hillary and Neil Armstrong, resonate particularly well with male readers. On the one hand they thrill and enthrall readers about places and exploits too extreme for the average person; on the other they provide a cathartic release to those who are frustrated with the mundaneness of everyday life. They are particularly appealing to men who are troubled, bored, and need a taste of excitement. Adventure tales speak to men in ways that their normal lives can not. The main character in Robert Cohen's *Amateur Barbarians*, Teddy Hasting, is going through a "mid-life crisis." When he reads, he looks for excitement:

> He liked material of an extreme nature. The radical solitude of the desert, the dank resistance of the jungle, the flare and assault of tropical heat. Already that year he'd sailed up the Gambia with Mungo Park, floated down the Nile with James Bruce, crossed the Horn with Richard Burton, galloped the Levant with T. E. Lawrence.[1]

Teddy Hasting is looking to read about others experiences with risk and danger, conquest and difficulty. One of the reasons that heroic archetypes endure is that they serve as a counterpoint to the humdrum and mechanized life that has characterized modern society. They provide adventure, fantasy, exoticism, and release in large doses.

This is exactly why books such as Sebastian Junger's *The Perfect Storm* and Jon Krakauer's *Into Thin Air* were bestsellers and continue to attract readers and imitators. The activities of everyday life do not allow for extremes in performance and most men simply do not have the time to engage in activities that provide thrills. Modern society does not give men the chance to test themselves in ways that historically could be said to have been a part of the masculine experience. "Within this culture," writes Mark Gallagher, "accounts of survival amid extreme danger affirm the possibility of unmediated experiences of physical punishment and triumph."[2]

Within this realm there can be the enormously potent loner or the duo, in partnership. Whether it is an Eastwood-like hero who prefers to work alone as in so many examples, or a tandem, there is the opportunity to showcase divergent qualities and differing aspects of character. This is particularly pronounced in a duo where one member is learning from the older one. Pairings of famous men dot history and literature and provide for a richer explanation of narrative and allow for more variety in action. In some cases, without a partner there is no adventure, no process of discovery. Paired with a partner, Robinson Crusoe and Don Quixote are capable of much more on their quest or journey.

American literature is exceptionally robust in its offerings of crucial examples of manhood and potent illustrations of masculine endeavor. Many of the most significant characters created by writers as diverse as Mark Twain and James Fenimore Cooper celebrate the individual freedom of male culture. As well, lesser contributors to the pantheon of American fiction, from Horatio Alger to the characters created by Zane Grey also focus on these themes. Whether it is an Owen Wister "cowboy" or a Jack London animal tale that celebrates freedom, the structure and the characters of the works are often entwined with nature. This is another common theme in American literature, the connection between rural and natural society and the ability of men to be free in nature. This is often juxtaposed with urban society, both historically and in contemporary terms, which is portrayed as having a tendency to hamper male endeavor and to shackle natural masculine freedom.[3]

John Kasson suggests that the outdoors or nature has been a constant trope as a fictional testing ground. It always provides an antidote to the sterility of the mechanized white-collar environment. "The desire," he writes, "for unmediated contact with nature and occasions to test oneself against it constitutes and overriding element of American masculine identity."[4] It does not necessarily have to be the land, per se, but the sea, the river, and the lake as well. Whether the quest for *Moby Dick* or a sojourn down the Mississippi, the water is just as potent as a testing ground. One of the reasons that Hemmingway's stories and some of his novels are still so popular is that they were written for boys and men and served as a series of masculine proving grounds, often in natural settings. Whether it is in the bullring, hunting big game in Africa, or fighting it out with a Marlin, a male engages with nature to see of what he is made.

The content of Hemingway was one version. But a whole century of popular tales in the form of comics, penny dreadfuls, inexpensive re-prints, dime novels, and later on in movie serial and television format, provided a wealth of information to those who read and later, watched about how a real man was supposed to comport himself. One is stunned at the influence of works that were often dismissed as trash by some critics. James H. Maguire writes that dime novels "glorified the exploits of frontier heroes such as Daniel Boone and Kit Carson and reduced the elements of frontier narrative to a simple formula."[5] Their accessibility and relative ease of absorption and at times, the excellent stories and high quality writing, made them and still make them very popular for men. Naturally, the crime and detective novels that line the bookstore shelves are much more in tune with contemporary society.

Many of these popular versions also had their high-brow corollaries. Elements of popular fiction have become a seminal and significant staple of mass culture and demonstrate an enormous durability and pliability. What starts off as a form of base construction can eventually mature into something quite sophisticated. Genre need not be low brow, as Stephen King, who now graces the pages of *The New Yorker*, can attest.

The bestselling adventure stories such as *A Perfect Storm* and *Into Thin Air* recast the attempts to master nature in a manner similar to the stereo-typical memoirs and accounts from 100 years ago. Attempting to scale Mount Everest is something that many men wish to read about, but not necessarily undertake. Personal challenges and masculine excitement provide thrilling reading. Recounting the trials of a severe storm or a mountain-climbing expedition are important voyeuristic fantasies that serve as key stand-ins for the real thing.[6]

Men enjoy reading about the adventures and exploits of other men— especially if they are famous. Since the turn of the twentieth century, the popularity of biographies has reinforced this connection. Sporting figures and successful businessmen have always held fascination as subjects. Me-moirs are also very attractive, especially when they have something out of the ordinary to say. Anthony Swofford's memoir of his stint as a Ma-rine became a bestseller and a successful movie because of its unparal-leled insight and penetrating front-line access. *Jarhead* was a candid and frank look at Marine combat during the Gulf War and while many read-ers had no desire to go to Iraq, they were quite willing to be thrilled by his exploits. The fact that the book is exceptionally good does not hurt. It is engrossing and at times, riveting, capturing the age-old appeal of the military with its mixtures on insights into the Marine Corps with tactics on fighting and fitness. The gung-ho machismo of the group is balanced with the horror and tragedy of war as waged today. Yet despite the tough content, one can't put it down.[7]

Biographies on sports figures and autobiographies consistently appeal to men and specifically to male readers. Over the past few years, a number of very popular releases have appeared, by and on football coaches, wrestlers, NASCAR stars, and baseball players. In Canada, Stephen Brunt was especially successful with his book on Bobby Orr and a follow up on Wayne Gretzky. Jon Krakauer scored with his work on Pat Tillman, the NFL superstar who died tragically of friendly fire. Works on captains of industry, from Rupert Murdoch to robber barons such as Carnegie, Rockefeller, and Vanderbilt have also been popular.

In fiction there is no end of titles that touch on masculinity and manliness. From classics and mid-century gems to works by established masculine purveyors and examiners like Bellow, Updike, and Roth, variations and experimentations abound. There are major contributors, for example, Caputo, Ellroy, Irving, and Denis Johnson to younger writers such as Benjamin Kunkel, Keith Gessen, and Scott Mebus. Some, like Nick Hornby have carved out their own turf and speak to an audience of men that normally don't read fiction. The realm of the graphic novel has expanded enormously the boundaries and acceptability of various forms of masculine portrayal and this sophisticated genre has enormous potential if David Mazzucchelli's *Asterios Polyp* is any indication.

Crime fiction and police stories, detective tales and who-dunnits are still among the most popular fictional stories that men read. Many of the most successful writers of the past ten years have been scribes who deal in murder and mystery. This long-standing appeal has allowed the arena to grow and to accommodate a wide array of guys.

Much of contemporary and to some extent, post-war fiction that deals with a male protagonist is in some form influenced or affected by the world of the "hard-boiled" masculine character. One is tempted to assign the suffix "detective" to that term, but that is not always the case. This "cultural fantasy" was created in the years after World War I and matured into a specific literary archetype during the 1930s. Dashiel Hammett's creations stand out and have been lauded as one of the first truly unique versions. By the early World War II years, it had become a staple of "high culture" in its leanings and was eventually to find a prominent place in film noir.[8] According to Christopher Breu the name "hard-boiled" was suggestive in that it defined a man who possessed a "tough, shell-like exterior" who was "detached" and did not say much. The "hard-boiled" character was extraordinarily blasé and straddled the cusp of individualism and autonomy.[9]

All of these features define the dominant male literary archetype—albeit with slight variations. By the dominant literary archetype, what is suggested is that this template exuded enormous influence in both fiction and nonfiction formats. Acting in a certain way reflected the power of the hard-boiled character and could be applicable to virtually every facet of society. A number of decades after the distillation of the hard-boiled typology variations could include a more sensitive and emotional selection.

In three short story collections, Thom Jones has reinvigorated the supremely masculine archetype, especially a variation on the hard-boiled. In *The Pugilist At Rest*, the protagonists of many of the stories display hyper-masculine attributes and indulge in traditional active male vocations. From the boxer to the caretaker, men perform as men. Many, if not most, exhibit raw emotion and extreme character flaws. As with much of American manly fiction, Vietnam figures heavily as a problem. The boxer of the title story is burned out, busted, and broke. But being a man, he has to rise to the challenge. Paralleling Susan Faludi's thesis in *Stiffed* Jones writes,

> I was twenty-seven years old, smoked two packs a day, was a border-line alcoholic. I shouldn't have fought him—I knew that—but he had been making noise. A very long time before, I had been the middle-weight champion of the 1st Marine Division. I had been a so-called war hero. I had been a recon Marine. But now I was a garrison Marine and in no kind of shape. [10]

A number of novelists and short story writers, diarists, and raconteurs have won great fame and fortune by detailing the various guises of masculinity. From the works of Hammett and Chandler through Mickey Spillane, to Graham Greene, Kingsley Amis, Ian Fleming, and Norman Mailer, various versions of masculinity have been depicted in their novels and character creations. Some are pathetic and broken, while others stand tall and proud.

The work of John Irving, a first-rate literary novelist has often been suffused with a variety of masculine themes and a range of masculine characters. Irving himself embodies a very smart type of robust masculinity. A former collegiate wrestler, he was inducted into the wrestling hall of fame, as listed on one of his dust jacket blurbs, alongside mention of his National Book Award, Guggenheim and Oscar. Many of his characters exhibit a quiet and secure masculinity but also a strong form of sensitivity as well as duty and honor. His characters have interesting relationships with women and minor and major characters are often intertwined with women in very profound ways. In some cases, the men he creates are almost unable to act without some form of female intervention, and are thus paralyzed without a wife or a mother.

Irving's early *The Water-Method Man*, published before his break-through *Garp* novel, details a protagonist who cannot urinate properly. According to Sally Robinson, the theme in this early novel is one where "women" "aim to block the free flow of male sexual energies and to acculturate the men into mature and responsible manhood." This involves engaging in the emotional attributes of the "seventies new man," the male who has experienced feminism and is capable of displaying all sides and emotion. This means that the men are required to "communicate openly, experience, express, and share their emotions—as long as those emotions are 'soft' and 'safe' and *not* an expression of male priority, privilege, or power."[11]

Robinson suggests that males in fiction are often forced to take on the dual and contradictory roles of being both strong and silent as well as open and emotional. She feels that much of this dichotomy is based on the reactions to feminism and the bourgeoning writings about men, for men, that started to appear in the late 1970s and reached a crescendo in the 1980s. Destruction, both open and outward and inwardly directed is often at the core of the male image created in this manner of fiction. Pain and emotional blockage also define these protagonists, according to Robinson. And at the core is the contrary dialectic,

> The image of a simmering male body whose psychophysical energies are always circulating and recirculating in an effort to avoid both destruction and self-destruction constructs a masculinity that embraces pain as a manly credential even as it threatens to release those natural male energies that cause pain to others. Men *must* restrain their dangerous impulses, but men *cannot* restrain them; men *must* release their blocked emotions, but men *cannot* release them.[12]

Robinson assesses the results of the above by their acceptance in mainstream culture as morphing into a kind of normality. In turn, this leads to a wounded form of reactionary masculinity that surfaces. This is pronounced in the works of Pat Conroy. In *The Great Santini* and *The Prince of Tides*, the pressures and problems of adaptive masculinity often center on the fact that men can't express emotions. Tom Wingo, according to Robinson, the main character in *The Prince of Tides*, is a strapping athlete who is completely unable to give voice to his emotions, many of which are long suppressed. Both the book and the film chart his journey toward emotional health, meaning his ability to shed tears and confront his past along specific lines. This is placed in the context of a "post-liberationist America" where men are "marked" for their privileges and their burdens.[13]

The upheavals in the economy and the fracturing of the glory of the American dream have taken their toll on the men who populate contemporary fiction. No longer do they just zoom to the top and no longer are they guaranteed to succeed. Success has become a major plot device; even those that achieve some measure of material comfort are either never really secure, or else they are afflicted with an array of issues and problems that not only impact the narrative but the mental health of the reader as well. Richard Ford has won great acclaim for his *Sports Writer*, Frank Bascomb, in both the self-titled original and most recently in *The*

Lay of the Land. The latter features Frank as a successful real estate agent recovering from prostate cancer. Like so many of his contemporaries, from Philip Roth's creations to younger versions imagined by David Foster Wallace, Rick Moodie, and Jonathan Franzen, this male protagonist is wounded and conflicted and very introspective about the state in which he finds himself.

Phillip Roth's creations straddle the varied nature of contemporary masculinity and mirror North American society's preoccupations with sex, accomplishment, affluence and angst, race and America. His protagonists, David Kepesh, Peter Tarnopol, Nathan Zuckerman, Mickey Sabbath, Swede Lvov, Coleman Silk, Ira Ringold—to name but a few, exemplify and illustrate the varieties of post-war masculinity and stand for different points on this compass. Many are self-absorbed and selfish as creations yet they draw on the expansions and contractions of American society, both rural and urban. While inner focused in many respects there is a male universalism to his characters, perhaps exaggerated and extreme, but relevant and understandable. Far from being the cut out and one-dimensional stock figures of American mass culture and far from bordering on the literary stereotypes from Miller to O'Neal, there is a caustic depth to Roth's male creations. The anxieties and worries of death and dying jostle front and center with the possible decline of American might and justice. Like the country, his men end up alone.

John Updike was a wonderfully vibrant creator of men who stood as barometers of masculinity in changing times. Like Roth's characters, Updike's ministers, car salesmen, and writers sought success and sex as touchstones of their version of America. Doubt and release occupy the many masculine worlds of Updike, from *A Month of Sundays* to *Memories of the Ford Administration*, and of course the antics and thoughts of Rabbit Angstrom.

The most complex male heroes in the post-war fictional world were those created by Saul Bellow. Augie March stands supreme as an original American masculine creation. But Moses Herzog, Charlie Citrine, Eugene Henderson, and virtually all his male characters function and strive on multiple levels. Interesting too is their vanity; Bellow's creations care about how they look and what they wear. Consumption is a part of post-war American success and males must adopt the trappings appropriately. This is not as pronounced in certain books—Herzog is a slob, as is the Hemingwayesque Henderson—but it is important and manifest in *The Dean's December*, Augie March, and definitely *Ravelstein*. Below the surface of Augie March's Chicago, he adopts and chooses, selects and models. Like the best of America, he refines and absorbs. He is Gatsbian and not too proud to associate with those a little rough around the edges to prove he is a man and to learn what he is about.

The creation of the gangster or mobster as a faction staple and later as fodder for film allows for an interesting form of masculinity to emerge.

This was not a genteel and refined series of creations, but a rough template hewn from the immigrant masses that came to America's shores. The creation of the American gangster provides a template of masculinity that is visceral, violent, and independent. The most obvious and well-known version is Mario Puzo's *The Godfather*. Different from *Scarface* and other sagas, this is a unique construction. Popularized by Francis Ford Coppola's films, the story details the evolution of a mob family and the forces affecting its rise. It resonates with traditional Italian masculinity transported into the new world. Within the book as well as within much of stereotypical Italian culture, there is a focus on action rather than words. Key values from the old country are transplanted into the American context and these focus on honor, respect, and protection of one's family.[14] Accordingly it is vital, as Fred L. Gardaphe suggests, for Michael Corleone to demonstrate that he is a man by performing in public. He is deemed "a man" once he kills the enemies of his family.[15] What Gardaphe dwells upon in his examination of *The Godfather* is not necessarily the ability to engage in violence, but the underlying threat to use it. Violence is a controversial and key characteristic in the appeal of the novel, but also in the standing it has as a masculine attribute.

The willingness to be brutal and vicious is a staple of most gangster films and much of hoodlum culture. From the street gangs of L.A. to the historical roots of the mob, violence was part and parcel of criminal culture. Its unique resonance in mafia/mob interpretations gives it an edge. The legacy of the Italian-American gangster and his interpretations of masculinity have permeated much of American popular culture. What is acceptable as a man and what is proper and right as far as actions that are performed saturate popular mythology. From *Goodfellas* to *The Sopranos* to *Married to the Mob*, elements of masculine bravado and the good life often collide with more traditional expectations of society.

Another category that one must consider in the sliding scale of literary heroes has to be the intellectual as hero. Whether detective, investigator, or sleuth, this has been a very fertile trope in popular literature. Rex Stout's Nero Wolfe, gargantuan in appetite and in taste was a key American creation in this arena. There have been dozens of intellectually inspired sleuths since *Fer de Lance* and they have set the tone for an array of detectives who use their heads as opposed to their fists. Even something as popular and pedestrian as *The DaVinci Code* has a protagonist who is a scholar of religion and iconography. He is able to find things out and to solve the puzzle because of his learned capacities. Brawn and strength are still valued, but it is the educated man in this book and these kinds of works that is successful.

The novels of Elmore Leonard, many of which have been made into movies, merge a tough guy with a man who thinks. Whether it is Chili Palmer, La Brava, or some other unique creation, Leonard's fictional heroes—even many of his western characters—are thinkers who often find themselves in problematic situations. They inevitably come out all right, thanks to a plan, a woman, and some luck. Leonard's stories have gleeful-ly carried influence on everyone from George Clooney to Quentin Taran-tino in marking out a set of masculine guidelines for American men to read. They are street-smart toughs who don't like to fight, and they are also quite comfortable moving to and from the seedy side to the luxuri-ous worlds of Palm Beach and Bel Air.

The self-made businessman has long been a staple of modern litera-ture. The self-made man in general, as embodied by some Horatio Alger type who makes something of himself in the world, holds enormous appeal for boys and men. James V. Catano asserts that the appeal in the traditional and contemporary versions of this kind of "entrepreneurial masculinity" is the fact that success is predicated on "access to real mas-culinity."[16]

During the 1980s and 1990s, the variation on the masculine business-man was the corporate raider. Despite Michael Douglas' portrayal of Gordon Gekko as a nasty type, men still found much to admire in these heavy weights. Whether it was Carl Ichan, T. Boone Pickens, or even a Milliken, these wheeler-dealers—some of whom landed in jail—made so much money so quickly that they were seen as quintessentially heroic in the classic American sense. In Tom Wolfe's expose of a businessman's fall, *The Bonfire of the Vanities*, we witness a cool and collected captain of industry move from crisis to crisis without batting an eye. Then his world falls apart and he in turn collapses on a grand scale. Both *Liar's Poker* and *Barbarians at the Gate* were huge nonfiction bestsellers that shed light on the high-stakes world of big business. Written by talented writers, they provided insight into the exciting world of enormous money.[17]

Novels and writings that feature men who are consistently striving upward are also a part of the American landscape. These works and in particular, their main characters, personify a need to succeed and to hold in to the trappings of success. From Jay Gatsby to Babbitt in the 1920s, a template was cast, especially in the visible display of wealth. James D. Riemer, in discussing Sinclair Lewis' Babbitt does not focus on the tradi-tional element of conformity. Rather, in reading this 1922 novel from the vantage point of a men's studies perspective, Reimer suggests that Bab-bitt's actions are efforts designed to "reaffirm a sense of manliness in a changing social and economic environment."[18] What Reimer finds is that the culture that Babbitt is a part of no longer defines masculine achieve-ment through a sense of character, but rather, it has been replaced, or was in the process of being replaced, "by monetary wealth as the measure of the masculine idea." Riemer intimates as well that "conspicuous con-sumption" in turn becomes the yardstick for validating masculinity. Thus Babbitt and men like him utilized consumption and the avenues of striv-ing upward as pathways to exercise their masculinity. Babbitt finds con-stant opportunities to link his daily routine toward a series of tropes that speak to a historical masculinity that once mattered; dealing in real estate becomes a battle; driving his automobile, an adventure.[19]

The idea of equating masculinity with economic wealth has a long history in the United States and in Canada. This becomes especially glaring in the post-industrial world, where working with your hands came with a surrogate sense of masculinity. Moving ahead seventy years from Lewis's *Babbitt* to David Mamet's *Glengarry Glen Ross*, one sees the acceleration of this process as well as its nefarious impact. In both the play and the early 1990s film version, whoever makes the most sales wins. Their identity as men, as providers, and as humans is tied to how successful they are in selling questionable real estate. To make matters worse and possibly, more dramatic, the salesmen who populate Mamet's world are pitted against each other and their performance is publicly displayed; humiliation and shame result for the losers. The film is a particularly cutthroat portrait of capitalism and allows for a playing out of the most base and unchecked male passions. Women are completely excluded from this world—as they are in many of Mamet's works—primarily because they exhibit characteristics that threaten men and their values. As Andrea Greenbaum has remarked, there is no room for compassion or nurturing in Mamet's worlds.[20]

The movie version of *Glengarry* is almost noir-like in its impact: dark and rainy, bars and offices, trench coats and cars, pepper the film to create a very unpleasant and claustrophobic atmosphere. The content picks up from *Death of a Salesman* but expands on Miller's focus to implicate more than one man. Surprisingly, what *Glengarry Glen Ross* alludes to is *Fight Club*. It prefigures the stresses and pressures oriented around commerce and the sales racket and there is also an enormous amount of macho posturing. Language is extreme and men are, plain and simple, not happy in a society that forces them to make a living in often demeaning ways. Performance in almost Butlerian terms is a key feature in both works. Not being able to perform creates a barrier; it excludes those who can't close and thus can't succeed. *Glengarry* and *Fight Club* offer hints and generalities of this situation, glimpses of men unable to fulfill this masculine expectation. Perhaps the most bizarre version of masculinity—the final stage in its mediated destruction is found in *American Psycho*.

One of the most disturbing characters created in the past few decades is Bret Easton Ellis's Patrick Bateman. In his 1991 book, *American Psycho*,[21] Ellis presents a despicable and evil construction, which ranks as a memorable look at the excesses of the previous decade. The book is a shopping list of 1980s excess, complete with every designer and shop in existence in New York. The book is also a satire and celebration of over-the-top capitalism, the triumph of money, and the constant desire to spend. The characters are vacuous and shallow, but successful and young. They are obscenely rich and spend money on expensive dinners, fancy clothes, and the latest clubs, which cost a small fortune to enter and indulge.[22] Not one of the characters in Bateman's circle is likeable; no one has any redeeming qualities; no one has compassion or sympathy. Unlike, for example, Ellis's fellow Young Turk, Jay McInerny and *Bright Lights, Big City*, his people and his New York are devoid of humanity completely. Ellis creates a world that is fully self-absorbed, rude, conniving, and shameless. The way they talk about women and to women and the manner in which they treat those less fortunate, from cab drivers to the homeless, is exceedingly offensive. In essence the book creates a world of monstrous excess where not one male character is even gracious.

Prior to publication the book had already generated a firestorm of controversy.[23] Critics and cultural commentators, novelists and clergy, all sounded off on the horrors depicted in the book. Many felt that the content was too excessive and that it would compel some readers to copy the violence described in the book. Naturally there were those who pointed out the issues with this argument but, given the revelations of Paul Bernardo's horrific actions in Ontario, many were to say the least, disturbed. Many wondered why an author would even create such an odious incarnation.

The question most readers asked was, what was Bret Easton Ellis thinking? This chronicler of the young and pretty in New York and L.A. had go to an unsettling length to be overt in his descriptions of murder. Was he motivated by a desire to shock and to compose such an unsettling account for intellectual reasons? Or was he trying to simply create a book that would sell and make him rich? According to Richard Bernstein, "Ellis apparently allowed himself to imagine what is absolutely the worst that one human being can do to another and then described it in stomach-churning detail."[24] What confounds the reader in the most gruesome sense is the horror of mass murder juxtaposed with luxury and beauty in the form of clothes, furniture, and grooming. Some have suggested that this is a plot device designed for any number of complex reasons. Others have pointed to the violence inherent in consumption and the rise of both the global image market and the globalization of trade.

The first mention of murder and violence occurs quite innocuously and suddenly—a throw in, possibly—on page 52: Bateman, the narrator says, "I have a knife with a serrated blade in the pocket of my Valentino jacket and I'm tempted to gut McDermott with it right here in the entranceway, maybe slice his face open, sever his spine . . . " It comes out of nowhere. We know that Bateman and his group are rude and selfish, obnoxious and offensive, but the severity of the comment causes one to stop and gasp at the hostility. If we did not know about the book's contents and the surrounding controversy over the movie, it would indeed be a puzzle.

A little while later, on page 63, another casual remark is made. Bateman states: "I flossed too hard this morning and I can still taste the copper residue of swallowed blood in the back of my throat." Then, on page 76, the reader gets his first clear indication of Patrick the serial killer, the deranged murderer. He states, "I come to the conclusion that Patricia is safe tonight, that I am not going to unexpectedly pull a knife out and use it on her just for the sake of doing so, that I am not going to get any pleasure watching her bleed from slits I've made by cutting her throat or slicing her neck open or gouging her eyes out." He is truly deranged and totally unhinged. The man is, in fact, a monster.

The question is, what kind of monster? Is he someone beyond control or is he responsible? Everyone would agree that he is a classic psychopath and like Norman Bates, the character from Hitchcock's film *Psycho*, he is mentally deranged. Yet he is very much a part of his cultural moment—the 1980s—and cannot be divorced from it.[25]

Bateman is excessively vain. He constantly preens in front of the mirror and is obsessively concerned about every facet of his appearance. The time, money, and energy applied to his face, his hair, his nails, and his cleaning rituals are obscene.[26] One could argue that all this attention to excess and appearance, to grooming and to how one looks—a seminal pattern in the novel—is part and parcel of the culture of monstrosity. The Latin word *monstrare*, means to show.[27] According to critic Russell Kilbourn, the "monstrous is always in some sense concerned with representation, and by the same token representation is always in some sense monstrous." Key to this analogy is the fact that the monstrous, in this case Bateman, is always compared to established standards of beauty and especially to humanity.[28]

Think of any horror film monster or any physically repulsive creation and the fact is the "monster" does not *fit* in. It is "other" to the established norms of aesthetics and of course, to the established codes and conventions of how and what we define as human.[29] Whether it is Frankenstein, The Wolf Man, Leather Face, or some other creation, we know that this monster does not belong and cannot fit into society. The monster or the American Psycho creates havoc, kills, tortures, rapes, and maims—accordingly—because it or he cannot be a part of society no matter what steps he takes to blend in. Regardless if the monster tries to mask—a key idea—his appearance—he cannot ever become fully human and cannot fully integrate.

This is disturbing for a number of reasons. To some extent it grants an allowance for antisocial or psychopathic behavior. In our post-modern world, we want everyone to have a chance, even the monster. The reader never pities Bateman in the same way or on the same level that one feels a touch of compassion for Frankenstein. We do not feel empathy or sympathy for Ellis's creation. Mark Storey, borrowing a platform for Thomas B. Byers, suggests that this nefarious construction is the consequence of the fear of things "falling apart." Byers terms this "pomophobia" and implies that this is not so much about the "implications of the crisis for constructions of masculine identity," but rather, a redefining of the definition of masculinity.[30] Ellis's creation takes the reader to the awful extremes of male behavior. Whether or not this is a detailed satire or a complex, Dantiesque imagining is not the point. It is about the postmodern analysis of the "monstrous heart of masculinity."[31]

That of course is the extraordinary extreme; *American Psycho* presents a narcissistic personality at the edge; and it is overblown and gratuitous. Yet it speaks to a fascination with the culture of consumption and in particular, elements within that culture such as male vanity, body image, and obsession with fashion. Most do not go anywhere near that level of mania but there are many who are enormously concerned about image, style, and appearance. The interest in books for men, specifically here, "how-to" manuals, has exploded in the past ten years. Searching through the style section of a large bookstore yields dozens of titles on how men should dress, what they should own, and what they can do to improve how they look. A quick glance at Amazon.com brings up numerous books on virtually every facet of dress, from cuff links to shirts. It was rare a decade ago to see books on these topics and if you wanted to find them, you had to dig deep. Alan Flusser's two volumes were the standards, and to some extent still are. The explosion on dress, style, and comportment books for men now covers virtually every budget, scenario, and environment. The Christmas catalogue for one major Canadian bookstore chain had a full page devoted to these offerings. Some were quite serious and worthy, while others were forms of miscellany and compendium-like.

Russell Smith's *Men's Style: The Thinking Man's Guide to Dress*, is a very detailed examination of how to dress properly and what kinds of clothing to buy. One of the dominant points that Smith attempts to get across the fact that it is proper and almost artistic for a man to be well-dressed. "There is," he writes, "nothing unmanly about a proud and meticulous dress."[32] Smith goes into a fair amount of detail in his attempt to convey the importance of aesthetics and style, class and art, in the way a man chooses to adorn himself. Chapters in his book cover shoes, suits, ties, shirts, scent, and hair.

Michael Flocker's *The Metrosexual Guide to Style* encompasses virtually every facet of behavior and deportment ranging from grooming and fitness to home décor. Like Smith's guide, there is also a serious attempt to set the record straight about proper overall style. It is something to be considered and not to be dismissed as trivial. Flocker writes:

> The new breed of man is one of style, sophistication and self-awareness. He is just as strong and confident as his predecessor, but far more diverse in his interests, his tastes and most importantly, his self-perception. Secure in his masculinity, he no longer has to spend his life defending it. He has options.[33]

Somehow there was an increasing gap between style and sophistication and how men were supposed to capture those qualities. Perhaps in the past one's father mentored one in the art of dressing and looking good, but this must have skipped a generation or two. Books on style, design, and taste, specifically directed to men, are a growing market. In the preface to Thomas Fink's 2006 *The Man's Book*, the point is made in the first sentence:

> *The Man's Book* is the authoritative handbook for men's customs, habits and pursuits—a vade-mecum for modern-day manliness. It comprehensively examines the elements of a man's life and provides a guide to the year ahead.[34]

Men now need manuals to learn how to act manly and guides to look things up, books to peruse, and almanacs to consult. While in some way or form these have always existed, their presence today speaks strongly to the fact that men are in need of guidance. It is not guidance on how to be more humane or more moral, but guidance on how to be more masculine. Interspersed throughout Fink's book are constant references to the James Bond ideal; malt scotch selections and notations on chivalry that hearken back to Castiglione. Anachronistic episodes include pipe and cigar information as well as a passage on different hairs for shaving brushes, of which badger hair is the best. These antiquated references parallel the big push toward sophisticated technology in the form of the Braun electric self-cleaning razor, which accordingly, is pretty much the most amazing piece of technology one can bring close to the skin.

It is important to note that the counterpoint to so many books and manuals that focus on grooming are volumes that relate tales of how pathetic and sad it is to be a man in contemporary society. Codicils to these are memoirs of some masculine experience or undertaking, designed to detail a test of one's strengths.

A recent spate of books also seeks to examine the masculine condition from an ethnographic point of view. Charlie LeDuff's *US Guys* is a standout. A *New York Times* columnist, LeDuff takes a rollicking tour of the United States and relates the bizarre variety of masculine experiences he encounters. LeDuff details extremes in masculine behavior and the tough time most men are having just making do. He profiles men at a gay rodeo, Detroit homicide cops, and arena football washouts. The common element is a sense of frustration and desperation; that there is no hope but one must still try. LeDuff's book is almost old-fashioned in its use of colloquialisms and its jargon. That is, perhaps the point. In attempting to harness some semblances of the past, perhaps some of that historical dignity and success can also be recaptured.

LeDuff does not like what is happening in the contemporary United States. He is attempting to speak for many men who have been marginalized. He is angry that there are very few opportunities left to work, to succeed, and even to get by. The anger is tangible, visceral, and pointed. It is directed at wealthy America and at large corporations, governments, and those who have let their people down. He hates the fact that men now have to perform rather than just be. They have to be like women in his interpretation. "A new masculine myth," he writes, "is emerging in an ultra-competitive city (New York) with an ultra-competitive job market and men are being told that brains and charisma are no longer enough; they must now look the part as well if they're going to get the *edge*, whether it be in the boardroom or the bedroom." [35]

This is something that women have had to do for quite some time. Now men have to do it as well. In his profile of the editor of *Cargo* magazine, LeDuff is told that men's vanity is the new "gold rush." [36] A traditionalist who rejects the superficiality of consumer culture, LeDuff and others like him have a hard time understanding the changes and adapting to what is expected of them. That is why all of this is so troubling and so foreign: they have to buy into the process of looking good and being fit. What he hits at is the fact that now they are not only expected to provide—an issue in itself—but be "on" and up-to-date as well.

And this is perhaps the main reason why so many men seek to embrace things other than what is celebrated by male vanity culture, especially in the realm of reading. Perhaps they want an antidote to the perceived softness of contemporary culture and in terms that are reminiscent of *Fight Club*, they want to reject the culture of creams and moisturizers that so bother LeDuff. For him, these are not real things and they gloss over the true things that make a man and that define one's character. It is why *Fight Club* and *The Perfect Storm* are perennially popular. It is why war memoirs and adventure stories still resonate. But that is not the whole story. While these offerings continue to thrive, they do exist with other versions of masculinity, which speak to other segments of the male population who want to indulge in something new and wish to go beyond variations of the old templates. Men who read these novels and non-fiction offerings on a whole series of topics may be just as willing to embrace issues of the new style and comportment.

There has been a recent wave of books for boys—and men—that have a more sensitive hero at the core. He is usually motivated to do well in a way that differs from the Victorian, Edwardian, and pulp-styled heroes of old. There is much more of an emphasis on emotion and caring, sympathy, and feeling than in previous groupings. From mysteries to science fiction, memoir, and high-brow leanings, a generous hero is now almost natural. Whether in the work of Gordon Korman, Louis Sachar, or any number of the now burgeoning array of writers for boys, there has been a renaissance in the adventure story. And what is interesting is the fact that while the hero is now a much kindler and gentler individual and the content of many of these stories is often eco-friendly, the diametric opposite is at work in the world of video games and online combat. Violence and killing are the order of the day in virtually every popular game that is released.

NOTES

1. Robert Cohen, *Amateur Barbarians* (New York: Scribner, 2009), p. 7.
2. Mark Gallagher, *Action Figures: Men, Action Films, and Contemporary Adventure Narratives* (London/New York: Palgrave Macmillan, 2006), p. 22.
3. John F. Kasson, *Houdini, Tarzan, and the Perfect Man: The White Male Body and the Challenge of Modernity in America* (New York: Hill & Wang, 2001), p. 211.
4. John F. Kasson, *Houdini, Tarzan, and the Perfect Man*, p. 211.
5. James H. Maguire, "Fiction of the West," in *The Columbia History of the American Novel* (New York: Columbia University Press, 1991), p. 438.
6. Mark Gallagher, *Action Figures*, p. 22.
7. Anthony Swofford, *Jarhead: A Marine's Chronicle of the Gulf War* (London: Scribner, 2003).
8. Christopher Breu, *Hard-Boiled Masculinities* (Minneapolis: University of Minnesota Press, 2005), p. 1.
9. Christopher Breu, *Hard-Boiled Masculinities*, pp. 1, 2.
10. Thom Jones, *The Pugilist at Rest* (Boston: Little, Brown, 1993), p. 20.
11. Sally Robinson, "Men's Liberation, Men's Wounds: Emotion, Sexuality, and the Reconstruction of Masculinity in the 1970s," in *Boys Don't Cry?* ed. Milette Shamir and Jennifer Travis (New York: Columbia University Press, 2002), p. 220.
12. Sally Robinson, *Marked Men: White Masculinity in Crisis* (New York: Columbia University Press, 2000), p. 152. Italics in the original.
13. Sally Robinson, *Marked Men*, p. 180.
14. Fred L. Gardaphe, *From Wiseguys to Wise Men: The Gangster and Italian American Masculinities* (London: Routledge, 2006), pp. 15, 16.
15. Fred L. Gardaphe, *From Wiseguys to Wise Men*, p. 34.
16. James V. Catano, "Entrepreneurial Masculinity: Re-tooling the Self-made Man," *Journal of American and Comparative Cultures* 23, no. 2 (Summer 2000), p. 1.
17. John Micklewhait and Adrian Wooldrige, *The Company: A Short History of a Revolutionary Idea* (New York: Modern Library/Random House, 2003), p. 141.
18. James D. Riemer, "Rereading American Literature from a Men's Studies Perspective: Some Implications," in *The Making of Masculinities: The New Men's Studies*, ed. Harry Brod (Boston: Unwin Hyman, 1990), p. 294.
19. James D. Riemer, "Rereading American Literature from a Men's Studies Perspective," p. 294.
20. Andrea Greenbaum, "Brass Balls: Masculine Communication and the Discourse of Capitalism in David Mamet's *Glengarry Glen Ross*," *Journal of Men's Studies* 8, no. 1 (October 1999), p. 34.
21. Bret Easton Ellis, *American Psycho* (New York: Vintage, 1991). Subsequent page numbers are to this edition.
22. Russell J. A. Kilbourn, "American Frankenstein: Modernity's Monstrous Progeny," *Mosaic: A Journal for the Interdisciplinary Study of Literature* 38, no. 3 (September 2005), p. 169.
23. Meg Cox, "More Protests Seen as Psycho Nears Release," *Wall Street Journal*, February 22, 1991.
24. Richard Bernstein, "Shocked by the Printed Word," *Vancouver Sun*, January 19, 1991, p. D3.
25. See Mark Storey, "'And As Things Fell Apart': The Crisis of Postmodern Masculinity in Bret Easton Ellis's *American Psycho* and Dennis Cooper's *Frisk*," *Critique* 47, no. 1 (Fall 2005), note 3, and Russell J. A. Kilbourn, "American Frankenstein," p. 169.

26. Russell J. A. Kilbourn, "American Frankenstein," p. 169.

27. Cited in Russell J. A. Kilbourn, "American Frankenstein," p. 169.

28. Russell J. A. Kilbourn, "American Frankenstein," p. 170.

29. Russell J. A. Kilbourn, "American Frankenstein," p. 170.

30. Mark Storey, "'And As Things Fell Apart,'" p. 57.

31. Mark Storey, "'And As Things Fell Apart,'" p. 58.

32. Russell Smith, *Men's Style: The Thinking Man's Guide to Dress* (Toronto, ON: McClelland & Stewart, 2005), p. 11.

33. Michael Flocker, *The Metrosexual Guide to Style: A Handbook for the Modern Man* (New York: Da Capo Press, 2003), p. xiii.

34. Thomas Fink, *The Man's Book* (London: Weidenfeld & Nicolson, 2006), p. ix.

35. Charlie LeDuff, *US Guys: The True and Twisted Mind of the American Man* (New York: Penguin, 2006), p. 175.

36. Charlie LeDuff, *US Guys*, p. 176.

FIVE

History Revisited

At least two generations of men have grown up very comfortable with the power and presence of women in all spheres of western life. At work, in particular, this is less and less of an issue. One idea that makes this so relevant has been the rise of the single parent household, where women are the dominant caregivers. Men grew up seeing the woman/mother being the definitive voice and were not uncomfortable with this process in the public sphere. As more and more popular culture products were devoted to this theme, its acceptance permeated much of western society. From television shows, greeting cards, and novels to movies and music videos, the saturation by the mass media of this pronounced place of women seemed carried across generations. Yet, if David Brooks, Michael Kimmel, and Gary Cross—among others—are to be believed, there is a seeping out of the qualities that men have been suppressing, which leads to the cyclical crisis of masculinity.

One could argue that any attempt to decipher the complexities of male history owes much to the women's history movement. "As women's studies brought women into history, men's studies began to as how men had experienced history as men, as carriers of masculinity." Those who study the history of men are aware that the assumption of masculinity, that of having a "particular psychological identity, social role or cultural script" is a product "not of God, not of nature, but of historical process-es."[1] What is significant in this respect according to Catherine R. Stimpson, is that "most scholars in men's studies have concluded that gender, our sense of being masculine or feminine, is as much a human construct as the pyramids or pewter. Like all human constructs, gender systems can change."[2]

Perhaps the best way to understand the fact that male experience was a historically gendered issue is to look at one particular era of history which seems to encapsulate all of the societal forces "threatening" men. What is meant here is that men were having trouble meeting their male role demands: as husband, provider, warrior, or capitalist. Importantly, there was a residual concern about young boys and their traditional roles and paths to manhood.[3] This was the era that saw the rise of everything from the western novel to the creation of Tarzan. It was the heyday of the imperial adventure story and the incorporation of Darwinist principles into social discourse. It had Buffalo Bill, Teddy Roosevelt, and the modern Olympics as part and parcel of its culture. Movies were on the horizon, as were magazines and newspapers with comic strips, half-tone photographs, and photography. Organized sports and professional sporting contents, football, boxing, and baseball came into being during this period as well, giving men numerous surrogate activities, both as participants and spectators, to test themselves.

This is the period from 1870 until just before the outbreak of World War I. Academically, it was a time that "triggered an interest in the historical meaning of masculinity." Over forty years ago, an essay by John Higham set the tone for much future debate and discussion over the male experience. Higham, looking back at this period, pinned the growth of sports, the rebellion against the routine of industrial urban culture, and the rise of jingoism as "indicators" that provoked a changing interpretation about the issues surrounding masculinity.[4]

In the final decades of the nineteenth century men were confronted with forces that provoked them to question their role and to rethink their place in society. A reorientation of the male experience began, one that was a backlash against the erosion of the traditions that had been in place and as well, a reaction against what was being perceived as a feminization of society. Men sought to reinvigorate their masculinity in numerous ways, both consciously and unconsciously, based on the fear that they would have to share what had taken so long to achieve. As well, they attempted to transfer this to their sons. The wave of newness, foreignness, and plain change were acting against most men who could not readily comprehend the modifications expected of them. Nonetheless, they made valiant attempts to prevent being swallowed up by industrialization and modernity. Within this time frame, throughout the English-speaking world, the most tangible element of vulnerability seemed to be their "manliness." Bombarded, threatened, cajoled, and in many cases, made redundant, whether in reality or in misguided impression, men sought to rejuvenate their vitality and soul by action and by pronounced contemplation, by deed and design, through dream and reality.

War was always the definitive barometer in defining the epitome of masculinity. The U.S. Civil War in particular had been a gut-wrenching, soul-destroying, and nation-bifurcating event that left a legacy of hatred, injury, and death, but for those too young to have participated, a gaping hole in the opportunity to test oneself. War, despite being increasingly mechanized and much more destructive than in the past, still held enormous attraction for men and boys. It was a testing ground and a proving ground for the ultimate virtue. According to Waller R. Newell,

> of all the traditional virtues, none is more directly connected with manhood than courage in war. Indeed, in both ancient Greek and Latin, the words for courage are synonymous of the words for manly virtue in general. *Andreia*, the Greek word for courage, is derived from the word for a "manly man"—*aner*, somewhat like the Spanish word *hombre*.[5]

Newell makes it clear that it was understood that when classifying someone a "manly man" it was quite obvious that this man was different, in essence "a manly man is understood in contrast with a mere 'human being.'" The mere "human being" was part of the "undistinguished mass of mankind, including women, children" and others who could not participate in war by bearing arms.[6]

As I have detailed in a previous book, going back in time to retrieve the essential ingredients of what was threatened, the most common and potent spice is through war or some approximation of it. This involved a noble tradition, a time-honored brotherhood, and an essential form of camaraderie and was deemed both invigorating and healthy for men and their nations. It appealed to all the dulled senses in a most bracing series of ways. War, or at least the thought of it, would be the supreme test of one's manliness and an emblem of character of the highest degree. But if there were no actual wars to fight, then suitable alternatives would have to do. These would provide the exercises, the mental and physical training grounds that would sharpen the skills and hone the traits necessary for combat of any kind—should the need arise. The definitive statement and testament of masculine endeavor up until quite recently was participation in war. For most of western history war was the supreme test of masculinity and in the period between the late reign of Queen Victoria and the outbreak of World War I, this continued to be the case despite the perceived erosion of established conceptual interpretations of war.[7] This is perhaps why the training of boys in sports and other proxies receives such an inordinate amount of attention.

One of the most interesting investigations into the above combination is Ray Raphael's examination of the content and effect of war, coming of age, and socialization on young men. "In most cultures," he writes, "boys must repudiate their prior vulnerability and aspire to a matrix of personality traits more appropriate to manhood: strength, endurance, courage, confidence and self-reliance."[8] This is a trying period in a boy's life and the implication is that in order for a boy to move into manhood, he must begin to "deny his childish past." This is problematic in a culture that is increasingly oriented to keeping men boys as long as possible. But in attempting to negate his former identity and create a new one, he often latches on to or is told to follow a suitable model or comport himself in a specific way. Sports stars, military heroes, and powerful men in general often serve as the ideals. Structured initiation rites aid in this process by helping the boy to overcome formidable obstacles. Drama and difficulty are often aspect of the test, which can take the form of hiking, climbing, or succeeding in a sport. The above has been the subject of countless movies and TV shows, from *Stand By Me* to *The Bad News Bears*; many Hollywood products attempt to trace the evolution toward manhood, with all its trials and tribulations.

The "dominant paradigm" for understanding male experience has been the theory of male sex-role identity, (MSRI). The theory suggests that,

> For individuals to become psychologically mature as members of their sex, they must acquire male or female "sex role identity," manifested by having the sex appropriate traits, attitudes, and interests that psychologically "validate" or "affirm" their biological sex. However, many factors conspire to thwart the attainment of healthy sex-role identity, especially for males.[9]

Regardless if this is now being challenged, the fact remains that men, in seeking to redefine, validate, or recapture their threatened masculinity, look toward various agencies and time frames to choose appropriate models. An attempted revival of masculinity in its various guises was a definite way to attain what was perceived as a "healthy sex-role identity." The enormous effort at channeling resources in the direction of boys, only buttresses this fact.

In the pre–World War II period things became blurry. The Great Depression had pummeled male initiative, enterprise, and ego. Once again though, the specter of war offered up limitless potential, just as it did in the pre–World War I era. The success of the warrior male during World War II, at least in the United States, was significant.[10] There was a robust confidence on the American scene, a chance once again to test their unlimited national muscularity. With the outbreak of war, all the armed services and the vast might of the American economy geared up for this huge undertaking. Once it began, it picked up enormous momentum and seemed nearly impossible to stop. Virtually every facet of society was recalibrated toward the war effort and it grew to unheard-of proportions. There was little room for introspection and less for alternatives. In some ways this syndrome bottled some of its most explosive forces, to be opened after the cessation of hostilities. The factors devoted to the creation of a supreme masculine archetype during World War II resonated into the post-war period and continue to impact contemporary American culture half a century later.[11]

One dominant archetype in the period in and around World War II— one which would served as a point of departure for many others, was the "loner" as hero. Constructed in part from the popular culture of the time, this autonomous individual—whether cowboy, detective, soldier,or superhero—seemed to reaffirm for many men the importance of masculinity in a time when technology was taking over.[12] Whether exceptional as loner or part of a group composed of those from different backgrounds with different skills, this archetype came to the fore and exemplified a way to conduct oneself as well as a model to aspire. He lingered on in the postwar period as a fantasy element for men to summon when involved in the drudgery of the organization or when trying to adapt to the post-war environment.

The 1950s were a time of enormous ambivalence for the male. On the one hand there was the affirmed stereotype of the supremely masculine male as defined by the soldier and in most cases, from the cinematic soldier in many war and western films. This military man was ideally expected to lay down his arms, put his nightmares away, and adopt the customs and conventions of the period. For many this meant making the transitions to the new suburban male. On the other hand, alternative male role models started to come into being, thanks in many cases to the mass media. These could range from the innocuous father to the beatnik to the rebel. In some instances, maleness and masculinity were defined by rejecting bourgeois values and embracing alternative lifestyle choices. These could be as diverse as the motorcycle gang member, the hot-rod-der, or the man who rejects the city for the country. There was extraordinary fragmentation in certain geographic locales and in media reports of what was happening. In order to feel somewhat useful and possibly artistic, the handyman was an appealing, if slight, pose for certain men to adopt. The focus on literature and poetry that the Beats' projected was grandly appealing in that it provided a virile masculinity that was totally non-traditional. The artist, whether painter or writer, was adopted by magazines and newspapers as a new role model for men. Profiles and pictures of Jackson Pollack and Ernest Hemingway implied that not only was it okay to be creative, but that one could be supremely creative and excessive in one's masculinity. Both the painter and the writer exuded a unique American masculinity that left no doubt that they were, at least to the readers of *Life* magazine, definitively male.[13]

Pollock has been typecast as the epitome of the masculine artist. He was drawn to create art so different and so unique that perhaps the only way to retain his edge was to adopt a severe "macho pose." Commenting on the pictures that appeared in *Life* in 1949, critic Peter Schjeldahl suggests, "his helplessly photogenic, clenched features, broadcast by *Life* in 1949, made him a pinup of seething manhood akin to Brando."[14] One could compare him to the equally famous Picasso, but as far as their masculine appeal, Pollock wins by a large canvas. Picasso seemed to be about quantity, both in women and in output.

The *Life* profile presented an image of the artist as robust and manly. Pollock was in reality intensely depressed and often insecure. Yet the picture that the media created of him was that of a definitive man, one comfortable and at ease with life and the creative process. Coming from Cody, Wyoming only added to the masculine allure trumped up by the media. Pollock was presented as a man capable of a form of artistic independence that was fully harmonious with a statute of masculinity to which many Americans could relate. Deborah Solomon sums up the famous photography shoot and the resulting article in very interesting terms:

> In a denim jacket, blue jeans, and paint-spattered work boots, he crouched on the floor and ran earth through his fingers, giving a performance as the rough, rugged all-American genius of his ambitions. [15]

Pollock posed as a working man who knew his way around a farm and was equally comfortable in the world of abstract art—a movement that most people possessed little in the way of understanding. He adopted the persona of a cowboy and implied through demeanor and gesture a level of confidence that was absent from his true self. One could even suggest that he was leading the way into the 1950s; performing as a supremely confident man, one who could be an artist, yet hiding so much anxiety and fear.

Both Pollock and the even more famous exemplar of American artistic masculinity, Ernest Hemingway, owe much of their popular public persona to the fact that they were profiled by *Life* magazine. The power of *Life* during the 1940s and 1950s to enshrine a specific image in the collective mindset of American and world audiences was almost unrivaled. Henry Luce's American Century idea actually worked as a promotional device; and even while television began to make inroads into the magazine's power, it still retained influence that was unparalleled. It did not matter that some liberties were taken; a few facts stretched, or in Hemingway's case, elongated to the point of fable, for people wanted to see and read about these heroes. [16]

Pollock never left the United States. His counterpoint was the older, worldlier writer. As a larger-than-life creator, Ernest Hemingway was even more prominent on the world state as a hallmark of American masculinity incarnate. Despite being afflicted with a variety of ailments and psychological issues, he came to stand as the quintessential embodiment of the American artist. He grew up hunting and fishing and reached some level of heroic fame as an ambulance driver during World War I. He roamed the world as a foreign correspondent, saw violence in the form of war and killing, indulged in excessive drink, and hobnobbed with a who's who of the twentieth century, from Charles de Gaulle to Gertrude Stein. Hemingway's writing broke new ground in the same way that Pollock's painting did. It was fresh, startling, and wholly modern. It was stripped of adornment and superfluous words, standing alone as a unique American creation. [17]

In his profile of Hemingway, Paul Johnson summarizes his impact and his worldview by concisely detailing Hemingway's essence, which was intertwined with who he was:

> Hemingway saw the Americans as vigorous, active, forceful, even Violent people, doers, achievers, creators, conquerors and pacifiers, hunters and builders. He was a vigorous, active, forceful, even violent person himself.[18]

"Action was his theme," writes Johnson,[19] physical, visceral, wide-ranging actions. He chose a course that was not necessarily original, but one that spoke to him in an almost kinetic way. Killing, roving, and moving, fighting, fishing—all came to be dominant themes in his writing and his life. Hemingway felt the compulsion to act and to try something, regardless of the outcome. And this translated into his mythology and his appeal among readers. There was also the public fascination with the growing legend and the increasingly iconic stature. Again, Johnson is dead on in highlighting Hemingway's appeal:

> The essence of Hemingway's fiction is observing boxers, fishermen, bullfighters, soldiers, writers, sportsmen, or almost anyone who has definite and skilled action to perform, trying to live a good and honest life, according to the values of each, and usually failing.[20]

This was as applicable to his life as it was to the characters he created. His persona merged with his creations and his characters. He became Hemingwayesque; he wore the safari suits, grew the beard, was tanned, and appeared virile. He had his photographs taken at the right time, with the dead game or the once struggling marlin, always posed in a way that said "I did this." Even his Karsh photograph implies a magnetism and a dynamic essence.

Hemingway became the mold and the template for the masculine, active artist. He lived the life of action and sport and expended his enormous talent. Others often tried to follow suit. Norman Mailer and a host of imitators tried also to be larger than life and to balance the image that Hemingway made almost impossible to follow. For most men though, it was a pure fantasy, something to be dreamed, not attempted.

Glancing at a book of advertisements from the 1950s, one is struck by the tableaux of men hanging out together in a defined form of male space. Whether it is the workshop or the den, the garage or on a golf course, one sees numerous clusterings of men together. Often in these advertisements, a beverage is prominently displayed. The men are relaxed, at ease, and visibly comfortable. They are glad to be there. They are listening to one of their group talk and are interested. Whether drawn in an illustration or photographed for a glossy magazine, the dominant message is one of calmness and security. The men in these staged depictions obviously feel good being together. Perhaps it rekindles their experience in the army. There is no posturing, no strutting. Another series of images that populates the pages of magazines from this era are a sequence of advertisements featuring a father and son working together, sitting side by side, or simply in close proximity. The family in this instance is a man and a boy. Yet the family, whether shown or implied, is key. Numerous advertisements also featured a comfortable family setting. Everyone is happy or content and there is no strife. The residence or space in which the members are situated is important. In and around the home or near by, it functions as a significant symbol. [21] This point was hammered home throughout the 1950s. According to the dominant narrative of the time—and excluding the *Playboy* exceptions—men were supposed to be married, were supposed to be home and were supposed to be good and active fathers. The advertisements in these magazines and sometimes on television reflected values that Elaine Tyler May has suggested were essential to combating "internal subversion." Normal, heterosexual behavior that exuded maturity and responsibility was fundamental and at times suggested to be almost vital in maintaining the core values of American society. [22] The father had to stay home and was supposed to perform his role as a respectable husband, loving father, and breadwinner. Popular culture has long perpetuated this ideal—situation comedies most notably come to mind: *Leave It to Beaver* of course, but films and advertising also conveyed this idea.

The problem was that the above was illusory. Men were often not too happy to be home. Many were discontented and disgruntled and dreamed of getting out—both literally and figuratively. [23] This explains the resurgence or focus on things that were specifically oriented towards men, a form of nascent "guy culture" that was beginning to be enormously popular in the 1950s. There was a strong pull among many men to do away with responsibility and to chuck it all and roam. Jack Kerouac picked up on this, as did other elements of popular culture.

The motivation to want to opt out and to almost regress and hang out with other guys is a strong element within many western cultures. That is why pubs and pool halls exist as predominantly male spaces. Men often want to forget the pressures and complexities of being a father and husband and move into a zone where they perceive their lives to be quite carefree. One of the notable changes that have occurred in recent years is the desire to prolong the benefits of being a guy without the responsibilities of accepting manhood. Unlike during the 1950s, some have speculated that there is now a protracted extension of male adolescence, which many men gleefully jump into. The space devoted to glorifying youth in popular culture and mass media has a tendency to trickle out into everyday life. [24]

In many instances, men choose, deliberately, not to grow up and to avoid responsibility and commitment. There is also a concomitant desire to isolate themselves from the pangs of intimacy. A great deal of thought was expended on this subject in the 1950s. Men who deliberately chose to avoid the necessary precondition of acknowledged maturity—that is, marriage—were looked upon as being a trifle suspect. Whether their masculinity was questioned or their selfishness was raised, the man who knowingly wished to stay unencumbered by marriage and the obligations of fatherhood was attacked as being deviant, among other things.

Eventually, this marked deviance evolved from a pathological condition to a popular affliction. The name for this syndrome—the one that eventually stuck and became part of contemporary parlance was derived from Dan Kiley's 1983 book, *The Peter Pan Syndrome: Men Who Have Never Grown Up*. This catchy title and catch-all book was a harbinger of the self-help, bifurcated gender discussion industry that was to reach its crescendo in the 1990s. A bestseller when it was released, Kiley's book spoke to the lackadaisical way many men were raised—without any real commitment to anything substantial. Importantly, men who were reared in the 1960s and 1970s never had to work for what previous generations had to struggle for. According to Kiley, things were simply too good and life too carefree for hard work and any form of commitment. Things in this affluent, leisure-based society came too easy and thus, there was no need for men to grow up and shoulder real responsibility.[25]

Although there is a new version of this treatment every few years, the essential ideas hold currency and are often reworked every once in a while for further popular consumption. One way that this comes out is in the endless relationship material that circulates in press and online. This is accented by a movie version of some man who refuses to grow up and accept responsibility by getting married and fathering and rearing children. Often he is tricked into being mature by having to care for someone thrust suddenly into his life, such as an orphan or an aging parent.

The notion of the double-bind, commented on earlier in this work, invites confusion and seems in many cases to send out a variety of mixed messages. This conflicting duality, where men are expected to be everything at one and the same time has, of course, its feminine parallel. One of the reasons that the "Beauty and the Beast" dichotomy comes up so often is in fact because of its longevity as a staple in the realm of masculine deportment. Historically, the fairy tale from which it is derived has been around in various versions for hundreds of years and has served as a significant pedagogic template for boys and girls. Jack Zipes intimates that whether it is Perrault's version or someone else's, there is a definite civilizing process involved with a healthy dose of domestication. In essence, for moral, social, and societal reason, the man must be tamed and taught.[26]

Susan Bordo's analysis of the Disney version of the fairy tale, *Beauty and the Beast*, points to numerous contractions about masculine behavior. On one hand, the Beast is an animal with urges and a temper, but on the other he is gentle and an intellectual. He is contrasted with Gaston the hunter, who looks normal but is in reality a true beast.[27] According to Henry Giroux's reading, Belle is capable of civilizing the Beast by teaching him the fundamentals of etiquette, such as learning to eat properly and the social graces involved in dance. As a result, she "turns this narcissistic, muscle-bound tyrant into a 'new' man, one who is sensitive, caring and loving."[28] Yet another interpretation of this movie and it moral suggests, "maleness is associated, both metaphorically and literally, with beastliness."[29]

Disney has been one of the most successful corporations in the United States for a long period of time. Beginning with animation and moving into merchandising, theme parks, feature film, and television, its hold on the popular imagination is immense. The versions of films, specifically animated, that they produce, often have the power to supplant the traditional source of the tale. By modifying the content of an established fairy tale, the Disney version reigns as definitive for most viewers. "So, when offering time-tested mythic material," observes Richard Schickel, "Disney was careful to present it in every day, down to earth artistic terms, that offered no difficulties of understanding to the large audience . . ."[30]

Gaston, the most obvious character in *Beauty and the Beast*, is not part of the original story. But it is Gaston in particular who exudes the most venal of masculine characteristics. Not only is he shallow and vain, but he is also ignorant. A hyper-masculine caricature, he hunts and drinks, fights and spits, bullies and lies. He also utters the most anachronistic nonsense heard on the screen for quite some time.[31] Gaston consciously seeks out male social contacts and male gatherings as spaces where he cannot just relax but exercise his status as an alpha male. He lives outside and publicly. Gaston may look good in the "Tom of Finland" sense, in that he possesses the physique of a bodybuilder, but it is a fantastic and overblown exaggeration.[32] Gaston spends his nights at the bar or pub and regales his fellow drinkers with his exploits. The Beast, on the other hand, is confined to his castle. He cannot go out and he most certainly cannot go out with the guys. He reads, we are to assume, based on the library in his castle, which becomes both his refuge and his connection to Belle.

For many men, getting together for a golf weekend or a hunting trip is often motivated by the desire not just to be away or to get away, but substantially, to be away from women. The presence of women acts as a form of surveillance and as a "moderating influence" on men's behavior. Banishing the women does not necessarily alleviate their spirit, for as Jake MacDonald writes, "even when they're not on the scene their absence is a kind of presence."[33] Guy's weekends and being with men only rekindle a time in a man's life when he was surrounded by men and women were a different form of influence. In essence, for many men, it brings them back to their youth.

Many men are attracted to the notion of staying young and as often as possible, recapturing anything that rekindles the glory days of youth. We pay for, buy, and, of course, consume so much that gives us the illusion of staying young in some way or form. Even working out is much more than a health orientation. One of the reasons why there has been an explosion in sales of retro games and knick-knacks and authentic products from past decades is that grown men are buying these items as a way to forget about being grown up but in particular, they wish to recapture something special from their past. As Gary Cross notes,

> In many ways, but especially in our nostalgia for the commercial culture of our youth—in collecting our childhood toys or restoring our teenage cars—we literally bought back our youth. [34]

Sometimes it is hard to separate the period of adolescence from adulthood. The boundaries are increasingly blurred and undefined. Aging used to be a natural process and part of the life cycle. Advertisements in prominent publications for everything from workout equipment to supplements attempt to banish these distinctions. One ad features a seventy-year-old man with a physique that rivals most body builders. It is quite bizarre to look at the photograph of Dr. Life and see that he has stopped time. The incongruence of what used to be an advanced age with this "young" physique takes a lot of getting used to. It has the same impact of seeing someone you know is quite old, after a successful plastic surgery procedure.

It is certainly not just about men. Society in general seems to be focused on the recapturing of youth and has set up a vibrant and lucrative "nostalgia" industry with that specific purpose in mind. Hobbies and collections that would have been deemed problematic, had they been in the open a few years ago, now seem quite common. Lego now has a sizeable adult consumer base, known as Adult Fans of Lego, or AFOLs, which not only makes a fair amount of money for the company but is vital in stimulating interest in the building blocks. In his book about the culture of adult LEGO enthusiasts, journalist Jonathan Bender relates the fascination with building towers and other sculpture with a rekindling of the childhood memories of wanting to build and building with his father. He writes,

> For the true fan of Lego the bricks can never be put away forever. People have built their entire careers, relationships, and lives around this toy. They have developed a language and commerce, all in celebration of pursuing a childhood passion together. And I wanted in to that world. I wanted to build like they build. I also wanted to recapture what I used to feel as a child, while building. [35]

Christopher Noxon has coined the term "rejuvenile" to characterize this process. Noxon suggests that this phenomenon has taken on extremes in its boundaries. He intimates that it is no longer necessary to grow up and give up all the trappings that were once the hallmark of being a kid. Noxon cites statistics and figures to buttress his thesis: the average age of those watching cartoons is well over eighteen; the plethora of cartoon characters found in offices and on desks is quite high; and, just to hit the point home, living at home is far more common among those aged twenty to thirty-four. All of this implies that there is a marked and conscious attempt to identify with the "kid inside." [36]

Noxon implies rather strongly that the appeal of shows like *The Simpsons* and the sustained popularity of the *Star Wars* franchise is in much more than commercial. It is oriented around a desire to both stay and feel young, mentally and physically. If you do not take part or at least feign an interest then it quickly becomes obvious that you lose the capacity to interact with those who do, regardless of age. From a marketing point of view, you can become redundant if you don't pay attention. [37] Given the fact that so many "rejuveniles" are affluent, the marketing aspect is significant. But it is not everything. A substantial part of the appeal in fact is the orientation around recapturing all that that means to you, to different people and the enormous impact of the nostalgic component in their collective memory. Most wish to mentally touch some element of their youth as Bender implies with Lego.

No matter who you are, when you think back to your formative years as a young person, things seem to come out as clearer and much simpler than life is to you in contemporary terms. As referred to earlier, there are constant attempts to recapture spirits and essences that many feel were better "way back when." This is exactly the same process that propels the cyclical reexamination of the men's movements and the crises that are touted every few decades. Beginning in the late 1980s, the problems affecting the role of the man in society and the changes "threatening" traditional masculinity were articulated in a series of books that sold extremely well and were featured throughout the media. Three in particular attempted to define and map pathways back to recapturing the essence of traditional masculinity. Robert Bly's *Iron John* became the primary text in this movement, followed closely by Sam Keen's *Fire in the Belly* and Moore and Gillette's *King, Warrior, Magician, Lover*. [38]

What all three of these books had in common was that they were designed as manuals for men to take up or find a more natural form of masculinity, one that had been lost to industrialization, feminism, and urbanization. Similar to the movements that led to the attempt to recapture masculinity at the end of the nineteenth century, these late-twentieth century endeavors were about reclaiming what had been lost. The impact of emotion and sensitivity in relationships was especially singled out in these literary Viagras.

Going out and literally being with other men is a key element of masculine culture. It is more acceptable than staying at home and playing shooter games or surfing the Internet for porn. Whether the pub in Britain, the sports bar in the United States or Canada, or simply having a coffee in Italy or France, the all-male grouping is a significant feature of being a man, socializing with other men, and exhibiting masculine, public behavior. There is a long tradition that runs from the coffee houses of the seventeenth century to the science salons of the eighteenth and nineteenth centuries. All male gatherings, whether fraternal in composition with organizations like the Elks and other monikers,[39] or juvenile such as the Boy Scouts, or educational such as fraternities, have provided a safe zone away from women and their influence.

One of the reasons men congregate with each other has a lot to do with creating a security zone that allows them to push away the pressures of being the breadwinner or the stoic rock and regress back to certain levels of immaturity. Why men desire to get away with other guys has a variety of possible explanations. The motivation for the weekend retreats that were popular a couple of decades ago and which coalesced around the "Iron John" movement were based on these. The "Burning Man" pyrotechnics held in Nevada are just the latest manifestation.

Extreme versions of all-male, ritualistic bonding took hold during the late 1980s and attempted to address a variety of concerns such as visceral masculinity, Christian manliness, natural masculinity, and archetypical masculinity. From wearing war paint to dressing up in costumes to screaming and hooting, these gatherings were taken seriously by many men. Similar to the late 1960s and early 1970s pop-therapy conferences and retreats in a number of bizarre ways, these conglomerations spoke to many men. As Michael Kimmel has observed,

> These men were conducting their own quest for their lost "deep" manhood in weekend retreats and workshops across the country. By donning totemic animal symbols and reclaiming ancient myths of male bonding, those weekend warriors hoped to tap into some primitive stream of essential masculinity, long buried by the feminizing worlds of work and home.[40]

Like the books that inspired the questing movements, many of these gatherings were designed to be primal and primeval in order to stimulate or more accurately, jump-start masculine culture on the right path. These types of movements gave rise to a variety of more sectarian versions, such as the Million Man March and the Christian-oriented Promise Keepers. Yet they burned out and fizzled after a time and were replaced by other versions of masculine activity. These were often located closer to home and required less of a commitment to a group or club that was formalized and codified.

The "do-it-yourself" movement of the 1980s spearheaded by Home Depot and other entities was designed to recapture the spirit of building and the sense of accomplishment that comes from constructing something yourself. In American (and North American) culture, the ability to exercise one's manliness has often been tied to building and to erecting things of stature and importance. As less and less of one's sense of masculinity is tied publicly to the brawn-based orientations, the domestic or private version still exudes appeal. The espousing of a variety of avocations that allowed men to feel that they could build things, in this increasingly pre-fabricated world manifests itself in a number of ways. From hobbies to home repair, to tinkering with the car to puttering around in a workshop, men have attempted to keep this culture alive by working out in the back, building things, fixing things and indulging in a micro-version of what was once a substantial part of the economy and their lives.

The move to suburban housing allowed generations of men to have a space to work in and to stock this area with tools and furnishings that gave a tangible feeling of need and essentialness. Workshops, hobby areas, the garage, and tool sheds sprung up in these communities as both a need and a validation. The fact that so much of this do-it-yourself community was based on slick marketing that pandered to men's desire to accumulate tools was irrelevant given the crucial place of tools in both the masculine mindset and in American culture. This desire and need was summed up at the end of the 1940s, on the cusp of the suburban home boom, in the iconic *Death of A Salesman*. This complex and timeless work that among many things, marks the transition from the war generation toward something new, carried a message that still resonates today. In Arthur Miller's seminal and disturbing play, the tragic (and pathetic) Willy Loman states: "A man who can't handle tools is not a man,"[41] providing a mantra for future generations to think about and to aspire toward. Regardless if this statement was meant as a smoke screen or a validation is open to interpretation but it suggests that men were grasping at ways to reaffirm who they were.

A key linkage to the past that fuses the modern world to the heritage of many cultures is the tool. Tools have yielded results for their users from the ancient world on through the Middle Ages. They were important, tangible, and cherished items of value. They held a pride of place and were graciously passed down through generations among stone workers, blacksmiths, and a host of other craftsmen. They have been termed extensions of man and have allowed him to modify his environment. Tools have also been seen as definitive masculine accessories and de facto appendages to men. Even in a culture sated with electricity and technology, the simple power of a hammer or an axe is regarded as impressive. With the introduction of power machines, the possibilities seem endless.

Whether one was a mason, a carpenter, or later on, a plumber, there was a feeling of communion with material and a brotherhood in working with one's hands. It set you apart from the menial day laborer, unskilled and transient, and marked you as part of an elite. For the working class,

this was important in the implication that it allowed for a sense of fraternity and comradely feeling.[42] Having their own space, so to speak, was
vital in establishing a sense of self and a notion of worth in society. This
was increasingly juxtaposed with the upper classes and beginning during
the mid-Victorian period, with the white-collar worker.

Throughout the nineteenth century there was a backlash, especially in
middle-class periodicals, against the use of tools. They were deemed inappropriate for those who aspired to a higher station in life and beyond
the bounds of acceptable things to use for those of a certain class. By the
end of the nineteenth century, many commentators were torn between
recommending the use of tools as a wholesome activity, especially for
boys, and the association that tools could have for reinforcing gender
types. Social commentators eventually started pushing the use of tools on
boys as a way that would keep their hands busy and allow them to learn
a useful and practical skill, one that could lead to some form of handi-
ness, if not an outright profession. Significant also was the fact that
fathers were no longer at home and around to help out. As men became
more immersed in the world of work outside of the home, their ability,
time, and inclination to engage in the domestic sphere deteriorated, no
matter what they did.[43]

During the early years of the twentieth century the cellar in the house
evolved into a basement. As the decades moved on, the basement became
more hospitable and functional and it was divided into rooms. An extension of the area in the basement led to the creation of a "men's territo-
ry"—because of "the labor necessary to shovel coal and ashes," which in
turn gave rise to the workshop. This area began to fill up with benches
and tools, racks, and shelves that contained all that was necessary to fix,
build, and repair. Influential magazines such as *Popular Mechanics* and
Popular Science encouraged these zones as masculine spaces and offered
advice as to how to set one up and what to stock it with.[44]

Hobbies were often slighted as being child's play but with the cost
and time involved, they were much more sophisticated and required an
inordinate amount of money. Time and skill were involved, which differ-
entiated model-building, stamp collecting, and railroading from mere
play.[45] Part of the appeal was the nostalgia factor in attempting to recapture one's youth, but also the enormous creativity involved especially in
the creation of micro worlds. It allowed men the option to use their skill-
building talents and gave enormous satisfaction to men who no longer
could, in fact, build. If they could not participate in actual construction,
these model surrogates would have to do.

The construction worker or the "hardhat" had surpassed the factory
worker as the icon of working-class embodiment during the early part of
the twentieth century. The drudgery of the assembly line and the lack of
freedom granted to factory workers held little romantic appeal. The confinement to indoor hells of heat and stifling conditions did not lend itself

to any form of glorification. The macho independence of the man working on the scaffold, outside, and free of the rote mechanics of industrial mechanization remained purer to the spirit of all that was thought noble in the realm of the masculine proletariat. As Joshua Freeman puts forward, there was nobility within the "hardhat," one that was glaringly absent from the toil and obligations of the assembly-line worker. This process gained in prominence as a kind of linchpin masculinity during the second part of the last century. In particular, the 1960s and 1970s saw the "hardhat" emerge as everything from an icon symbolized in popular culture to a political force to be reckoned with. One of the reasons why this template of masculinity is so resonant even today is because of the essence it conveys—through advertising and media—in accessible ways as a stereotype for masculinist shorthand.[46]

Whether in truck commercials or most ubiquitously, beer commercials, the construction worker is featured prominently as an easily understood masculine archetype. It is interesting to speculate on this influence in so many facets of North American life. It runs the gamut from the model for "do it yourself" and has antecedents to the lineage of the cowboy. The construction worker ethos means independence and raw, untamed masculinity but within an urban environment. It is also about knowing how to handle oneself in dangerous situations, being brave, and being able to wield a tool with skill.

One of the reasons why baseball still carries with it an enormous weight of the past is that the men who play the game use tools in an ersatz pastoral or pseudo-agricultural frame of reference. The bat and the ball, as well as the gloves, are emblematic of the past and of the origins of baseball. It is significant as well that at the professional level, the bat is still made of wood and very often, handmade.[47] Unlike in tennis, technology has not fundamentally altered the game. With the adoption of steel, aluminum, and finally composite racquets, tennis evolved into a very different kind of sport from when it was played with wood. The point for many sports is to find the proper equilibrium; there has to be a balance between change and tradition. What this suggests as far as tools is that, ideally, they should embody both the past and future. Nowhere is this more pronounced then in the realms of the home workshop and in the plethora of tools available for do-it-your-selfers.

In the post–World War II era there was a well-orchestrated move for men and some women to build things with their own hands. Inspired by the fact that many manufacturers were shifting toward a consumer economy, this dovetailed with the emergence of the middle-class home and the leisure industry. As well there was an attempt to link building things to the agrarian past where men were encouraged to get back in touch with what their forefathers had done.[48] Suffusing magazines, books, and other publications with promulgating this message, the focus was oriented on recapturing an independent, masculine ethic that could be exercised by working with tools.

During World War II, the influx of women into the traditional spheres of masculine work—from welders to electricians to tool and dye to machinists of all kinds—demonstrated that women could do the work of men as well, if not better.[49] The returning veteran was in some ways egged on by a variety of industries to reassert his rightful place as the prime handler of tools and as the individual responsible and adept in building, even on a small scale. Advertisements from the era began to reinforce this bifurcated role and to instruct on the appropriate ideology: when rigid divisions were broken, this caused stress to individuals and the system.[50]

The growth of big box stores such as Home Depot and other outlets that offer products and services for independent craftsmen and individuals who wish to work on their own has come with an overt rule. In order to really be a man (and increasingly, a competent woman) you have to be able to make something from scratch. These stores run seminars on constructing a deck for the back yard, painting the living room, and wiring speakers. One's masculinity used to be in question if he could not wield a tool with the proper authority or did not know the different gauges of measurement or other information necessary for building. In essence, if you were not interested in building a treehouse for the kids, and further, if you did not know how, there was an implication that there was something wrong with you. Hobby culture was also tinged with these assessments and evaluations. Men had to have some kind of hobby, no matter how seemingly trivial, or else there was too much idle time.

Men's hobbies have always straddled the fine line between the perception of feminist influence and the reorientation of masculine identity. During the nineteenth century, there was much discussion over the "manliness" of selected hobbies. In harmony with the growth of the imperial mentality and accumulation of great wealth in the west, there was the creation and rise of a veritable array of hobbies, many of which involved the mania for collecting. It also witnessed a clearly delineated selection of hobbies for boys and those deemed appropriate for girls. As boys aged, their leisure time was specifically channeled toward the pursuit of specific hobbies and diversions that were focused on masculine arenas.[51]

As more people were able to afford homes, men gravitated toward outlets that defined their space in the domestic sphere. A similar process, to be discussed later, can occur in micro environments such as the home office or the den. In the first part of the century, the move toward woodworking was designed to visibly demarcate a masculine element within the increasingly feminized domestic sphere. Because of the increasing move toward office routines and the gradual disappearance of working with tools and the disappearance of older forms of employment, the connections were stressed in the home zone. With the end of the war, one of the definitive spaces for men in the home became the workshop. Whether it was located in the garage or in the basement or even in a shack behind the house, its purpose allowed for a masculine space in an increasingly feminized domestic zone.[52]

Collecting and building things such as model trains and other kit-like products also fused a number of central masculine attributes into full-fledged hobbies. Trains illustrated mobility, the transfer of goods and people, and the colonization of nature. Locomotives were powerful and strong, capable of pulling mighty loads. The train enthusiast could create miniature masculine environments that spoke of the past, the present, and at times, the future. From intricate detailing to elaborate cities and landscapes, the hobbyist could make his own world and define the boundaries on specific scales. The building of model cars, with blueprints and glue, could be combined with one's son for a male bonding activity.[53] But perhaps this is more the mediated version than the actual reality. Gary Cross observes that although hobbies were supposed to be a retreat, they

> let men and boys share in a boy-man world escape from the expectations of maturity in the modern world. Despite ads showing father and son happily playing together with Lionel electric trains, making model airplanes, or even working together in home workshops, hobbies didn't necessarily promote cross-generational togetherness.[54]

Since the late-Victorian period, men have attempted to collect for a variety of reasons. There has been the idea that stamps and coins mimic a colonial desire for ordering the world in a micro form and there is also the notion that collecting was a masculine version of the desire to fill the middle-class home with clutter and chintz. It was an acceptable way to masculinize the domestic sphere. Men could be just as proud to display their coins, trophies, and stamps as women could of their weaving and china figurines. There was a serious focus devoted toward the building of the collection; this generally was not something trivial. It also provided a wonderful way to use one's time in the proper pursuit of leisure as opposed to the more salacious public amusements. During the depression, the popularity of hobbies and collecting increased as many men either had no work at all or were forced to work much shorter hours.[55]

Model building became a significant activity during the Depression and generated both huge sales for manufacturers and stores as well as enormous interest that affected magazines and hobby clubs. This new activity, which held appeal to men and to boys, became quite sophisticated in its evolution. Whether building boats, cars, or airplanes, this hobby became quintessentially associated with masculine accomplishment. As Steven Gelber writes,

> The constructed model was a testament to the skill of the builder, and the functional versions could stand in for their makers in head-to-head

contests to determine dominance. Furthermore, model airplane building provided the sense that hobbyists were participating on the cutting
edge of scientific advancement.[56]

Model trains did not have the same impact as the new airplanes and sleek
military models that were quickly released. They harkened back to a
different time and a different era.[57] This continues to be a feature in
building models to this day. There is the quaint, nostalgic feature to
trains that is also found in baseball card collecting.

During the 1970s and 1980s the eruption in popularity of baseball card
collecting reflected an interesting surge in nostalgia, which often embodied the desire to recapture a tangible material piece of one's youth.[58]
What was once a hobby or a focus that appealed to young boys became a
full-blown activity oriented around connoisseurship, auctions, and very
high costs. Middle-aged men became the primary movers and shakers in
this explosion. John Bloom raises the question of why men would be
interested in this varied activity, especially "one that they remembered as
exclusively male and relatively homogenous." He suspects that much of
the interest that is not oriented around profit has to do with recapturing a
significant place and time, when men were boys and felt safe and secure.
For men of a certain age in the 1980s, it was the 1950s. Bloom relates that
the attraction focuses on recapturing the times when boys played together without any competition and without any pressures. Part of the issue
was that one had to divest oneself of what was deemed a hobby for
young boys and for a while, collecting cards as an adult was problematic
as far as appearances.[59] The collecting of toys also serves a variety of
similar functions. It is heavily influenced by men and in some cases has
become a very expensive hobby. Many men like to possess what they
could not have as children and, as with baseball cards, the monetary
value of an original GI Joe or a Matchbox car in mint condition is extremely attractive.[60]

The other significant activity that men and boys are oriented around,
especially as a media-derived rite of passage, is camping. While not a
sport but more than an activity, it can be termed a hobby. Unlike garden-
ing or more specifically, cutting the grass, it is about interacting and
engaging with nature on a very unique scale. Canoeing can be a part of
this as well. In his wonderful essay on camping and kayaking, "The Boys'
Trip," Rich Fairbanks makes numerous references to movies and novels
that feature a hardy masculine protagonist interacting with nature. He
refers to Hemingway and Jim Harrison, John Wayne, and Clint Eastwood
as models and inspirations. "The Boys' Trip" is an annual canoe and
backpacking excursion by men. Fairbanks and his buddies embark on
this expedition into nature with the intensity of young men, although, as
he makes clear, age is catching up with them and the arduous terrain and
physicality forces them to tone down the scale as each year goes by.

Somewhat like children, the new camping and hiking toys are a big part of the trip and all the gear, from a French coffee press to GPS units must be accounted for. Yet, despite the shopping and the accumulation of all their cool stuff, the experience is still a key masculine undertaking, one to be savored and one that never fails to revitalize them. Notwithstanding carrying the trappings of "civilization" into the wilderness, the salubrious impact is rejuvenating. "Even when I paddle with the boys," he writes, "I spend long hours in silent, almost meditative paddling."[61]

Hunting has always resonated with a definitive masculine sense of security. Hunting has also been seen as a close approximation to soldiering. During both world wars this equation became linked and especially during World War II, the connections between hunting and militant masculinity were firmly meshed.[62] Throughout the 1950s and into the 1960s, hunting increasingly came to stand for a supremely masculine outlet and was often juxtaposed against or with "feminized anti-hunting campaigns." It was consciously defined as an activity to exclude women, and through magazines such as *Field and Stream*, came to stand as a "quintessential masculine practice."[63] In her analysis of periodicals such as *Field and Stream* and *Outdoor Life*, Andrea Smalley finds that in the post-war period there was a massive growth in the popularity of sport hunting that was tied to the culture of war. Specifically, Smalley suggests, the editors of these magazines made a conscious attempt to position hunting not as "mere recreation" but "as an essential source of gender identification for all men."[64] This process is buttressed by research undertaken by Lisa Fine that focuses on the blue-collar culture of Michigan in the post-war period. Accordingly, men were supremely tied to the culture of hunting and all its trappings in very specific and potent ways. It was both a defining ritual and a key masculine touchstone.[65]

One of the problems today in many social groupings is the fact that hunting resonates with as negative a series of connotations as does smoking. In certain parts of the United States and Canada it is considered an acceptable activity, but move to a big city and many people are aghast when a man says that he hunts. Given the influence of anti-meat culture, respect for the environment, and the taboo against gun culture in many parts of North America, the forces against hunting are great.[66] The upper-crust British mania for fox hunting is not the same as an annual deer hunt or a weekend up north hunting moose. As James B. Twitchell remarks, "most men don't even know how to dress a deer anymore."[67] Hunting is still around and celebrated in different regions. But over the years, the forces opposing the killing of creatures have grown. Target shooting, skeet shooting, and other firearm-oriented hobbies have come into being as a replacement. That being said, there is still an enormous industry behind hunting: from television shows and crossbows to cookbooks focused on game. A segment of the population readily gravitates toward hunting. As a popular culture touchstone, and not just in the

United States, it still holds appeal as a definitive feature of masculine proficiency.

For decades, a hallmark of masculine competence has always been the ability to repair a car. To tinker with the engine in order to make it go faster, to fix what is broken, or to simply change the oil, have all been key demonstrations of one's masculine technical standing. As cars become more oriented around the computer, it is no small thing to be able to fix one, and increasingly, a benchmark of expertise in the masculine imagination, is disappearing.

Within the world of car customizing and urban drag racing, having the right vehicle gives a young man both a sense of pride and masculine power. What accents this process and elevates it is the ability to work on the car yourself. As Amy Best relates in her study of "fast car" culture, "Boys who pay someone else to customize or modify their cars accrue less status than those boys who are able to work on their cars themselves, because they are seen as imposters."[68] This process harkens back to many masculine endeavors in that it is ingrained as a feature of tradition and popular culture lore. As Best suggests, there is enormous credibility and respect bestowed upon those who can work with their hands, and who can, literally, do it themselves.

To the man who can achieve this there is the element of reverence, but one can also surmise, a significant amount of independence of spirit is captured.[69] The tactile and visceral components necessary in working with one's hands suggest that this has a powerful appeal to so many males searching for true masculine experiences. This is especially pronounced in a world increasingly defined and dictated by technology and legislation, not to mention changing values. In subgroups that are marginalized or discriminated against, this ability to assert their masculinity through hard work is particularly rewarding. This has had a spill-over effect in a number of ways, one of which is a move toward a marked and defined hands-on movement. Similar to the arts and crafts movement of the late Victorian period, there is increasingly a popular move toward working with one's hands. Numerous organizations are now propounding the effects of getting back to basics and building furniture or customizing your car. All of this seems like a back lash against the prepackaged designs and what-you-see-is-what-you-get products, which leave little room for tinkering. And, because of the diversity of areas involved, there is something for almost everyone.

Unlike so much of the contemporary world that is bought, pre-designed and specifically designated, the ability to rework, modify, or build retains its appeal in the masculine universe. The manly man can do his own repairs and fix things, whereas the man too dependent on the absolutes of appearance won't stoop to get his hands dirty. The capital of respect given to the man who can do his own repairs is both blurred and admired. The fact that women are just as proficient makes it less of a masculine achievement as does the fact that even fixing and building has become prepackaged and abutted by so much technology. Surveying the men on 1980s and 1990s home renovation shows, one is struck by their androgynous appeal. They were not the burly men who came to your home in the 1960s. Although there are no shortage of women on these shows, often as hosts, there now seems to be a return to the traditional stereotype of the manly do-it-your-selfer who exudes, like Mike Holmes, a comfortable confidence and a wisdom that seems more in tune with the times than brawn.

NOTES

1. Catherine R. Stimpson, "Foreword," in *The Making of Masculinities: The New Men's Studies*, ed. Harry Brod (Boston: Unwin Hyman, 1990), p. xii.

2. Catherine R. Stimpson, "Foreword," p. xiii.

3. Joseph H. Pleck, "The Theory of Male Sex-Role Identity: Its Rise and Fall," in *The Making of Masculinities: The New Men's Studies*, ed. Harry Brod (Boston: Unwin Hyman, 1990), p. 22.

4. See John Higham, "The Reorientation of American Culture in the 1890s," in *Writing American History*, ed. John Higham (Bloomington: University of Indiana Press, 1970).

5. Waller R. Newell, *The Code of Man* (New York: HarperCollins, 2003), p. 55.

6. Waller R. Newell, *The Code of Man*, pp. 55–56.

7. See Mark Moss, *Manliness and Militarism: Educating Young Boys in Ontario for War* (Toronto, ON: Oxford University Press, 2001).

8. Ray Raphael, *The Men from the Boys: Rites of Passage in Male America* (Lincoln: University of Nebraska Press, 1988), p. x.

9. Joseph H. Pleck, "The Theory of Male Sex-Role Identity," p. 22.

10. Christina S. Jarvis, *The Male Body at War: American Masculinity during World War II* (Dekalb: Northern Illinois University Press, 2004), p. 4.

11. Christina S. Jarvis, *The Male Body at War*, p. 4; Susan Faludi, *Stiffed: The Betrayal of the American Man* (New York: Morrow, 1999), p. 16; and Donald J. Mrozek, "The Military, Sport, and Warrior Culture," in *The Columbia History of Post–World War II America*, ed. Mark C. Carnes (New York: Columbia University Press, 2007), pp. 131–136.

12. Leo Braudy, *From Chivalry to Terrorism: War and the Changing Nature of Masculinity* (New York: Knopf, 2003), p. 495.

13. Leo Braudy, *From Chivalry to Terrorism*, p. 507.

14. Peter Schjeldahl, "American Abstract: Real Jackson Pollock," *New Yorker*, July 31, 2006, p. 80.

15. Deborah Solomon, *Jackson Pollock: A Biography* (New York: Cooper Square Press, 2001), p. 193.

16. See Joe Moran, *Star Authors: Literary Celebrity in America* (London: Pluto Press, 2000), p. 25. Moran comments that through a series of clever connections, such as the one between life and art, a unique image surfaced. In Hemingway's case it centered on the creation of an active, manly man.

17. See Carlos Baker, *Ernest Hemingway: A Life Story* (New York: Collier/Macmillan, 1969/1988).

18. Paul Johnson, *Intellectuals* (New York: Harper & Row, 1988), p. 150.

19. Paul Johnson, *Intellectuals*, p. 151.

20. Paul Johnson, *Intellectuals*, p. 152.

21. Doug Owram notes in *Born at the Right Time: A History of the Baby Boom Generation* (Toronto, ON: University of Toronto Press, 1996), p. 7: "The idea of home, really an emblem for a million personal recollections of friends, family, and normal daily activities, seemed much more immediate and emotionally meaningful than abstract concepts like democracy, or faraway places like Poland . . . In fiction, magazine articles, poems, and newspaper stories, the vision of 'home' was re-created with hundreds of variations. Coca-Cola ads showed returning soldiers and sailors coming back into the embrace of the family."

22. Elaine Tyler May, *Homeward Bound: American Families in the Cold War Era* (New York: Basic Books, 1999), p. 82.

23. "Dreamed," was the operative word. Divorce was not a common or pleasant option. In 1948, according to Donald Katz, "the director of the American Institute of Family Relations, Paul Popenoe, contended that 'no one can escape the conclusion that the divorced population represents to some extent a biologically inferior part of the population." *Home Fires: An Intimate Portrait of One Middle-Class Family in Postwar America* (New York: HarperCollins, 1992), pp. 34 and 35.

24. Michael Kimmel, *Guyland: The Perilous World Where Boys Become Men* (New York: HarperCollins, 2008), p. 6.

25. Dan Kiley, *The Peter Pan Syndrome: Men Who Have Never Grown Up* (New York: Dodd, Mead, 1983).

26. Jack Zipes, *Fairy Tales and the Art of Subversion* (New York: Routledge, 1991), pp. 31–37.

27. Susan Bordo, *The Male Body: A New Look at Men in Public and Private* (New York: Farrar, Straus & Giroux, 1999), p. 243.

28. Henry A. Giroux, *The Mouse That Roared: Disney and the End of Innocence* (Lanham, MD: Rowman & Littlefield, 1999), p. 100.

29. Paul Nathanson and Katherine K. Young, *Spreading Misandry: The Teaching of Contempt for Men in Popular Culture* (Montreal, QC, and Kingston, ON: McGill-Queen's University Press, 2001/2006), p. 161.

30. Richard Schickel, *The Disney Version: The Life, Times, Art, and Commerce of Walt Disney* (New York: Touchstone/Simon & Schuster, 1985), p. 194.

31. Paul Nathanson and Katherine K. Young, *Spreading Misandry*, p. 163.

32. Edisol Wayne Dotson, *Behold the Man: The Hype and Selling of Male Beauty in Media and Culture* (New York: Harrington Park Press, 1999), p. 67.

33. Jake MacDonald, *With the Boys: Field Notes on Being a Guy* (Vancouver, BC: Greystone/Douglas & McIntyre, 2005), p. 1.

34. Gary Cross, *Men to Boys: The Making of Modern Immaturity* (New York: Columbia University Press, 2008), p. 142.

35. Jonathan Bender, *LEGO: A Love Story* (Hoboken, NJ: Wiley, 2010), p. 8.

36. Christopher Noxon, *Rejuvenile: Kickball, Cartoons, Cupcakes, and the Reinvention of the American Grown-up* (New York: Crown, 2006), pp. 1–5.

37. Christopher Noxon, *Rejuvenile*, pp. 12–13.

38. Robert Bly, *Iron John: A Book about Men* (Reading, MA: Addison-Wesley, 1990); Sam Keen, *Fire in the Belly: On Being a Man* (New York: Bantam, 1991); Roger Moore and Douglas Gillette, *King, Warrior, Magician, Lover* (New York: HarperCollins, 1990).

39. See James B. Twitchell, *Where Men Hide* (New York: Columbia University Press, 2006), pp. 60–64.

40. Michael S. Kimmel, *Manhood in America: A Cultural History*, 2nd ed. (New York: Oxford University Press, 2006), p. 208.

41. Arthur Miller, *Death of a Salesman* (New York: Viking, 1976), p. 44.

42. See James B. Twitchell, *Where Men Hide*, pp. 184–185, and Craig Heron, "The Boys and Their Booze: Masculinities and Public Drinking in Working-Class Hamilton, 1890–1946," *Canadian Historical Review* 86, no. 3 (September 2005), p. 411.

43. Steven M. Gelber, *Hobbies: Leisure and the Culture of Work in America* (New York: Columbia University Press, 1999), pp. 183–185. Gelber writes, p. 186, "It is possible

that middle-class men only a generation or two removed from the farm may have feared a loss of status if they did manual work around the house."

44. Steven M. Gelber, *Hobbies*, pp. 207–208, and Gary Cross, *Men to Boys*, p. 89.

45. Gary Cross, *Men to Boys*, p. 88.

46. Joshua B. Freeman, "Hardhats: Construction Workers, Manliness, and the 1970 Pro-War Demonstrations," *Journal of Social History*, Summer 1993, p. 725.

47. See Michael Mandelbaum, *The Meaning of Sports* (New York: Public Affairs, 2004), p. 177.

48. Carolyn M. Goldstein, *Do It Yourself: Home Improvement in Twentieth-Century America* (New York: Princeton Architectural Press, 1998), p. 38.

49. Carolyn M. Goldstein, *Do It Yourself*, p. 69.

50. Carolyn M. Goldstein, *Do It Yourself*, p. 68.

51. See Steven M. Gelber, *Hobbies*, and Howard P. Chudacoff, *Children at Play: An American History* (New York: New York University Press, 2007).

52. Carolyn M. Goldstein, *Do It Yourself*, pp. 76, 77.

53. Steven M. Gelber, *Hobbies*, pp. 232–234.

54. Gary Cross, *Men to Boys*, p. 90.

55. Steven M. Gelber, "A Job You Can't Lose: Work and Hobbies in the Great Depression," *Journal of Social History* 24 (Summer 1991), pp. 741–743.

56. Steven M. Gelber, *Hobbies*, p. 232.

57. Steven M. Gelber, *Hobbies*, pp. 232, 233.

58. John Bloom, "Cardboard Patriarchy: Adult Baseball Card Collecting and the Nostalgia for a Presexual Past," in *Hop on Pop: The Politics and Pleasures of Popular Culture*, ed. Henry Jenkins, Tara McPherson, and Jane Shattuc (Durham, NC: Duke University Press, 2002), p. 67.

59. John Bloom, "Cardboard Patriarchy," pp. 67, 76, 77.

60. See Christopher Noxon, *Rejuvenile*, pp. 100–114.

61. Rich Fairbanks, "The Boys' Trip," in *Eco-Man: New Perspectives on Masculinity and Nature*, ed. Mark Allister (Charlottesville: University of Virginia Press, 2004), pp. 111–125.

62. Lisa M. Fine, "Rights of Men, Rites of Passage: Hunting and Masculinity at REO Motors of Lansing, Michigan, 1945–1975," *Journal of Social History*, Summer 2000, p. 810.

63. Andrea L. Smalley, "'I Just Like to Kill Things': Women, Men, and the Gender of Sport Hunting in the United States, 1940–1974," *Gender and History* 17, no. 1 (April 2005), p. 184.

64. Andrea L. Smalley, "'I Just Like to Kill Things,'" p. 187.

65. Lisa M. Fine, "Rights of Men, Rites of Passage," pp. 805–823.

66. See James B. Twitchell, *Where Men Hide*, p. 39.

67. James B. Twitchell, *Where Men Hide*, p. 39.

68. Amy L. Best, *Fast Cars, Cool Rides: The Accelerating World of Youth and Their Cars* (New York: New York University Press, 2006), p. 96.

69. See Matthew B. Crawford, *Shop Class as Soulcraft: An Inquiry into the Value of Work* (New York: Penguin, 2009).

SIX

The Impact of the 1950s

The Slacker, the Dude, and the Rebel

The 1950s held up many diverse models of masculinity for men to use as templates on which to model their behavior and gauge their manliness. It was a decade characterized by extremes in politics and culture and in turn, these extremes found their way into the fabric of media portrayals of masculinity. One thing that is certain is that the "preoccupation with masculinity" during this decade, was, as James Gilbert has remarked, rooted in the fact that "the period followed wartime self-confidence based upon the sacrifice and heroism of ordinary men." Like other periods in modern history, there may have been a corresponding "male panic" also known as a crisis of masculinity, but what made this period particularly potent in its male self-assessment, was that many academics were singling out a variety of forces that were affecting or harming men. A "tough guy masculinity" permeated discussions on foreign policy, and the fear of being labeled a homosexual—"the lavender scare"—was enough to polarize and promote a certain way of acting. To make matters more volatile, Gilbert singles out the mounting conflict between traditional, virile masculinity and the "new forms of masculinity based upon notions of companionship and cooperation within the family and workplace."[1]

One of the stressors that impacted men was that during the war, women had filled a variety of roles that men had traditionally performed. The fact that they did these jobs and had been able to make do, relatively speaking, put enormous pressure on men to return to work and to reassert their roles as bread winners while at the same time, coax women back into the home.[2] This accounts for the emphasis on the family as a significant social and economic unit in the 1950s.

The family in the United States, Canada, and Britain became infused with importance in the post-war period. Elaine Tyler May suggests that it was seen as a safe and loving antidote to the fears and horror of a nuclear war.[3] The supremacy and sanctity of the family and the patriarch could be found in many places during the 1950s and on television, the rise of prominence of the family with the father in his role as head of the household became a common feature of popular culture.[4] Despite numerous forays into humorous situations, the father was depicted as a figure to be respected and one who possessed wisdom.

Barbara Ehrenreich has suggested that the importance of the family and of men, marrying and being committed had as much to do with personal fear as with public displays of commitment. In *The Hearts of Men*, she intimates that the red scare and the lavender scare propelled men toward the legitimacy of the family structure. Commenting on Ehrenreich, Bill Osgerby indicates that being married and being a provider was both an obligation and a duty. "To stray from this norm," he writes, "was to court suspicion. Failure to conform to the breadwinner ethic could cast doubts on both a man's sexual identity and his social status."[5]

By the end of the decade, the pressures to conform and the expectation to be a provider fractured masculine obligation into a duality. Some men hung in while others looked for options. Some of the alternatives came in the form of the visible presence of rebels on the screen, Marlon Brando and James Dean in particular.[6] In other ways, it was more subtle. The major publishing successes of the time singled out the rebellion against conformity in careful and analytical terms. *The Lonely Crowd*, *The Organization Man*, and the novel, *The Man in the Grey Flannel Suit* all suggested that being too willing to adopt all the mannerisms of the institutional structure of corporate America was taking its toll on men.[7]

The equation of communism with homosexuality during the 1950s is part of a long-standing historical pattern of linking perceived differences and deviance with a threat to established norms and to societal stability. Witches were burned because they offered alternatives in behavior and deportment, and women in general who refused to play roles assigned to them have been persecuted. Blacks in the American south, Jews in all parts of the world, and other minority groups within majority cultures have also been subjected to this treatment. The fear is based on the perceived threat to the status quo. Michael Rogin terms this "political demonology"[8] —a process where "sexual fear and fantasy have often underlain the demonization of those imaged as threats to order and civility in America." The fear this time was that homosexuality was on the rise and would permeate mainstream American manhood.[9]

In terms that can only be described as ironic, it was World War II and its massive demand for men to move around that may have unleashed the modern gay (and lesbian) movement. In pre-Stonewall days, bringing thousands of men together in an institutional space may have facilitated the pursuit of the ability to have same sex relationships.[10]

The offerings available in port cities or sophisticated urban environments such as Los Angeles, San Francisco, and New York were also significant in creating more visible homosexual communities. The Kinsey reports seemed to give concrete validation to the rise of homosexual activity and were unsettling to the mainstream for this reason, among others.

By the 1960s, this was to change. When in doubt, many men look backward to times that seem simpler. In order to counter this perception there was an attempt to return to masculine models that had impeccable credentials. One masculine archetype was the hard-boiled detective, a tough guy who upheld the law. The other was the cowboy.

Perhaps the dominant model of the 1950s, more so than the cinematic rebel, was the cowboy as defined by Hollywood. This archetype had been used since its popular inception by writers such as Owen Wister and Zane Grey and never really disappeared from the popular imagination.[11] During the 1950s the western was resurrected with a vengeance. As Michael Kimmel has noted, the western was perhaps the prevailing genre of the decade. It dominated films, television, reading lists, and popular material culture.[12] The model of the cowboy stood out with almost glaringly regularity and was both inspiring and frustrating to men who may have been searching for molds of masculinity to fashion for themselves. Interestingly, it was at this time that the formation of one of the embodiments of 1980s masculinity started to appear: future president Ronald Reagan. A related phenomenon that accentuated the western ideals—or at least the nostalgic, mythologized version—came in the form of toys. In particular, toy guns seemed to be everywhere. As Thomas Newkirk relates, many of these toys were related to the cowboy mania: "We couldn't pinpoint the exact year," he writes,

> But I must have received my Easter gun around 1955, the Eisenhower years, a time of extraordinary domestic tranquility. Yet toy guns were everywhere—small cap pistols, bigger .45 replicas with holsters, plastic army rifles. We still have some embarrassing pictures of my cousin and me in cowboy hats and chaps, each of us with a holstered gun.[13]

Newkirk ties the popularity of guns to their prevalence on television. As far as content goes, by the end of the 1950s and into the 1960s, westerns were a dominant staple on television. Shows such as *Gunsmoke*, *Bonanza*, and *The Rifleman* were enormously popular with a wide cross section of viewers.[14]

Perhaps the prevalence of guns in 1950s popular culture served to prepare American men for the coming of the next conflict. While the cold war developed, its primary symbols seemed to be too intellectual or too technological for most people to comprehend in tangible terms. Guns seemed to be reassuring and familiar as well as something to which most men, having served, could relate. Like tools, they were seminal masculine artifacts. Although they were lethal, they had grand appeal to young boys. What seemed to be needed was a bridge between the two. In the early 1960s, that link was found in the form of an action figure, GI Joe. The significance of this creation stretched over three generations and had added resonance in that the toy was based on the idea and contributions of real life soldiers.

The Joe doll has proven to be quite adaptable as a masculine icon. It has continuously been remade to pander to the different trends affecting American culture. During the late 1960s, when opposition to the Vietnam war was quite vocal, the Hasbro Corporation refit Joe to be a member of an "Adventure" team rather than part of a military unit. The Adventure team went on missions that were more holistic as opposed to militaristic, and the accessories that Joe carried were more in line with the nature of this evolution.[15] As a consequence of the OPEC-inspired oil crisis of the mid-1970s, Hasbro, in dealing with a product made from petroleum-based chemicals retooled the Joe figurine so that its cost was affordable. As Karen Hall writes, "The new muscle torso used less plastic and gave Joe an exaggerated, sculpted musculature, ironically inflating Joe's body, and by extension, his strength and invulnerability at a time when economics was making him morally vulnerable."[16]

Joe consistently served as a connecting figure for boys who were not sure of their place in society. While they played war and other aggressive games many came to learn that perhaps there were problems inherent with war and soldiering. The narrative surrounding the figure placed it in the context of World War II,[17] as opposed to Korea or Vietnam. World War II was about victory and the rise of a "masculine nation" that saw itself ready to assume control of the world through its dominant masculinity.[18] The foot soldiers, so to speak, that would initiate this dominance were the GIs who had served as both the heroes and the participants of that war.[19]

The bridging of World War II culture with the 1950s and eventually the 1960s was significant in a number of seemingly contradictory ways. According to Susan Faludi, there was the Common Man, who was communal in his contributions, and then there was the jingoistic representative of the American Century. Faludi suggests that it was Henry Luce and his Time/Life Empire that best espoused the latter view,[20] that America was "a masculine nation whose manifest destiny was to loom like a giant on the global stage." Accordingly, America had to be involved on the world rostrum, and had to "mix it up" lest it become weak and impotent. The dichotomy between the two positions is summed up in the following:

Did an American man establish his merit by nursing his nation's people or by goring the world's? Was he Daniel Boone come home to tend
to his community's affairs or Davy Crockett sallying forth to take his
pelts?[21]

The average male, concludes Faludi, was much more concerned with his
community and his own world, than with the machinations of foreign
affairs. The fact that dads were staying home and that community clubs
such as Little League and the Scouts blossomed in this period to some
extent confirms this. On the other hand, after years of being away, they
had no choice. Yet something about this life did not satisfy all.

In Francis Ford Coppola's movie *Peggy Sue Got Married*, the title character is transported back in time—to the early 1960s. One of the characters that Peggy Sue encounters is a poet, a literati, who wears a leather
jacket, listens to jazz, runs like an athlete, and drives a motorcycle. In
sum, he is cool, detached, and hip like all James Dean/Allen Ginsberg
clones are. Peggy Sue drops him, though, when he reveals his misogyny
and his underlying biases despite his sartorial sense and his not-too-deep
rejection of conservative culture. But what is interesting about the character is that his coolness derives from the fact that he loves literature; he is
passionate about novels and poetry while still being a rebel—at least on a
superficial level. In fact, he is a Beat. Donning the leather jacket gives the
viewer a strong cue that he is not a conformist and that he's not going to
fit into some large corporate structure. He is disillusioned and angry, but
he is, after all, a teenager.

Many things can define the idea of the teenager and specifically the
male teenager; these involve age, demographics, and assorted classifica-
tions such as consumerism and social psychology. But there was something else, more potent and much more glaring as a reminder of what the
teenager resembled and how he acted. A specific look, derived from a
number of sources, but clearly the cinematic images of James Dean and
Marlon Brando, were most important. Donning leather jackets and other
symbols such as white t-shirts and blue jeans, this new grouping suggested a subculture that was unhappy with the status quo. The leather
jacket "became a gleaming second skin for the new generation. It originated," writes G. Bruce Boyer, "both practically and symbolically, as protection, but quickly grew into a revolutionary attitude of insolent dissent,
one which stated that rebellion for the sake of rebellion had its own style
and importance."[22] They sought to rebel, albeit, via masculine lines,
against the perceived sterile world of adults, many of which they also co-
opted.[23]

The leather jacket, t-shirt, and jeans, as well as a number of other
fashion artifacts coalesce around individuals to form a uniform. Uniforms often symbolize specific roles and places. They serve as defining
statements about what a man does. In a significant way, uniforms serve

to tell the outside, non-uniformed world, that "this is who I am or" in certain cases, "what I was." In many instances, there is a "proto-military aspect" to the donning of standardized clothing.[24]

Uniforms, especially the military variant, are also appealing to young boys. In many ways, they are cool and signify power and maturity. They also reflect both belonging and being apart. The uniforms of old are resplendent with their starchy formality, places for medals, and crisp appeal. Today, what passes for the uniform, the Desert Storm look of the multi-pocket camouflage pants, appeals in another way. They reinforce the macho look so ingrained in movies. Seeing the soldiers in Iraq or Afghanistan or seeing the private contractors from Blackwater is like seeing a Hollywood movie version of what it—soldiers, modern combat, war in the desert—is often supposed to look like. As well, like a sports team, the keen observer can immediately decipher the nationality of the soldier by the emblems and patches.[25]

Another version of the "proto-military aspect" of clothing has been the militarization of men's fashion. The wearing of military dress and military clothing—all the time—is the most common attribute of this phenomenon. The standard variation is the adventurer/explorer look. As with other masculine trends, this began during the Edwardian period. During the late Victorian and early Edwardian period, when imperial and militaristic fervor was at its height in Britain, the population was fascinated by the overseas exploits of military campaigns and was eager for news about virtually every battle and every imperial outpost. A steady stream of reports, fictions, speakers, and adventures kept the population up-to-date about colonial doings. It was the Boer War, (1899–1901) where British forces adopted the color khaki in their uniforms; from there, an embracement by civilians of a military look took hold. There was a wide-spread movement by manufacturers to market military-styled clothing and products to the civilian population. According to Brent Shannon, shop windows and department store displays were filled with "elaborate military and patriotic themes." Shannon suggests that the "most enduring fashion to come out of the Boer War was the adoption of khaki fabric and colors for civilian fashions." Khaki became an unprecedented occurrence in consumption, trend-setting, and importantly, masculine clothing. Shannon writes that it was durable and rugged, ideal for athletics and everyday. Accordingly it was the first military/masculine style embraced by the male population as a whole. And when a man wore something constructed from khaki, the military overtone was constantly present.[26]

Clothing that was worn by military personnel became much more accessible after World War II thanks to enormous quantities in circulation that had been produced for the army, especially in the United States. The leather pilot's jacket, produced for the Air Force as well as the khaki trousers, also produced for the armed forces, sold in the thousands and was a uniform for those who had been demobilized as much as for those who had served. The boots and pea coats, hats, and other products entered mainstream culture as a consequence of their wholesale sell-off and availability from surplus stores.[27] What makes this clothing phenomenon interesting is that until the 1950s, what people wore was often dictated from the upper classes and versions of it "filtered down as clothes were handed from master to servant." Now, as G. Bruce Boyer remarks, a modern version was at work from the bottom up. As Boyer observes,

> Instead of filtering down from the court and the manor house to the servants and peasants, fashion would now bubble up from the streets. Street clothes, i.e. those work clothes worn by ex-GI's, cowboys, farmhands, and industrial and outdoor laborers, and ethnic dress assumed by second-generation working-class immigrants—army surplus, cowboy gear, gangster suits, bowling shirts, mechanic coveralls, sweatshirts and warm-up jackets, lumberjack shirts and farmers' field coats, navy peacoats, campaign boots, garrison belts, olive drab T-shirts, CPO wool shirts, watch caps, bomber jackets, cargo pants, ranch jackets, carpenter pants and baseball caps—have all proved fertile ground for designers. And in this respect, the invention of casual clothes within the American lifestyle was partially a product of the section of the postwar generation that felt alienated from the dominant society.[28]

The complete and significant series of post-war fashion trends, especially for youth and in the realm of everyday clothing, were accordingly set by Army/Navy/Air Force surplus and their distillation throughout society via their relative cheapness. For those who did not wish to indulge in this standardization there was always the traditional elegance of the suit. This height of fashion statement was given its modern impetus by the Ian Fleming creation, James Bond, and especially the sartorial impact on screen by Sean Connery.

The most durable male icon to emerge from the 1950s was the character created by Ian Fleming. Bond, in book form or played by Sean Connery and later by others, such as Pierce Brosnan and most recently, Daniel Craig, embodied two seminal features that were of enormous appeal: the merging of sophistication with brawn; an impeccable appearance with the lethal ability to get the job done. Although part of a large organization and patriotic to boot, he is given a fair degree of autonomy in his job. In the culture of the 1950s, James Bond was not quite The Organization Man and his worldliness and success with women were very appealing to male readers and later on, viewers of the films. During the late 1950s, dashing John F. Kennedy was one of the first to admit his attraction and devotion to such a role model. David Lubin suggests that

> Bond was a fantasy figure for those like Jack Kennedy who had the wherewithal to emulate his social and sexual savoire-faire and for a wide array of other men during the cold war era. The Bond movies (*Dr. No* came first in 1962, followed by *From Russian with Love* in 1963 and

Goldfinger in 1964) extended the impact of the imaginary secret agent
on the run-of-the-mill male fantasy, setting the hearts of boys and men
aflutter with Bond on-screen.[29]

The Bond ethos and all that it meant is still a prominent cinematic franchise today. Many of the more extreme and chauvinistic elements have
been refined and tempered, yet other aspects of the character's style and
behavior have remained. The various actors who have played James
Bond may differ in their physicality, but all exude the same coolness and
the same masculine sophistication. The films and the character have been
able to keep pace with the varieties of masculine experience and have
consistently reached out to boys in many places.

For certain boys, those inordinately concerned with "coolness," James
Bond and all that he stood for was almost revolutionary in the sense that
he was supremely masculine but handsome, strong, and well-dressed.
He was, as Jay McInerney remembers, the type of man who could do it all
and look great. "Connery's Bond," writes McInerney, "provided a kind
of role model that hadn't existed in the U.S. before —a cultured man who
knew how to navigate a wine list, how to field-strip a Beretta, and how to
seduce women."[30] This last point was particularly important and probably quite damaging to a generation of boys.

While Bond may be the epitome of sartorial elegance and while he
may possess knowledge of wine and women that is unparalleled, to some
extent his polar opposite is not or was not the effeminate sissy man, but
rather a new breed of males who were extraordinarily masculine but
extremely aloof. One element of the binaries of 1950s and early 1960s
culture that sums this up is Gary Willis's idea of the period being "John
Wayne's America." This stoic masculinity was imbibed by millions of
boys who could watch him at the movies and later on, see him on television. Wayne's version of masculinity fit in with the anti-communist hys-
teria of the 1950s. Wayne, through his westerns, gave the impression of
holding one's ground and that as a man, he would not back down or
show weakness. This dovetailed with the obsession of not appearing soft
on communism, which permeated the cultural and political discourse of
the era.[31]

During the 1950s it was vital for political leaders not to give the impression that they were soft on communism. In turn, this carried over
into how men conducted themselves in a variety of situations. What
made appearing tough on communism important was that it seemed to
buttress the idea that the west had gone soft. Related to this was the fear
that once again there was a crisis of masculinity, and as well, a fear of
widespread prevalence of homosexuality. To some extent, as was referenced earlier, this was confirmed by the important role that women had
played domestically during World War II and as well, the female orientation around the home.[32]

Why both James Bond and JFK appeared so significantly masculine is because they seemed to counteract this trend. JFK, at least on the surface, appeared to be a proud father and a devoted husband. He still managed to exude a sophisticated and comfortable level of masculinity. Bond, in print and later on the screen, took this to completely new heights and to new levels. His unabashed desire for women and for adventure, for action and heroism, resonated with men eager for something completely and utterly different.

Yet in keeping with the increasing applicability of diversity in the masculine appearance, both in the media and in everyday life, there was a potency and cache to the anti-hero or rebel who was also capable of conveying a series of essential masculine vibrations. The Beats and their descendants provided a wellspring of difference and a series of challenges to masculinity that the media used and in turn popularized. This made the 1960s a different climate. Despite the strictures and biases put in play during the Cold War, the excitement and innovation in art and culture, poetry and literature, film and music, hinted at something bold and new. As W. T. Lhamon Jr. suggests, "the consequence was a period with an uncommonly high proportion of embattled and daring works."[33] Lhamon proposes Robert Rauschenberg, Kerouac, Mailer, Ginsberg, Chuck Berry, Myles Davis, and Tennessee Williams as examples of the creativity unleashed. It would take a while, but many of these artists became part of a suburban middle brow acceptance and were in turn, co-opted by the media machine. The Beats, as purveyors of a new cultural voice, has an appeal to many in numerous ways. Ginsberg and Kerouac may have been radicals who rejected traditional notions of stability and the family, but despite their subversiveness, many middle-class men were attracted to their writings and their messages via the media.[34]

The upheavals caused by World War II generated a period of readjustment in North American culture that was extraordinary in many ways, one being its lack of success. Damaged men who served and nonconformist males who did not made up a sizeable proportion of the population. The biker, the Beat, and the surfer came to be versions of a new male archetype. At the core of this typology was an unwillingness to be a part of mainstream culture. They exhibited their aversion to the conformity of the 1950s by retreating into all-male fraternal groups, by wearing clothing that was in complete contrast to the button-down, "grey flannel" look, or in the case of California beach culture, wearing little but swimming trunks. The Hawaiian shirt, the leather jacket, jeans, and white t-shirts came to be seen as uniforms for the set that did not wish to don the clothing of corporate consumer culture. But more than their wardrobe—or lack of one—was the attitude.

In most societies, there is a universal equivalent to the biker, the Beat, or the surfer; an outsider of some social force who is both derided and grudgingly respected. Within the history of the United States, and thus arguably through its popular culture's influence, the notion of "rebel masculinity" has a long history. Many of the major figures of American literature and American history are defined in rebel-like terms. Daniel Boone and Buffalo Bill are two prominent versions of these figures. These men lived off the environment or utilized nature and had the ability to survive and thrive in their chosen milieu.[35] They are admired and respected as outsiders and their exploits are lauded. Much of the reason that they are held up as role models has to do with the War of Independence mindset and is also oriented around the importance of individualism in American culture. The fact that so many fictional characters exhibit similar traits: Tom Sawyer, Huck Finn, Jay Gatsby, and Holden Caulfield suggest key features in American culture have a tendency toward nonconformity and are created with a premium on individuality. According to Gary Cross, the Beats saw themselves as "following the twisting river of Mark Twain's Huck Finn and thought of themselves as descendants of the ruggedly independent mountain men."[36]

Whether this individualistic demeanor was self-imposed or derivative of distaste with authority depends on the creator and the individual interpretation. In many cases, there is a propensity toward the adoption of peculiar habits. Leaving society as with Huck Finn or Thoreau removing himself and living by the pond or even adopting some unique look or uniform, form patterns in this archetype of American culture.[37] This is also the reason why so many "mavericks" are so prominent in American popular and established culture. From gangsters like Bugsy Siegel and Pretty Boy Floyd to the aforementioned radical artists such as Jackson Pollock and Ernest Hemingway, to rock stars like Dylan and the Ramones to stand-out athletes in the Ali mold, the ideal carries weight in interpreting masculinity.[38]

For a certain group of men, their clothes and overall appearance are not especially important. There is a tendency with these men to simply throw on what is around and to indulge in only the most basic grooming. They may show potential interest when women are involved, but their focus is not on how they look. In the 1995 Coen brothers movie, *The Big Lebowski*, Jeffrey Lebowski, who insists on being called "the Dude" is a classic anti-hero and a classic slacker. He lounges around all day in shorts and sandals, maybe donning his bathrobe, and drinks White Russians. He gives very little thought to his appearance and wears a selection of clothing that is positively bohemian and very eclectic. He goes bowling and smokes drugs and is content to live in a haze of removal from existence. This creation has become a full-fledged folk hero and is celebrated in festivals all over North America.

Younger versions of the Dude exist in a number of variations: the Seattle grunge dude and the surfer dude are just two. During the 1980s, variations such as these came to the fore with films such as *Fast Times at Ridgemont High* and *Bill and Ted's Excellent Adventure*. These films and their characters are distinguished by a nihilistic self-centeredness that in some ways is nicely resolved by the end of the film. This is accomplished through a quest or an experience that leads to some level of maturity. They revel in their inward focus and their rejection of obligation. There is a freedom in this but also an infantile lack of commitment. As John Troyer and Chani Marchiselli suggest, "Dudes are free from the responsibilities of a self-conscious adulthood." [39]

In film and on television, the slacker subculture and its elastic archetypical look flowered as a version of white masculinity during the 1990s as a consequence of certain factors. One was the popularity of the characters from *Fast Times* and *Bill and Ted* but there was a marked interest by mainstream men who adopted elements from slacker culture and made it, in a way, a part of the conventional. These were variations that could straddle being part of and withdrawn from various permutations within society: from a bourgeois glamour to a proletarian existence, they were always masculine in some way. In sports, vestiges of this look surfaced in the way certain athletes dressed and carried themselves on and off the field or the stadium. Andre Agassi adopted a version of this form of slacker-masculinity and made it work. [40] Kyle Kusz discusses the Agassi phenomenon in the context of a variety of other forms of sports which all shared a similar political and racial foundation. Kusz contends that the attitude of Agassi and the popularity of extreme sports, as variations on the slacker, nonconformist individual, were ways in which white masculinity and its supporting structures attempted to reassert hegemony in the domains of sporting and popular culture. [41] Agassi's looks, and in particular his hair, as well as his antics and his clothing combined with his rapport with the crowd were elements similar to what style mavens from the past had utilized. He shared much with teen idols from film and music in standing out and perfecting a unique persona. But he was also very successful on the court and very hard-working. [42] Agassi evolved from this version of slacker-masculinity to a hybrid version as his career progressed. Inherent in the later manifestation was his sensitive side, his caring and altruistic face that proved just as popular. As he became less glamorous and more professionally successful he still retained a sense of difference and exhibited a coolness that lingered through the remainder of his career.

Another established template of the slacker brand of masculinity is the surfer culture. Coming primarily out of a laid back sense of style from California, this variant merged and morphed continuously throughout the last few decades. The surfer culture, which is a multifaceted world, is appealing as a masculine-mediated template for a number of reasons. The freedom to surf, especially in far-off, warm, and exotic destinations is particularly appealing. While one can indulge in surfing in locales that are closer to where one works, it is a sport that requires complete and total submersion into its environs. The after-surf culture is also fun and involves a fair amount of indulgence in partying and beach life. Simply going to the major surf destinations means moving to someplace that is very different from a typical urban environment. Surfing culture is also oriented around a lack of concern with time and employment. In order to master the waves, one has to put in the time and surfers usually don't care about time.[43]

The guys who surf, the dudes who skateboard, and the males who indulge in rebellious, extreme sports, all adopt a pose that is anti-establishment, and one that is oriented around being extremely cool. In his essay on the origin of "cool," Rick Moody places the term in its modern context around Miles Davis and his creation of slow jazz. Cool is then picked up and refined by the Beats, in particular Kerouac, and given more currency.[44] The Beats have much in common with the slackers and dudes and The Dude. Their vision of life is slow, downbeat, and their outward appearance had been modified by their new vision. Like much of the varieties of post-modern masculinity, this comes out in a multiplicity of ways. It can be the skateboarders who frequent specific places and drink select beers and wear a special set of clothes, or it can manifest itself in a variation of Seattle grunge.

John Leland suggests that one of the first overtly "hip" and cool archetypes was the fictional detective. Within the realm of popular culture and its related impact on mediated masculinity much has to be taken from the quintessential character of the hard-boiled detective. Created out of the pulp magazines of the 1920s and streamlined by masters like Dashiel Hammet and James Cain, this heroic male icon was tough, smart, and a "figure of masculinity unbound."[45] On the surface, the hard-boiled detective exists in contrapuntal relationship to the slacker and the dude, yet what unites him with these more anti-establishment types is the streak of individualism as well as the recurring problems with authority and bureaucracy. He is usually on the fringe of society partially because of his natural tendency to work alone but often placed there by his inability to get along with power figures. A partner may have existed, but may have died or may have betrayed the detective, which is often the case with the women he encounters.

The significance of the hard-boiled detective as an outsider is, as with the slacker and the dude, his detachment.[46] This is a key masculine characteristic as well as a sign of his coolness. Although active and involved in so many dynamic pursuits, the detachment of the character makes him a magnet for women as well as other men. He is unemotional most of the time and stays above it all. Staying cool despite the fact that one's environment is disintegrating is especially important to the allure of detachment. John Leland suggests that this is a mask that one must wear to protect the self but also to give weight to the world to which the detective must descend.[47] Extensions of this include the trench coat or the uniform and even the costumes so favored by superheroes. The fedora and sun-glasses can also be material versions.

Trying too hard to be with it, to be hip, or in the know, erodes the coolness factor. Regardless of how one explains the current usage of the word, one just knows, or one should know, what is cool and what is not. The slacker does not care and that is why he is cool. It is cool to be on the cutting edge and to give the impression of not knowing or caring. Once corporations and the advertising they promote get into the act by appro-priating the lingo, the clothes, and the style, it is no longer cool to those in the know. By the time some facet of coolness is featured via a character on TV, the essence is lost to those on the cutting edge who have moved on. But for the great majority of viewers, it still holds resonance.

What unifies the slacker and the dude is the archetype of the rebel. However this is defined, what the fundamental nature seems to be is someone who is rebelling against the dominant norms and concepts in a given society. By choosing to do something different and to look so radi-cally uncommon, the individual has set himself apart. In recent years, advertising has coopted this notion and lifted this once marginal figure onto a podium on par with the successful conformist. Accordingly, it is now possible to be a rebel and to look the part yet at the same time be a good father and an entrepreneur. One does not necessarily exclude the other. Many business magazines feature these rebels in profiles and equate marching to your own drum as another successful business strate-gy.

Harley Davidson as a motorcycle and an image speaks to many men hoping to catch a touch of the rebel and the outsider; men who have the deep pockets to afford one. The Harley Davidson ethos is emblematic of the "compensatory consumption" thesis discussed by Douglas Holt and Craig Thompson in the beginning of this work. Building on the ideas of John Schouten and James McAlexander, Harley Davidson connotes rebel-liousness and an association with a series of rebel-like overtones. Al-though cost is a factor and thus available only to men with sufficient disposable income, the message conveyed in owning and driving a Har-ley is definitive in its masculine associations:

> The burgeoning community of mainstream Harley riders construct themselves as rebellious men who live for the autonomy of the open road. When riding these domineering machines, men experience a sense of liberation and personal autonomy from the constraints of po-lite society akin to the idealized frontiersman of the West.[48]

As one of the most defined masculine products, the Harley denotes free-dom and captures a key trope in American—and global—mythology; that of freedom and independence. It is also very potent in suggesting that the vehicle is the "antithesis of confinement." In real and semiotic terms, it allows for mobility and breathing space and is capable, so its owners believe; of liberating them form the constraints of modern society.[49]

NOTES

1. James Gilbert, *Men in the Middle: Searching for Masculinity in the 1950s* (Chicago: University of Chicago Press, 2005), pp. 2–3. For a description of an earlier crisis of masculinity, see my *Manliness and Militarism: Educating Young Boys in Ontario for War* (Don Mills, ON: Oxford University Press, 2001).

2. Patricia Vettel-Becker, *Shooting from the Hip: Photography, Masculinity, and Postwar America* (Minneapolis: University of Minnesota Press, 2005), p. xi.

3. Elaine Tyler May, *Homeward Bound: American Families in the Cold War Era* (New York: Basic Books, 1999), pp. 17–18.

4. See Lynne Spigel, *Make Room for TV: Television and the Family Ideal in Postwar America* (Chicago: University of Chicago Press, 1992) and Ella Taylor, *Prime-Time Families: Television Culture in Postwar America* (Berkeley and Los Angeles: University of California Press, 1989).

5. Bill Osgerby, *Playboys in Paradise: Masculinity, Youth and Leisure-Style in Modern America* (Oxford, UK: Berg, 2001), p. 68.

6. See G. Bruce Boyer, *Rebel Style: Cinematic Heroes of the 1950s* (New York: Assouline, 2006), pp. 5–8.

7. Bill Osgerby, *Playboys in Paradise*, p. 72.

8. Michael Rogin, *Ronald Reagan, the Movie: and Other Episodes in Political Demonology* (Berkeley: University of California Press, 1987), p. xiii, cited in K. A. Cuordileone, *Manhood and American Political Culture in the Cold War* (London: Routledge, 2005), p. 70.

9. K. A. Cuordileone, *Manhood and American Political Culture in the Cold War*, p. 70.

10. K. A. Cuordileone, *Manhood and American Political Culture in the Cold War*, p. 71.

11. See Michael S. Kimmel, *The History of Men: Essays on the History of American and British Masculinities* (Albany: SUNY Press, 2005), pp. 32–33, and Jane Tompkins, *West of Everything: The Inner Life of Westerns* (New York: Oxford University Press, 1992), pp. 4, 145.

12. Michael Kimmel, *Manhood in America: A Cultural History*, 2nd ed. (New York: Oxford University Press, 2006), p. 252.

13. Thomas Newkirk, *Misreading Masculinity: Boys, Literacy, and Popular Culture* (Portsmouth, NH: Heinemann, 2002), p. 8.

14. Thomas Newkirk, *Misreading Masculinity*, pp. 8–9.

15. Karen J. Hall, "A Soldier's Body: GI Joe, Hasbro's Great American Hero, and the Symptoms of Empire," *Journal of Popular Culture* 38, no. 1 (August 2004), p. 37.

16. Karen J. Hall, "A Soldier's Body," p. 38.

17. Tom Engelhardt, *The End of Victory Culture: Cold War America and the Disillusioning of a Generation* (New York: Basic Books, 1995), p. 175.

18. Susan Faludi, *Stiffed: The Betrayal of the American Man* (New York: Morrow, 1999), p. 16.

19. Susan Faludi, *Stiffed*, p. 17.

20. This point is confirmed throughout Alan Brinkley's work. See *The Publisher: Henry Luce and His American Century* (New York: Knopf, 2010).

21. Susan Faludi, *Stiffed*, pp. 21–22.

22. G. Bruce Boyer, *Rebel Style*, pp. 9–10.

23. Doug Owram, *Born at the Right Time: A History of the Baby Boom Generation* (Toronto, ON: University of Toronto Press, 1996), pp. 146–150.

24. Leo Braudy, *From Chivalry to Terrorism: War and the Changing Nature of Masculinity* (New York: Knopf, 2003), p. 366.

25. Natalia Aspesi, "Military Style: The Reappearance of Uniforms in the Icon of Masculinity," in *Material Man: Masculinity, Sexuality, Style*, ed. Giannino Malssi (New York: Abrams, 2000), pp. 148, 150.

26. Brent Shannon, "Refashioning Men: Fashion, Masculinity, and the Cultivation of the Male Consumer in Britain, 1860–1914," *Victorian Studies* 46, no. 4 (Summer 2004), p. 605.

27. G. Bruce Boyer, *Rebel Style*, pp. 13, 14.

28. G. Bruce Boyer, *Rebel Style*, pp. 15, 16.

29. David M. Lubin, *Shooting Kennedy: JFK and the Culture of Images* (Berkeley: University of California Press, 2003), p. 109.

30. Jay McInerney, "How Bond Saved America—and Me," in *Dressed to Kill: James Bond, the Suited Hero*, ed. Jay McInerney et al. (New York: Flammarion, 1996), pp. 13–36, cited in Bill Osgerby, *Playboys in Paradise*, p. 163.

31. Gary Willis, *John Wayne's America: The Politics of Celebrity* (New York: Simon & Schuster, 1997).

32. See K. A. Cuordileone, *Manhood and American Political Culture in the Cold War*, pp. 9–18; James Gilbert, *Men in the Middle*; and Bill Osgerby, *Playboys in Paradise*.

33. W. T. Lhamon Jr., *Deliberate Speed: The Origins of a Cultural Style in the American 1950s* (Washington, D.C.: Smithsonian Institution Press, 1990), p. 7.

34. Gary Cross, *Men to Boys: The Making of Modern Immaturity* (New York: Columbia University Press, 2008), p. 67.

35. Douglas B. Holt and Craig J. Thompson, "Man-of-Action Heroes: The Pursuit of Heroic Masculinity in Everyday Consumption," *Journal of Consumer Research* 31 (September 2004), p. 427.

36. Gary Cross, *Men to Boys*, p. 68.

37. Daniel S. Traber, *Whiteness, Otherness, and the Individualism Paradox from Huck to Punk* (New York: Palgrave Macmillan, 2007), p. 6.

38. Douglas B. Holt and Craig J. Thompson, "Man-of-Action Heroes," p. 428.

39. John Troyer and Chani Marchiselli, "Slack, Slacker, Slackest: Homosocial Bonding Practices in Contemporary Dude Cinema," in *Where the Boys Are: Cinemas of Masculinity and Youth*, ed. Murray Pomerance and Frances Gateward (Detroit, MI: Wayne State University Press, 2005), p. 267.

40. Kyle Kusz, *Revolt of the White Athlete* (New York: Peter Lang, 2007), pp. 22, 24.

41. Kyle Kusz, *Revolt of the White Athlete*, pp. 1–20.

42. Kyle Kusz, *Revolt of the White Athlete*, pp. 27–30.

43. See Tom Lutz, *Doing Nothing: A History of Loafers, Loungers, Slackers, and Bums in America* (New York: Farrar, Straus & Giroux, 2006), p. 256.

44. Rick Moody, "Against Cool," *The Best American Essays: 2004*, ed. Louis Menand (Boston: Houghton Mifflin, 2004), pp. 164–172.

45. John Leland, *Hip: The History* (New York: HarperCollins, 2004), p. 90.

46. John Leland, *Hip*, p. 91.

47. John Leland, *Hip*, pp. 91–95.

48. John Schouten and James McAlexander, "Subcultures of Consumption: An Ethnography of New Bikers," *Journal of Consumer Research* 22 (June 1995), pp. 52–55, cited in Douglas B. Holt and Craig J. Thompson, "Man-of-Action Heroes: The Pursuit of Heroic Masculinity in Everyday Consumption," *Journal of Consumer Research* 31 (September 2004), p. 426.

49. John Schouten and James McAlexander, "Subcultures of Consumption," pp. 52–55, cited in Douglas B. Holt and Craig J. Thompson, "Man-of-Action Heroes," p. 426.

SEVEN
Masculinity, Media, and Aggression

As women in the west reach levels of parity in the world of work, education, and income earned, it becomes obvious that the one area they will never surpass men is in violence and destructive behavior.[1] Violence and aggression are significant features in many men's communities and are celebrated in numerous media and popular culture portrayals. Whether through UFC bouts or the lyrics of music, the central feature of much of mediated culture involves violence and aggression perpetrated by men.[2] In the worlds of anthropologist Richard Bribiescas, "men make up about half of the human population, but they are involved in far more than half of humankind's destructive and violent behavior."[3] Before they were men, they were boys and much ink has been spilled on discussing what is right for boys and young men as far as media exposure and popular culture's impact.

All the research and all the time that has been devoted to creating a generation of boys who will grow into sensitive, nonviolent men, seems to come crashing down at specific intervals. Some authorities suggest that violence is a negative offshoot of aggression, which when harnessed properly, far outweighs its nefarious costs. What this means is that the inherent tendency of boys and men to participate in daring, aggressive, and often questionable behavior is part of their make-up. This is also why boys and men will watch shows that feature these extremes and listen to music that celebrates this propensity. Boys are taught that those who go the distance, take chances, and engage in risk are more likely to be successful. Boys and men who physically excel in certain arenas are more likely to be the ones who become leaders and who, in many cases, effect change.

Attempts to weed out destructive, aggressive, and hyper-masculine behavior seem to constantly fall by the wayside. In the introduction to her edited volume, *What Makes A Man*, Rebecca Walker has to deal with the real world of masculine culture closing in on her young son. Despite all the effort and all the attempts to raise a sensitive and passionate son, outside forces conspire to ruin the project. The traditional staples of sports and violence make in-roads on her son's sense of self, and simply put, he can not be accepted as a full-fledged member unless he participates in team sports, becomes an athlete, while at the same time, engaging in video games and computer simulations that involve killing. The pressure to conform to this world is immense:

> You don't understand, he said huffily. Boys talk about sports, like their matches and who scored what and stuff, or they talk about new versions of computer games or tricks they learned to get to higher levels. Tears welled up in his eyes. I don't have anything to talk about.[4]

Walker comes to the sudden and sad awareness that boys, in order to be considered full-fledged members of this male fraternity, only have two options: "fight actually in sport, or fight virtually on the computer." Regardless of who her son really is, in order for him to be part of the group and to be considered a member with "social currency," he had to join up and participate.[5]

In observing the diverse array of masculine images presented by the media, and factoring in the changes that have occurred over the previous two generations, one would think that the pressures to conform to traditional notions of aggressive maleness would have been severely dissipated by the growing acceptance of other behaviors. Yet as Walker's anecdote makes quite clear, large pockets of this culture of aggression continue to exist. In the extreme, as she observes, she wonders if he was being "primed for war," "primed to pick up a gun." Was this process inevitable? Were the pressures so extreme that in order to ward off the epithets of "fag, bitch, punk, pussy, homo, queer," he would have to go to war, literally and metaphorically? The demands of being a man, a "real man" she concludes, inevitably close in on the boy; extended this means that the subtle and not so subtle ways to act and comport oneself. The list this entails, if recited one hundred years ago, would have been considered a "manly" one, but in contemporary terms it reads like an embarrassing array of problematic and contradictory illusions that still find currency in modern day culture: "don't feel, take control, be physically strong, find your identity in money and work, do not be afraid to kill, distrust everything that you cannot see. Don't cry."[6]

William Pollack's observation on boys and the cultural wall, which prevents them from expressing emotion, coalesces around what he terms "The Boy Code." The pressure to not exhibit any emotional variables other than productive rage has "paralyzed" male culture and has "isolated" young men. Pollack cites one eighteen year old who likens this lack of visible emotion to donning armor: "You can never flinch. . . . Don't let your feelings show."[7]

In another essential feature of the "Boy Code" the most horrific insult is to be termed unmasculine. "The worst insult," writes Pollack, "a boy can experience is to be called a 'wimp,' 'fag,' 'homo,' or 'wuss.'"[8] The process carries over into adulthood. Young men and men in general never learn to deal with intimacy and fear, doubt, and genuine emotion. To Rebecca Walker, it seems as if these characteristics are killing men through heart attacks or destroying their souls through depression. Yet there are attempts to break these molds, to move in new directions, and to get men to deal with stress, to show emotion, and to alleviate aggressive tendencies in ways that are less taxing and less lethal.

Despite these attempts to make men more receptive to expressing themselves in positive ways, cultural constraints and the content of mass media still reinforce dominant codes of masculine deportment. Showing a crying man in a film is not as appealing as Clint Eastwood seeking revenge. The historical imprint, both in real and mediated terms, still wields enormous power on the popular psyche. Leo Braudy has discussed the pull of historical masculinity and in particular, how it exerts a lasting influence on the definitive masculine paradigm. Braudy makes an interesting series of connections in this regard:

> Cultures and individuals hang on to outmoded styles of masculinity in the same way that armies hang on to older technologies. In this sense there is a masculinity that is built on simple masculine myths: a bipolar difference between male and female: the decisive role of the body; male strength and male sexuality.[9]

Armies and military culture in general have a tendency to advertise specific forms of masculinity. If one looks at propaganda and recruitment posters from World War I, there is a focus on clean masculinity, a kind of "homey" and comforting portrayal of men in uniform that is often not threatening, but rather pure. During World War II, elements of hard-boiled masculinity are clearly discernable in many posters, complete with tight bodies and rock-hard jaws. Currently, looking at commercials for both the American services as well as the Canadian forces, a very different picture emerges. There is a stealth-like quality to many of the advertisements, which, as will be discussed, seems dependent on technology in very significant ways. This mirrors, or perhaps is mirrored, in many of the films made in the previous twenty years, which merge technologically sophisticated culture with an agile, quick-thinking man. As well, there is also the time-tested adventure aspect to advertising and marketing. Falling out of a plane or being dropped from a helicopter are features that appeal to a certain male demographic, in particular those that watch and participate in extreme sports and those who play specific video games.

Currently, this masculine matrix finds expression in very unique ways. The utilization of technology can devalue individual bravado and courage but as the content of at least a dozen Hollywood films suggests, the man still wins in the end. But in the real world, the integration of technology into spheres that are inherently dangerous, such as the battlefield or the deep sea, poses a problem for some men. If those are the places that were the traditional or last proving grounds and men are being substituted for machines, this is often seen as threatening. With electronic drones, deep-sea robots, and a host of other devices, the last bastion of masculinity's proving ground may disappear. Even in cutting-edge science fiction films such as *Avatar*, the machismo of soldiers and their ilk has to be accounted for despite the fact that technology has almost taken over. The thinking is that the body must remain supreme and vital to the mission. Heavily-armed troops now sport a variety of technological enhancements, prosthetic accoutrements to the traditional flesh and blood. From night-vision goggles to body sensors that can detect poisonous chemicals or radiation, these new "metamen" are enhanced by scientific developments. In a very short time there will be Terminators, Robocops, and Universal Soldiers.

The military has always been at the forefront of developments for its soldiers that will enhance their performance in the field. From sunglasses to sunscreen, Kevlar vests, and Humvees, innovations that inevitably find their way into civilian use are often the result of initiatives first asked for by military personnel. Video game technology is just the latest version.

To some extent men flock to electronic gadgets and like the synthesis of devices with their body that will allow them to perform better. Digital culture is at the cutting edge of this merging and video games in particular mark an enormously important element of this evolution.

From the Wii to virtual reality glasses to the X-Box, boys and men gravitate toward technologically based objects for a variety of reasons. They enjoy the tactile nature of holding them and they seem to be enthralled with the prosthetic-like extensions into universes or zones that are proffered up. The worlds of video games offer players an Ericksonian psychosocial moratorium. In essence, boys don't have to worry about failure and don't have to worry about being made fun of. They can master the game in private and then choose to display their prowess online. They can and do feel empowered and in many instances, video games are what they excel in as opposed to the public performance required in sport or even being cool. As two researchers have commented, "video-games are spaces where players can be successful in their endeavors."[10] The most popular games pander to traditional notions and ideals of masculinity with a heavy emphasis on violence. These include racing games and shooter games as well as war games. For older boys and men, sports games are extremely appealing and offer the chance to be successful on the field, to exercise some virtual physicality without being injured. Fantasy and creative construction games such as *Myst*, *The Sims*, and *Civilization* offer chances to build and construct as well as to be something one is not.[11] These later games exude a level of sophistication that does not mean that traditional male attributes are wholly dominant, but rather, that there is a merging of a collective and constructive intent that is essential for success. Trying on roles and adopting new characters has held appeal since *Dungeons and Dragons* was popular and the legacy of being someone else is especially enticing. As Kathy Sanford and Leanna Madill observe,

> Videogames provide players with spaces in which to experiment with identify: to safely resist traditional masculinities currently prevailing in society, or conversely, to demonstrate their heterosexual masculinity and resist connections to the feminine, and to challenge societal expectations of appropriateness regarding attitude, appearance, or behavior.[12]

What becomes clear is that through video games and their ancillary worlds, boys and men can experiment with a variety of scenarios: they can perform and win, be a hero and a leader. What often ends up happening is that the traditional role models are what men and boys try on. Video game manufacturers, designers, and marketers create the most dynamic and hyper-masculine roles for those playing them to get into. Just looking at the box gives one a sense of the potency, power, and appeal. The problem is that the focus is often on violence and destruction.[13] Although this is not confined to the video-game world, and there are other features that video games satisfy such as competition, it is significant.[14]

Video games, especially the violent and killing-oriented ones, owe much to graphic novels, horror movies, adventure stories, and a whole compendium of cultural artifacts that build on the male hero trying to outdo or fight a series of enemies. Interspersed into these narratives or surrounding them can be larger issues such as war, crime, and even existence. The player is significant in the sense that he is in charge and can utilize the created world to escape from reality, while at the same time he is enabled to be successful in the virtual world.[15] This is especially pronounced in the desire to be a winner and thus, a hero.

Adventure and war games are often the most popular. One of the reasons for the enormous and consistent esteem of video games with a war theme is that it harnesses the popularity of the soldier hero. Whether these games are oriented around battling terrorists, futuristic combat, refighting historical battles, or rescuing hostages, they involve utilization of the combatant archetype.

Perhaps the most consistently durable male image, the one that transcends time and space, is the warrior or the soldier and the variables derived from that symbol—the adventurer and the explorer. This variable archetype exerts enormous influence and has a staying power that is unprecedented. Through the Spartans, Rome, and into the Knights of the Middle Ages on through time, the soldier/warrior was present in a front and center model. Refitted during the early modern period and "rebranded" in the eighteenth and nineteenth centuries, the soldier/warrior was given added appeal with the development of sophisticated visual imagery utilized in advertising and media of the late Victorian period. According to Brent Shannon, during this era,

> Advertisers relied heavily on the conqueror image in the form of the soldier and quasi-military adventurer because it was a familiar Victorian icon that instantly evoked powerful jingoistic associations of British imperial might, high adventure in exotic far-off lands, and a rugged, unchallenged masculinity. The middle-class British male, these ads implied, could share vicariously in the enterprises of the British Empire by shopping for goods related to its exploration.[16]

The distillation of military imagery throughout British and other European societies is a key feature of militarism and further enhanced the popularity of the soldier. A similar process occurred in the United States. The enormous resources devoted, especially in propagandistic terms, from the Civil War and the Spanish-American War through World War I and into World War II, cemented the image of the soldier as hero in popular consciousness. The elasticity of appeal from the Doughboy to the GI to the grunt is remarkable.

The warrior, despite its increasing devalued status and often, its replacement by technology, continues to attract men and spawn metaphors. The first Gulf War and the most recent Gulf War were presented through television in a manner that mimicked sports and that utilized all the vestiges of athletic culture. Regardless of the morality of the war or the horror associated with it, watching men walk around in their desert camouflage and their heavy rifles, thick helmets, and large boots, provides a "cool" image to prospective boys and men wishing to emulate someone masculine or aspire toward some model of legitimate machismo. A news item once reported that even though Canada was involved in the first Gulf War, American recruiting offices were barraged with calls from across the border asking how and if Canadian men could sign up. This bizarre series of requests indicates that many men still respond to the traditional masculine association of the Army and further, that the American armed forces are truly the place to be as a pure militaristic masculine outlet.

Anthony Swofford's memoir *Jarhead* details his life and experiences as an elite Marine sniper sent off to fight in the first Gulf War. His book reactivates the once-dormant passion of young boys to enlist. He conveys the appeal with well-stocked anecdotes and crisp writing, over-the-top stories, subtle observations, and a coherent narrative filled with male bonding and patriotism. He recognizes the contradictions and the horrors of death and dismemberment and is very much aware of the liabilities, but is still proud of his commitment and feels privileged and unique for having served. The attraction of signing up and serving is problematic for some, but for him and those like him, it is a chance to demonstrate their maleness and to survey something most men won't have the opportunity to engage in. What passes for inappropriate behavior on the outside is glorified and encouraged within the brotherhood of the fighting man. In one passage, Swofford comments on the fact that in civilian life war movies are designed to convey a pacifist response; to suggest quite strongly that war is "inhumane and terrible." But in the Marine Corps and in the other services, soldiers and seamen,

> watch the same films and are excited by them, because the magic brutality of the films celebrates the terrible and despicable beauty of their fighting skills. Fight, rape, war, pillage, burn. Filmic images of death and carnage are pornography for the military man; with film you are stroking his cock, tickling his balls with the pink feather of history, getting him ready for his real First Fuck. It doesn't matter how many Mr. and Mrs. Johnsons are antiwar—The actual killers who know how to use the weapons are not.[17]

Men, soldiers generally, and Swofford and his comrades certainly embrace these images and often revel in the depiction of violence. Many cross over because they have to, to actual killing. The line between the reality and the fantasy is very thin for them. This is the anti-catharsis at work.

Armies, like sports teams, have a tendency to employ and utilize the divergences of masculinity in a number of ways. Being part of a cohesive unit, large or small, armies can impart a very specific message to its members; messages of patriotism and of defense can be harnessed to buttress morale and overall images and visuals can be effective as forms of propaganda both domestically and internationally. Protection of people and property also figures into the grand appeal of joining an army. Fighting, as if for the defense of ideals embedded in people and property, also serves to congeal around patriotic masculinity. Stefan Dudink and Karen Hagemann pinpoint an interesting connection where the above originated. During the American Revolution, the images, sentiments, and narratives produced a "multiplicity of masculinities" that has resounded to the present day. But what is unique is that the Americans were focused during the Revolution on a new form of masculinity that revolved around citizens and the guarantees inherent in freedom and property ownership. This militia myth of masculinity was positioned around a robust hardiness, which was in turn contrasted against the perceived unmanly spirit of the Red Coats and especially against the British officers. They write that George Washington himself celebrated the uncontrolled enthusiasm of a citizen army and its quest for manly independence.[18]

When it is not possible to be engaged in an actual war, surrogates have always served as acceptable facsimiles. Men get excited about guns, rifles, cross bows, and knives. Even the insignificant penknife can serve as a connector, a talisman reminding some men of their primitive skills. Hunting and the mythos surrounding weaponry usually meet this felt need, regardless of politics. The rise of militias is a problematic response to this situation and is an extreme reaction. Hunting as referenced earlier, despite its critics, is still a supreme masculine testing ground. David Mamet has written about the solitary and communal joys of hunting. This cerebral playwright details in minute fashion the key attributes of male cultural bonding as illustrated in hunting and the firing of weapons. He is attracted to both the paraphernalia of these masculine activities and the attributes of violent culture.[19] In his essay on a *Soldier of Fortune* conference held in Las Vegas, he tries to be critical and distant but descriptors of admiration and impressive wonder keep popping out. Mamet can't seem to stop himself from being swept away with awe when he is immersed with former air marshals and representatives from Heckler & Koch and other armament corporations. He is like a kid in a candy store, excited to be so close to hard-core masculinity. His essay clicks with posturing and attempted distance but there is no escaping the fact that he is impressed.[20]

Even normally liberal—extremely liberal Dan Savage, the openly gay syndicated sex columnist, gets excited about something as supremely masculine as firing a gun. In his rebuttal to right-wing commentators, who think that the United States is on the verge of a moral and social collapse, Savage investigates the seven deadly sins on a tour throughout the country. His chapter "Anger" focuses on his first attempts to fire a variety of different caliber guns in Texas. He's good. As the instructor tells him, "You're a good shot. It's a gift." He's thrilled that he is a natural at this lethal and manly sport.[21]

A problem here is the fact that very often these masculine gatherings involve not just the amateur rifleman or the sport shooter but rather, members of the extreme fringes of society. This means KKK members or militia recruits who are rabidly racist and anti-Semitic, and who are bent on the overthrow of the U.S. government. This extremist version of the macho gun enthusiast is confined to a small fringe, yet the antiquated and often misogynistic, homophobic, and fundamentalist ethos is disturbing and dangerous.[22]

Violence is celebrated, not discouraged, in much of contemporary popular culture. Whether high or low, popular or mass, visions of masculine success are often filtered through the lenses of violent programming, texts, and video games. Violence as a male outlet for emotion as well as a form of entertainment is much more sophisticated than simply the cause-and-effect type of explanation. To watch and to read and then, simply to act, does not hold up to scrutiny. There are divergent variants of violent entertainment, which run the gamut from comic book formats, to slapstick to documentary, all of which lead to the conclusion that it is too complex as a form of entertainment to be wholly causal. But certain entertainment offerings stand out as significant touchstones of violent entertainment. They are useful as examples because they are watched and often created by men. But violence is also so anomalous to the everyday. Commenting in the *New York Times*, Sam Tanenhaus writes,

> It is not news that so-called senseless acts often unfold along the coordinates of an inner logic. This is what makes criminal violence so attractive a topic for artists and thinkers. The Western literary tradition, from Shakespeare to Dostoevsky, teems with pathologically violent men. Norman Mailer and Truman Capote wrote nonfiction masterpieces about them. They dominate the novels of Don DeLillo and Robert Stone, not to mention films by Sam Peckinpah, Francis Ford Coppola and Martin Scorsese. [23]

In a number of places throughout this book, works such as *American Psycho, Fight Club,* and *Gladiator* have been referenced to discuss aspects of mediated masculinity. What they have in common is a heavy amount of violent content. Another seminal visual text of the nineties that deserves brief mention here is the 1992 Michael Douglas film, *Falling Down*.

What *Falling Down* illustrates is the impotence of the white male and his frustration at a system that has sold him out. Douglas's character had once been a successful defense industry engineer, with a wife and a child to complete the so-called perfect life. In the movie, he lashes out at society—immigrants, the rich, and women—who he believes have sold him out. Bill Foster, the character played by Douglas, represents the average guy who no longer has a part of the world and is increasingly removed from participating in what he was led to believe was his due. This sentiment and the subtext of the movie reflects the political and economic changes of the period, when cheaper jobs overseas inspired numerous American corporations to sell out their traditional workforce. With the decline of the Cold War, the once-lucrative defense sector was also reduced to a fraction of its former self, as the character in the movie demonstrates. A fair amount of resentment and bitterness is effectively confirmed through Foster's now superfluous role. [24] The only way for him to recapture some kind of dignity is to have him killed so that his insurance money can go to his child. This undercurrent of desperation is pervasive throughout the film and dialectic in its indictment of the "system." It is both glaring and extremely effective. What also adds to the irony is that the policeman who shoots him is on his last day of work, being put out to pasture as too old, and being forced to retire to spend his days with his annoying wife.

Falling Down typifies a string of films and novels devoted to the almost "masochistic" failings of men. Most of the blame is in some way or form put on the shoulders of the American economic system and its complete disregard for human capital. What results in fictional form, although quite often in life as well, is a backlash against the system where the protagonist resorts to either corporate sabotage as in the Jim Carrey movie, *Fun With Dick and Jane*, or flat-out violence or revenge against a corporate entity in order for the man to recover some shred of decency. In some manifestations, by acting out, he becomes a version of a folk hero or a rebel, based on a form of institutional victimization.

Both David Savran[25] and Lynn M. Ta—among others—have pinpointed this financial and moral failing as a crystallization point. According to Lynn M. Ta, as

> a slave to the economic system, the white male rebel must revolt against a dominant culture that has ostensibly pushed his masculinity to the margins. In the face of this social and economic disempowerment, he seeks recourse in victimhood, becoming the divided self who at once laments his victimization but also depends on it as a point of protest and identification.[26]

As juxtaposition to the film treatment of middle-class and working-class white men, there is the panacea of music articulated by Bruce Springsteen's lyrics. During the 1980s and well into the new millennium, his music came to embody an angry streak, which to some extent took the system to task. Ripe with factory layoffs and still reeling from Vietnam, Springsteen embodied a rejuvenated American masculinity that transcended class and held great appeal to men.[27] What Springsteen's songs were big on was respect. Getting it and maintaining it are important to his worlds just as they are in certain aspects of rap music.

One of the key attributes of manliness is the concept of respect. A manly man or a supremely masculine male is one to whom other men show respect. Lack of respect, especially in a public forum, is interpreted as a challenge to a man's authority and to his sense of masculinity. Whether it is boys on a playground, gang members in the inner city, competitors on sports fields, or the wrong comment in a bar, the challenge to authority and the visible posturing and audible impugning of one's character and/or masculinity, upsets the balance. For many men, this is when the fight begins. If it happens in a work environment, fighting is not an option and this can lead to displaced aggression. You are supposed to take it outside. Fighting videos are quite popular on video sharing sites such as YouTube.[28] In these cases they are not always provoked by disrespect but when they happen in a bar or in the schoolyard, they often occur for no reason other than boredom.[29]

Despite the fact that the influence of academic feminism has had an impact on the way boys are socialized, and despite the fact more fathers take an active role in the home, there are still enormous factors that contribute to the "boys being boys" notion. Beyond genetics and inveterate features, many are acquired socially. Most young children in a playground situation will group together by sex. The boys gravitate toward certain kinds of games and specific sports. The play engaged in is often very different; boys tend to engage in much more competitive and daring activities.[30]

As they get older, the differences become much more meaningful and begin to take on a pronounced importance. Adolescent boys and young men are very conscious of how they are perceived, either alone or in groups, and they are willful about their roles as masculine performers. The wrong move or the wrong choice of clothing can have dire consequences.[31] Yet in research conducted on the culture of young boys and masculinity, the issue of individuality and the assertion of independence from the dominant codes of masculine behavior does surface. At school, according to the authors of an article on this topic, anyone who is out of line with the dominant forms of gender appearance runs the risk of being labeled a "fag." A significant marker in maintaining a masculine pose in this context is the way young boys physically posture themselves, the manner in which they hold their bodies. Size and physical prowess in gym are also key features in accessing masculine privileges.[32]

The culture of sport, so closely linked to dominant masculinity and aggression, is intimately tied to "being a man." Although there are increasing exceptions to this, such as the move in certain school environments to be more tolerant of boys who do not wish to compete in sports and the issues surrounding bullying, there is still a significant thrust in this arena. If a boy is good at sports, he often has an easier time fitting in, being popular, and succeeding, at least socially as a teenager. The converse is also true.[33] Closely related to this is the obsession with body image. Boys, like girls, want to look good. Having a good, if not perfect body, is a very strong marker of fitting in.

Sport and jock culture emphasize everything from toughness on the field to being able to take pain. Internet videos constantly feature boys trying to test their strength in fights or in stunts that involve the ability to withstand punishment. The tougher one is the more credibility one has amongst one's peers. The ideal compilation is to be and act tough and to look like a bad guy.

It is almost a cliché to suggest that men are equally concerned about body image as women. Men are told through advertising and the plethora of action heroes, television shows, and fashion and design, that they have to be fit and ideally, possess "washboard" abs or an overall, perfect physique.[34] They can choose to have the powerful physique of an athlete or the sleek build of a model, but either way, the bar is set unreasonably high. This is why so many hours are spent in the gym, away from other activities, and this is also why the use of steroids provides such a popular shortcut. Men are also indulging in cosmetic surgery to whittle away the flab and men from a diverse variety of backgrounds eagerly seek this method out as a cure-all. Journalist Charlie LeDuff relates the following quip from a Manhattan plastic surgeon:

> The media is telling him he doesn't measure up, the doctor says. "It's not just the rich Park Avenue guy. It's cops and everyone else. I had a bus driver come in here and request liposuction. He says he feels self-conscious, that he thinks the women on the bus are staring at his love handles.[35]

What this points to is that many men are extremely concerned not just about how they look, but more to the point, about not measuring up to some new and almost impossible ideal. The boys on *Jersey Shore* spend an inordinate amount of time working out and tanning, not reading or trying to better the world. As a result, they look unreal; this, in turn, seems to bother men who work for a living. Gone is the idea that men simply don't care. Now, the connections between men and their bodies have undergone a huge transformation. The slick and tight look featured in so many advertisements and movies has had an impact on men.[36] The following lengthy quote from Guy Garcia sums up the situation and the problem:

> But Madison Avenue's fervid embrace of beefcake has cost men much more than a ballooning balance on their Macy's charge card. When Calvin Klein figured out in the eighties that eroticized images of muscular men would sell underwear to men and women, straight and gay, he not only let the macho gay aesthetic out of the closet and into the shopping mall, he opened the door to the not-so-brave new world of straight male neurosis. As it became acceptable for near-naked male bodies to be ogled in ads and in the media, most men only felt a creeping sense of self-consciousness and inadequacy. While images of men had changed, masculine codes of behavior and sexuality had not. Masculinity had been repackaged but not fundamentally altered: guys were still expected to act like men, but now they had to look like Olympic gods, too.[37]

While boys and young men have always been positioned at certain points as sex objects, the erotic qualities to these poster boys have always been rather tame—at least in the mainstream media and within the confines of heterosexual culture. In the 1990s, as extreme sexual of images of women, especially very young women, began to proliferate, a version of this came into being for men. This took the seemingly innocent firemen calendars to the highly suggestive images of the perfect man parading around in his underwear.

Since the 1990s, the depiction of the male body both as a sexual object and as erotic attraction has been growing as a commonplace attribute of visual imagery wit each passing year. Advertisements for cologne and men's wear from Ralph Lauren to Dolce & Gabbana are almost pornographic in their staging. The seeming regularity of nearly naked men in photographs and calendars, on TV and elsewhere, strips away the impact of the image, making it commonplace. Men who are featured are often in such good shape that this creates a paragon body image that becomes an ideal that is "mass produced, and then disseminated throughout the population."[38] The average man now feels inadequate and unmanly in comparison to the super-buff men in the world created in the media. This is one reason why steroid use and supplement abuse has increased.

The rise of "supermales" originally comes from the increasing use of steroids in major doses by bodybuilders and later, athletes from all sports. Chemically enhanced size as a consequence of artificial hormones and other substances came into use during the 1950s by eastern bloc weightlifters and other athletes. Once the results were seen, others jumped on the bandwagon until it became an ingrained part of competitive sports. Bodybuilders in particular took to steroids and increased muscle mass in proportions that were previously unheard of. As pictures of the enormous musculature became more common, others, wishing to gain muscle and mass as well as strength, resorted to steroids to attain the size that no amount of hard work could produce naturally.[39]

It is not just Hollywood movies and bodybuilding magazines that perpetuate this sense of hugeness that is both dangerous and unrealistic, not to mention detrimental, to a boy's psychological development. In harmony with the mass media, there are a host of ancillary avenues pushing this message. Vitamin and supplement manufacturers as well as diet and pseudo-health companies further the distorted message of size and strength in a bottle.[40]

The authors of *The Adonis Complex* also point to the fact that children's toys reinforce this message. Whereas the improbability of the Barbie body is one thing—this would give a real-life girl a sixteen-inch waist—the GI Joe and other toy versions of action figures have grown to enormous and outlandish muscular sizing. The current versions are hyper-muscular and defined to the extreme. They are literally steroid versions in plastic.[41] This exaggerated version of hyper-masculinity has resonance with young boys and with the bodybuilding community. It is not seen as obscene or completely abnormal. For some boys and some men, being as huge as possible is integral to their self-esteem. Although few men realistically compare themselves to these grotesque versions, the impact is still quite pronounced.

North American society puts a supreme emphasis on male strength. This is often complimented with large size and even the focus on height. Related to the grandiose focusing on strength is the opposite, weakness.

Weakness in sport, society, work, and relationships is of course relative and subjective as well as subject to a changing series of definitions. Not showing pain is one manifestation, as referenced earlier, and this attribute is all about not showing any weaknesses. To further add to the contradictions, so too is the obsession with risk-taking.[42] From the media, males learn to withhold any evidence of emotion that focuses on sissy-like behavior, but at the same time, they are expected to be in touch with their emotions.

NOTES

1. See "Sometimes It's Hard to Be a Man," *Economist*, December 22, 2001.

2. For some interesting commentary as well as facts and figures on the role of women in the traditional spheres, and examples of violence in popular culture, see Guy Garcia, *The Decline of Men* (New York: Harper Perennial, 2008).

3. Richard G. Bribiescas, *Men: Evolutionary and Life History* (Cambridge, MA: Harvard University Press, 2006), p. 1.

4. Rebecca Walker, "Putting Down the Gun," in *What Makes A Man: Twenty-two Writers Imagine the Future*, ed. Rebecca Walker (New York: Riverhead/Penguin, 2004), p. 2.

5. Rebecca Walker, "Putting Down the Gun," p. 3.

6. Rebecca Walker, "Putting Down the Gun," pp. 3, 4.

7. William S. Pollack, with Todd Shuster, *Real Boys' Voices* (New York: Random House, 2000), pp. 4, 5.

8. William S. Pollack, with Todd Shuster, *Real Boys' Voices*, p. 6.

9. Leo Braudy, *From Chivalry to Terrorism: War and the Changing Nature of Masculinity* (New York: Knopf, 2003), p. 86.

10. Kathy Sanford and Leanna Madill, "Resistance through Video Game Play: It's a Boy Thing," *Canadian Journal of Education* 29, no. 3 (August 2005), p. 219.

11. See Jeroen Jansz, "The Emotional Appeal of Violent Video Games for Adolescent Males," *Communication Theory* 15, no. 3 (August 2005), p. 219.

12. Kathy Sanford and Leanna Madill, "Resistance through Video Game Play," p. 297.

13. Jeroen Jansz, "The Emotional Appeal of Violent Video Games for Adolescent Males," pp. 219, 220.

14. Jeroen Jansz, "The Emotional Appeal of Violent Video Games for Adolescent Males," p. 224.

15. Derek A. Burrill, *Die Tryin': Videogames, Masculinity, Culture* (New York: Peter Lang, 2008), p. 2.

16. Brent Shannon, "Refashioning Men: Fashion, Masculinity, and the Cultivation of the Male Consumer in Britain, 1860–1914," *Victorian Studies* 46, no. 4 (Summer 2004), p. 605.

17. Anthoy Swofford, *Jarhead: A Marine's Chronicle of the Gulf War and Other Battles* (London: Scribner, 2003), pp. 6–7.

18. Stefan Dudink and Karen Hagemann, "Masculinity in Politics and War in the Age of Democratic Revolutions, 1750–1850," in *Masculinities in Politics and War: Gendering Modern History*, ed. Stefan Dudink, Karen Hagemann, and John Tosh (Manchester, UK: Manchester University Press, 2004), pp. 8, 9.

19. See David Mamet, "Deer Hunting," in *Make-Believe Town* (Boston: Little, Brown, 1996) and "Practical Pistol Competition," in *Some Freaks* (New York: Penguin, 1989).

20. See David Mamet, "Conventional Warfare."

21. Dan Savage, *Skipping towards Gomorrah: The Seven Deadly Sins and the Pursuit of Happiness in America* (New York: Plume/Penguin, 2003), pp. 258–259.

22. See Jon Ronson, *Them: Adventures with Extremists* (New York: Simon & Schuster, 2002).

23. Sam Tanenhaus, "Violence That Art Didn't See Coming," *New York Times*, February 24, 2010, online edition. Tanenhaus's article deals with the female mass murderer Amy Bishop.

24. Stella Bruzzi, *Bringing Up Daddy: Fatherhood and Masculinity in Post-War Hollywood* (London: British Film Institute Publishing, 2005), p. 154.

25. David Savran, *Taking It like A Man* (Princeton, NJ: Princeton University Press, 1998), p. 5.

26. Lynn M. Ta, "Hurt So Good: *Fight Club*, Masculine Violence, and the Crisis of Capitalism," *Journal of American Culture* 29, no. 3 (September 2006), pp. 269, 270.

27. See Eric Alterman, *It Ain't No Sin to Be Glad You're Alive: The Promise of Bruce Springsteen* (Boston: Little, Brown, 1999).

28. Michael Strangelove, *Watching YouTube: Extraordinary Videos by Ordinary People* (Toronto, ON: University of Toronto Press, 2010), p. 10.

29. Guy Garcia, *The Decline of Men*, pp. 54–58.

30. See Ioana Opie, *The People in the Playground* (Oxford, UK: Oxford University Press, 1994), pp. 7–8.

31. See Michael D. Kehler, Kevin G. Davison, and Blye Frank, "Contradictions and Tensions in the Practice of Masculinities in School: Interrogating Embodiment and 'Good Buddy Talk,'" *Journal of Curriculum Theorizing* 21, no. 4 (Winter 2005), p. 62.

32. See Michael D. Kehler, Kevin G. Davison, and Blye Frank, "Contradictions and Tensions in the Practice of Masculinities in School," pp. 63–65.

33. See Murray J. Drummond, "The Meaning of Boys' Bodies in Physical Education," *Journal of Men's Studies* 11, no. 2 (Winter 2003).

34. Guy Garcia, *The Decline of Men*, pp. 168–170.

35. Charlie LeDuff, *US Guys: The True and Twisted Mind of the American Man* (New York: Penguin, 2006), p. 179.

36. See Harrison G. Pope Jr., Katharine Phillips, and Roberto Olivardia, *The Adonis Complex: The Secret Crisis of Male Body Obsession* (New York: Free Press, 2000).

37. Guy Garcia, *The Decline of Men*, p. 163.

38. Edisol Wayne Dotson, *Behold the Man: The Hype and Selling of Male Beauty in Media and Culture* (New York: Harrington Park Press, 1999), p. 4.

39. Harrison G. Pope Jr., Katharine A. Phillips, and Roberto Olivardia, *The Adonis Complex*, p. 33.

40. Harrison G. Pope Jr., Katharine A. Phillips, and Roberto Olivardia, *The Adonis Complex*, p. 5.

41. Harrison G. Pope Jr., Katharine A. Phillips, and Roberto Olivardia, *The Adonis Complex*, pp. 42–45.

42. Margaret Carlisle Duncan and Michael A. Messner, "The Media Image of Sport and Gender," in *MediaSport*, ed. Lawrence A. Wenner (London: Routledge, 2000), p. 176.

EIGHT

Men and Technology

Open virtually any feminist tract on the subject of technology and inevitably there will be some potent reference to technology—machines, factories, and inventions—being a supremely masculine artifact or series of accomplishments. From the building of the great canals and bridges to everyday and mundane things, in some way or form there is a masculine imprint. The skyscraper to the train, the power station ot the computer, are all in some way linked to masculine vision. Whether on the inside with electronics or on the outside with design, technology is a surrogate for biological creation. Technology, in most of its manifestations, is what a man can do.

When pioneering French industrial designer Raymond Loewy immigrated to the United States, he was struck by the incongruities apparent on the inside of "things" and their ugly exterior. He could not comprehend how a society that was so efficient and so capable in the industrial realm could produce such ugliness on the outside of finished products and technology. Loewy set out to change the appearance of industrial products and in so doing, revolutionized how ordinary people saw and came to see the products of American industrial might. Prior to this time, it seemed almost okay to produce a highly efficient engine or a dynamo of grand power, and as long as it did what it was supposed to do, no one seemed to care what its "skin" or outsides looked like. But Loewy wanted to invert this process—to make the outside look clean and neat, sleek, and stylish. He was as concerned with the exterior as he was with the inside. While functionality had not been a problem, Loewy put an emphasis on outside appearance.[1]

On the other side of the spectrum stands both the architect and the engineer. The architect as builder, in all of his manifestations, is capable of creating and envisioning the impossible. Popular culture has created an image of the architect as a supreme creative genius. It is one area with a host of examples that are as American as they are international. From the fictional Howard Roarke to the real Frank Lloyd Wright, to I. M. Pei to Louis Sullivan, Louis Kahn, and Phillip Johnson, the architect is the embodiment of a level of craftsmanship and desire that is rarely seen in the everyday world. And now, in contemporary terms, there is the architectural equivalent of the rock star or superstar. Frank Gehry, Daniel Liebeskind, and Norman Foster are lauded the world over.

Superstar architects like Gehry, Michael Graves, Renzo Piano, and Liebeskind generally create buildings that are noticeable even in cluttered urban environments. They stand out and demand attention. The buildings that they create often don't fit into the feel of what is around them but nonetheless, "look stupendous" and create both a corporate image and buzz.[2] Sharon Zukin remarks that these superstars are very much akin to "a modern version of the Renaissance cult of genius," in that they outshine the successes of native architects and travel around from place to place designing and bringing their vision.[3]

Both the architect and the building itself fuse together to become and to be defined as embodying the "very essence of manhood."[4] Architecture has historically been about the outside; it is about the walls and the foundations and the external appearance. As Joel Sanders has observed, it is supposed to be about a manly form of construction that is genuine and stripped of feminine ornament.[5] Buildings, as definitive examples of masculine creations in the public sphere are often contrasted to and with the private realm, which has often been designated feminine. The city, and in particular, the modern metropolis, studded with buildings, has been held up as a supremely masculine achievement. The skyscraper in particular, and one can imagine the 1930s version, has come to dominate as a male archetype and symbolize masculine pride in the built environment. As Leslie Kane Weisman writes:

> From the corporate towers of the wizards of industry to the Emerald City of the Wizard of Oz, men have created the built environment in their own self image. The twentieth-century urban skyscraper, a pinnacle of patriarchal symbology, is rooted in the masculine mystique of the big, the erect, the forceful—the full balloon of the inflated masculine ego.[6]

The engineer holds a unique place in American culture. Engineering as a concept and ideal fuses the individualism of pastoral America with Yankee ingenuity and know-how. The lineage is one of the few facts that most Americans can recite. Edison, the Wright brothers, Bell, Ford, Land, and Lear and on, the achievements of the engineer stride above it all. They are enshrined in the history books, codified in museums, and their built legacies stand tall and firm. From bridges to dams to the products used in everyday life, there is something tangible and definitive about innovative and monumental engineering feats.

A specific version of the American entrepreneur and the self-made man is often focused on technology. More specifically it lingers around the appropriation of different kinds of technology in order to harness some kind of power. Henry Ford, John D. Rockefeller, Andrew Carnegie, and Thomas Edison stand aloft on these heights, but a variation can be found in entrepreneurs such as Steve Jobs of Apple and Pixar, Ted Turner of CNN, Phil Knight of Nike, Sergey Brin of Google, and Mark Zuckerberg of Facebook. All of these men created something from nothing and used technology in particularly successful ways. They are "renegades" to some extent but embodied a spirit of creation and drive that is highly admired.[7]

A related stream in this process involves self-modification. It can be found in men who rebuild or alter their cars in order to make them go faster and it surfaces in the pride one takes in successfully completing a home renovation. Tools are key in this process. Autonomy and making something different with one's own hands are also significant. But the attraction of men to machines is as clear as it is contradictory. In American culture, technology is balanced against nature to create a grand unproblematic paradox. As Mark Allister writes,

> This paradox is particularly acute within the power social construction of masculinity that the way to prove one's manhood is not to test oneself in nature but to destroy it. Many boys and men fantasize about controlling machines in the service of whacking around and altering the natural world.[8]

This is not always the case. There is increasingly a move to live within the boundaries of nature and to work within its dictates rather than to destroy it. Not to get too eco-emotional, but so much of the counterbalance toward technology and the extraction of fossil fuels has been about a masculine reorientation toward nature in a much more and productive way. But given the long history of exploitation, Allister's point still holds a lot of currency.

The natural world carries a particularly strong appeal to urban men who are confined to the office or the factory. The premium put on working outdoors and even being outside has become quite pronounced in contemporary culture. One of the hottest male trends of the last few decades was heading back to nature on a retreat and attempting to recapture the spirit of pioneer or cowboy associations with nature. These "rugged" masculine retreats were often attempts to commune with a particular version of nature, perhaps a mythologized version, where men did things with their hands without the pressures of modern industrial or post-industrial society. These retreats were highly popular because they did in fact offer a kind of natural, masculine therapy.[9] Nature, once again, could be used as a panacea, providing what modern society could not.

The outdoors offered a rejuvenating elixir for men who felt cooped up. So be it if men brought fancy gadgets and cutting-edge camping equipment with them. But what was and is most interesting in this version of nature-masculinity is the fact that so much of its success is dependent on technology. From GPS to high-tech sleeping bags, much of being outdoors involves utilizing the latest devices and materials. But getting there and in particular, driving a vehicle complete with all-wheel drive is still a necessity.

No object signifies its complex attachment to the world of men more than the automobile. For over one hundred years, the car has taken on a surrogate set of characteristics that make it much more than simply a means of transportation. It is something to be admired, to strive for in the realm of ownership, and often, it becomes a defining example of a man's identity or perceived identity. From the sleekness of a stylized coupe meant for speed to the rugged heaviness of a truck to the substance of a large family sedan, the automobile isn't just a car. For many men, the car is the most visible symbol of how they wish others to see them. It combines a self-perception quotient with a ready acceptance of the messages conveyed in the world of advertising. From very young ages, primed by images and toy versions, boys learn to covet the car as something special. The ultimate cars—Lamborghinis, Aston Martins, Bentleys—are akin to superwomen in their appeal, the desire to possess them, and they are outside presentation factors. They are meant to be shown, displayed, and ridden. For many men, the car has become a key masculine identifier.[10]

Historically, cars occupied a significant space in North American popular culture. Not only was it an industry of large proportions and significance, but also cars offered a way to personalize ownership of the vast space that made up the continent. As well, car culture was a significant aspect of television and film. Advertising in particular devoted enormous sums of money to creating commercials for car companies and in many instances, such as sporting events, advertising by car companies seemed synonymous with the events. Gary Cross argues that while a man's focus on clothing and appearance may be construed as trivial, his attention to the car was serious. Looking at car advertising from the 1950s, Cross writes,

> the real mark of maturity in men was competence, often technical. Since the beginning, car makers sold mostly to men, and their ads flattered male egos with amazingly detailed lists of technological innovations with very little explanation.

Men were supposed to know things such as torque, ratios of all sorts, and weight distributions.[11]

Different cars symbolized different things. Those who went after European cars such as Jags, BMWs, and Audis were sending a different message than those who drove the Cadillac or Lincoln. The Corvette occupied a seminal place in cool culture, as did the Jeep, for different reasons. Today, a hybrid of some form, whether a Prius or a Denali, conveys something else. The Hummer, currently the equivalent of driving the Space Shuttle to work, evolved out of a desire to drive a military vehicle. The size of the Hummer was part of its appeal, as was its paramilitary associations.

The car, specifically to North Americans, ties so much of what is deemed by advertisers as important—status, glamour, sophistication—together. But beyond that the car also captures essential elements of a national psyche. It provides for freedom, mobility, adventure, comfort, and independence. Perhaps no other invention has created such a liberatory impact as the car. Its place in culture was not just confined to speed and locomotion. As the engineer John H. Lienhard observes, "the automobile meant more than just movement; it meant *freedom* of movement."[12] For many in the United States and Canada, the car became a significant means of empowerment and autonomy, liberating them from the confines of place and time. It could take you somewhere and while on the way, an adventure could happen. Whether it was *Route 66, On the Road, Road Trip*, or numerous other movies or novels, the car is a key trope and the catalyst for copious stories. The drag race in *Grease* or *Rebel Without a Cause*, or the extreme version in *Death Race*, places the car at the center of the action. It is a vehicle that brings the *Beverly Hillbillies* and the Joad family west and a car that gets the attention in numerous television shows, from *Miami Vice* and *Magnum P.I.* to *Knight Rider*.

A sharp, curvy car can be sexual in its appearance. The many famous posters juxtaposing women and cars come to mind immediately. The car also provided numerous couples with a place or space for their first sexual experiences. The privacy afforded by the car was an unintended consequence that radically changed youth values and moral cores. Groups of boys cruising the strip, a staple of post-war society and a significant aspect of male teen culture also embedded itself into the fabric of mediated society from depictions in film and on television. The revving of the engine is now such a seminal aspect of collective memory; advertisers use it as a quick cue to convey a multitude of emotions.

The convertible was enormously significant in popular culture and cemented itself as the ultimate symbol of driving on the open road, evoking almost an appeal to the pioneer spirit. If movies, television, and advertising are to be believed, there is nothing like driving a convertible on a nice sunny day. This sentiment also has been a feature for countless movies and films and serves as a riveting opening sequence in everything from *American Gigolo* to *Banacek* to *Coupe de Ville*. And, until the iPod took over, there was music. Loud, blaring sounds, coming from primitive speakers were meant to titillate the driver and get everyone else's attention. Listening to tunes on the radio was an important addition to riding in the car. *American Graffiti* and other products made this point, which embedded itself into popular culture in some very unique ways.

Bruce Springsteen in particular has used the car as a masculine metaphor for virtually every accepted emotion. His lyrics fuse male desires with mobility and surrogate manliness. Whether it is the country-styled *Cadillac Ranch* or the much more potent lyrics of *Born to Run*, the car is often at the center of Springsteen's view of America. For Springsteen, the car, with all its intricate components and unique and customized features, often serves a means of escape, even if temporary. If provides a form of security and a form of a guarantee, provided it is tuned properly. It is a place for male bonding and cruising, an avenue that leads to women, a metaphor for heartbreak. The car, if it lasts and if it is fast will allow you to move; to get out of a particular place, perhaps one with bad memories to a new place with hope.

Going on the road is a quintessential American endeavor.[13] Taking a trip and even recording what occurs has always been a masculine outlet and endeavor. From Huck Finn on the river to Lindbergh in the air, movement and mobility has been a key stylistic and narrative device. It is the freedom or the potential freedom to travel, to move and to change that is significant. The fact that most can do it in a car accounts for its broad appeal and most men can in some way or form relate to this kind of journey. Either as a diversion or as an escape, with a buddy or with a girl, the road trip is a definitive American male rite of passage. And length doesn't matter here; it is not about how long, but the act of doing it. As a rite of passage the car trip occupies a key place in American—and Canadian—popular culture and historical precedent. The phrase "road trip" means much more than hopping into the car. Like a miniature Homeric odyssey, it is as much about finding out about oneself and exploring the world as it is about getting to your destination.

But often, in the American context, it is about seeing the country, exploring its geographic diversity and natural bounty. It is about exploration and adventure, chance meetings, and wonderful vistas. Ironically, it is the car that allows you to get back to nature. A number of years ago in advertisements for Nissan's Pathfinder, there was a wonderful semiotic connection displayed to the soundtrack of Lenny Kravitz's "Fly Away." The commercial suggested that the vehicle, the rugged, masculine, dirt-covered SUV, was what allowed one to get back to nature. You needed that car or truck in order to successfully navigate the trails and climb the mountains. This paradox of linking nature with technology does not pose a problem in advertising. It simply allows a man to feel free and importantly, to get away. As James J. Farrell writes,

In ads for men, nature tends to be distant and sublime, remote and challenging. In this advertising, nature is often where "real men" go to get away from civilization and from the civilizing women who stultify our manliness. Ads for SUVs especially seem fueled by testosterone dreams, evoking themes of escape and adventure, the sublime and the subliminal. In SUV ads—if not in SUVs themselves—we can escape the clutter and congestion, the rules and responsibilities, of our everyday lives.[14]

The linking of nature or going back to nature with retrieving one's masculinity or having a masculine moment is appealing to many men. It is also something that has a long history in American culture and importantly, in American literature. Yet using the big vehicle to get there is not as anomalous as it appears. It has been reconfigured to stand in for a canoe or a bush plane in order to take you someplace that is off limits to most. The apparent disharmony with nature is just one of those contradictions presented to men through media and one that is often not troubling to viewers.

The advertising for the SUVs and the names given to these large vehicles are quite suggestive. As stated above, part of the appeal is the ability to get away and the utility that these vehicles offer in going off the beaten track. But advertising attempts to also equate the SUV and its ethos with the heritage and lineage of archetypical masculine heroes and their endeavors. Whether a reference to travel and conquest, as in the Navigator and Explorer from Ford or a reference to the west in the form of cowboys and Indians as in Chrysler, Cherokee, and Durango, and the Tahoe from GM, there is a deliberate attempt to associate these vehicles, their images, and what one is supposed to derive by and from purchasing them with images of action and adventure.

Names go only so far. The actual image and its utilization in the media of the vehicle also accent owning the car. Movies and television shows have hooked on to this equation. From Steve McQueen's Mustang in *Bullet* to James Garner's Camaro in *The Rockford Files*, to the Batmobile and the Corvette, the car has become a supreme masculine emblem. The desire for Thomas Magnum's Ferrari or James Bond's Aston Martin or the Dodge in *The Dukes of Hazard* lingers on into adulthood for many men.

The remarkable explosion of interest in NASCAR over the past few years, making it one of the most popular spectator and attendance sports,[15] has a lot to do with the fundamental masculinity of cars. These stout, muscular vehicles differ considerably from the daintier look of the open-wheeled Formula 1 and CART cars. There is something quintessentially macho about the heaviness and grip of the NASCAR car that in a sense is hardy and nostalgic. Like steak and potatoes, it is down to earth and on a level to which most fans can relate. It harkens back to the early days of racing, when technology was not the key fact, the driver was.

According to LeRoy Ashby, NASCAR's popularity is literally off the charts. As of the last few years, Ashby states, "perhaps one-fourth of the U.S. population were NASCAR fans."[16]

One of the reasons, according to Ashby, for the enormous popularity of the sport is the fact that the drivers speak to the spectators and the fans. The latter are particularly devoted to the sport and orient their leisure time around big races. It was Dale Earnhardt who rose above the other drivers to become the sport's reigning superstar, eclipsing the King himself, Richard Petty. "He was," writes Ashby, "the stereotypical good old boy, the tough individual who would not let anyone push him around."[17]

One of the interesting items in the history of the automobile—at least the American car—is the evolution of the car as a bulky, hulking tank, to a muscle car and then to a sleeker version of the latter and then back to the muscle car. This parallels the bodies that men were seeking in the previous decades. In the 1950s it was heavy and robust, and beginning in the 1960s it got more muscled and chiseled in certain places; by the end of the 1990s, sleekness was desirable. The use of ornamentation in the form of fins and chrome added a pastiche of weight to the cars of the 1950s, a form of cumbersomeness seemingly inexplicable in a device meant to go fast. Stripped of its extraneous features, the car of the 1960s—the Corvette—was meant to go somewhere very fast. From the GTO to the Camaro and Trans Am, long-term stability at a fast pace seemed to complement the highways and freeways that were being built.[18]

One of the most notable developments of the last few years has been a return to the relative heaviness of the late 1960s and early 1970s in car design. Chrysler has been at the forefront of rejuvenating the muscle car in a number of variation but so too has Ford with its Mustang and GM with the Camaro. Despite the emphasis on better fuel consumption and the high price of gas, not to mention the environmental concerns, a large segment of males are purchasing these retro-statements.

Increasingly, it seems to be men going through a proverbial mid-life crisis who indulge in the purchasing of these retro-muscle cars. From the Mustang to the hefty new Camaro, what is suggested is a desire to return to a previous phase and a past stage. There is a desire among so many baby boomers and others to recapture some aspect of their youth, and one of the most potent ways is to buy the car that was once their dream car. When they were young they coveted this vehicle or a close facsimile, and now the chance to live out the fantasy is within their reach. Many of these men are buying a piece of their youth. This is similar to the mania for toy collecting, especially expensive toy collecting that involves painstaking research and a lot of money for everything from vintage Hot Wheels to tin soldiers. But cars are on another level.

Men who have the money to indulge in these purchases have been honed by thousands of pictures, movies, and advertisements that reinforce the seminal connection of mediated masculinity between cars and success. This is why so much money can be spent on vehicles and why the first thing most successful men purchase is an expensive car. The rarer the vehicle, the more exclusive the club. Rare car auctions are now televised and the thrill for the viewer is as exciting as it is for the purchaser. As well, in some cases vintage-racing vehicles can actually be raced on famous tracks. This kind of event is also televised and receives decent audience numbers.

The attraction to racing, to going as fast as one can, is an activity that perhaps is safest when attempted on a closed circuit or on a regulated track. Yet the appeal of street racing and all its ancillary components is vastly attractive to young men. The movie *The Fast and The Furious* opened a window on street racing subculture and fueled an interest in this dangerous activity. Every week, a news report seems to detail the problems and issues—even deaths—surrounding a street race gone awry. A major impetus behind the attraction is simple goading. Young boys cannot seem to pass up a chance to prove their worth and to respond to the challenge of a race. As sociologist Amy L. Best has detailed in her book *Fast Cars, Cool Rides*, this has evolved into a subculture of masculinity that deserves attention. According to Best, young boys and men engage in both street racing and car customizing in order to define who they are and to demonstrate their masculinity by using the car as a surrogate:

> Street racing and car customizing are activities shared among men—a set of social practices and relations from which young men work to construct and articulate coherent narratives that solidify a sense of being men. It is this heightened sense of competition that fortifies the enduring link between cars and masculinity. Perhaps this helps to explain why high-level risk-taking assumes such significance for these young men; the level of risk one is willing to take becomes the means to set oneself apart from other men.[19]

Like so much of contemporary masculine culture, the car and the racing of the vehicle still provide a podium for proving one's masculinity. The notion of standing apart has been a key attribute of public masculinity forever. In a world without as many opportunities to demonstrate uniqueness, the racing of a car and the winning of the race becomes a significant achievement, especially in the world that Best describes. Best suggests that these boys and young men engage in "risk narratives" in order to construct a defining script which allows them to be seen as definitively masculine and importantly, in complete control of their actions. "This is, after all," she writes, "the model of the autonomous, self-determining individual to which many Americans aspire and upon which masculine status rests."[20]

Within certain ethnic communities, both in the United States and in Canada, the culture of car customizing and speed resonates with masculine significance. It is, according to Best, one of the few prominent ways in which males can strut around in a form of hyper-masculine supremacy. It involves competence, daring, and a public display of cool-headed bravado. A successful race is a tangible masculine achievement to which all who are there or who heard about it can relate.[21] What is also quite significant among the Latin and Asian communities of boys that Best studied is the concept of respect. As often-marginalized and disenfranchised members of minority groups, the vestiges of fast-car culture provide a telling amount of reverence to those who are frequently bypassed in other realms. As Best remarks, "These boys invest in fast cars and this fast scene as they traverse a changing world in search of recognition, visibility and respect when the traditional way to gain respect as men is unavailable."[22]

This alludes to the props and trappings, physical and material, that increasingly appeals to men and boys as illusions, but still holds out concrete elements of masculinity. Whether trinkets or trophies, ersatz symbols often have to suffice.

NOTES

1. David M. Lubin, *Shooting Kennedy: JFK and the Culture of Images* (Berkeley: University of California Press, 2003), p. 131.

2. Sharon Zukin, *Landscapes of Power: From Detroit to Disney World* (Berkeley: University of California Press, 1993), p. 47.

3. Sharon Zukin, *Landscapes of Power*, p. 47.

4. Joel Sanders, "Introduction," in *Stud: Architectures of Masculinity*, ed. Joel Sanders (New York: Princeton Architectural Press, 1996), p. 1.

5. Joel Sanders, "Introduction," p. 3.

6. Leslie Kane Weisman, "Prologue: Women's Environmental Rights — A Manifesto," in *Gender Space Architecture: An Interdisciplinary Introduction*, ed. Jane Rendell, Barbara Penner, and Iain Borden (London: Routledge, 2000), p. 1.

7. Douglas B. Holt and Craig J. Thompson, "Man-of-Action Heroes: The Pursuit of Heroic Masculinity in Everyday Consumption," *Journal of Consumer Research* 31 (September 2004), p. 428.

8. Mark Allister, "Introduction," in *Eco-Man: New Perspective on Masculinity and Nature*, ed. Mark Allister (Charlottesville: University of Virginia Press, 2004), pp. 2–3.

9. See Russell W. Belk and Janeen Costa, "The Mountain Man Myth: A Contemporary Consuming Fantasy," *Journal of Consumer Research* 25 (December 1998), p. 221.

10. Cited in Amy L. Best, *Fast Cars, Cool Rides: The Accelerating World of Youth and Their Cars* (New York: New York University Press, 2006), p. 4.

11. Gary Cross, *Men to Boys: The Making of Modern Immaturity* (New York: Columbia University Press, 2008), p. 35.

12. John H. Lienhard, *Inventing Modern* (New York: Oxford University Press, 2003), p. 116.

13. See James B. Twitchell, *Where Men Hide* (New York: Columbia University Press, 2006), pp. 129–131.

14. James J. Farrell, "The Nature of My Life," in *Eco-Man: New Perspectives on Masculinity and Nature*, ed. Mark Allister (Charlottesville: University of Virginia Press, 2004), p. 262.

15. See LeRoy Ashby, *With Amusement for All: A History of American Popular Culture since 1830* (Lexington: University Press of Kentucky, 2006), pp. 471–472.

16. LeRoy Ashby, *With Amusement for All*, p. 471.

17. LeRoy Ashby, *With Amusement for All*, p. 472.

18. See Christopher Finch, *Highways to Heaven: The Auto Biography of America* (New York: HarperCollins, 1992), pp. 278, 279.

19. Amy L. Best, *Fast Cars, Cool Rides*, p. 86.

20. Amy L. Best, *Fast Cars, Cool Rides*, p. 89.

21. Amy L. Best, *Fast Cars, Cool Rides*, p. 89.

22. Amy L. Best, *Fast Cars, Cool Rides*, p. 89.

NINE

The Objects on Men's Desks

Looking through magazines such as *Architectural Digest* and *Forbes*, one often notices the desk of a man in either the background or foreground, cluttered with objects or clean with just a few things. Glancing at books in the design section of a bookstore one sees books, or at least book chapters, devoted to male spaces and specifically to male areas of the house. The movie *I Love You, Man* even celebrated the man cave as a total environment devoted to the peculiarities of bachelor culture. This focus suggests that men are both more comfortable with interior space and very much willing to display what they own or have garnered with unabashed pride. For quite a few decades, the office was thought of as a significant masculine space. It was cordoned off from the hub of activity that went on in the outside world and became an area of privacy and power. In the office, the central place of masculine identity is the desk.[1]

Within the home, which, in contrast to the office building, has always been assigned to the domain of women, a man's desk, whether in a library or study, often serves as the lone repository of masculine culture. Men's spaces are consequential to identify in this arena. During the Victorian period and well after, the specific masculine areas within the home were clearly demarcated and for all intents and purposes, off-limits to women.[2] These may have included the workshop, shed, garage, and much later, the den or trophy/game room. The desk seemed to stand out as significant. Whether a large desk or simply a corner roll-top, it was a place that could serve as a storage area of masculine traits through the objects that rested there.

When Tiffany & Company launched its Streamerica line of desk accessories in the early 1990s, the objects were weighted with masculine reference to a unique and central period of history. According to the brochure that accompanied the launch, these "desk accoutrements" were designed to remind one of the time "when the machine was the defining force in America and steel her most precious material." The advertising copy links the 1930s—the heyday of the skyscraper—with the masculine focus on building. As well, the objects—pens, watches, lighters, clocks, picture frames, letter openers, and ashtrays—are described as having a direct connection to Raymond Loewy, Henry Dreyfuss, and Norman Bel Geddes and their ideas of streamlining. These steel objects are described as powerful and possessing "graceful strength," conveying the ideas that not only are these supremely masculine but sophisticated objects as well.[3]

According to the popular anthropological point of view, consumption habits are very much oriented around gender. Significantly, men are large consumers of specific things at certain points in their lives—during adolescence and again during post-midlife. As James B. Twitchell has observed, "That's when the male collecting impulse seems to be felt. Boys gather playing marbles first, Elgin marbles later."[4] For men during the "Golden Age" of Dutch culture, it was important in their homes to display commissioned paintings and other luxury objects—in enormous variations and quantities.[5] As Thomas Hines comments on this historical epoch, with each passing year the "rooms in the paintings seem to fill up with more stuff. Bare floors give way to straw mats that are superseded by Persian and Turkish carpets, which have moved from tables to the floor. Chairs become softer, cabinets larger."[6] But this was a unique situation. While collecting had always been the province of the wealthy, it was not until the late eighteenth century that collecting became democratized and accessible to the rising middle classes. After this period, collecting and the display of a collection came into fashion as a proper gentlemanly endeavor.

Throughout the nineteenth century and into the current period—a large swath of time no doubt—the avenues and arenas for collecting and display have evolved into numerous outlets. From the personal collection to the private museum to the casual accumulation of specific artifacts, men have had many opportunities to possess and display their favorite items. Collecting and the amassing of objects began to be seen as a purely masculine venture and were viewed as a form of productive self-expression. Collection and display could in turn be excused as a challenge akin to the masculine indulgence to hunting and conquest.[7] As the rising middle class increasingly sought to mimic the consumption habits of the upper classes, a massive indulgence in the accretion of things came to define elements of masculine material culture. Motivated by the above desire to imitate, but also by prestige, control, and self-expression, men sought to buy and trade artifacts and to display them. This was also a tangible way to present one's taste, one's wealth, and even one's creativity.[8]

The accumulation and display of objects, regardless of merit, came to be fully accepted as a masculine enterprise. As well, concomitantly, the creation of the men's den or study in the Victorian home forged a new-found emphasis on the relationship between the display of objects and their meaning to men. By the early decades of the twentieth century, the proliferation of collecting could be expanded in myriad ways. *Things* rapidly multiplied and there was no end to what could be consumed and displayed. According to Donald Norman, there are between twenty and thirty thousand things or objects readily observable on any given day.[9]

One area of unique interest for the display of objects is the desk. By way of illustration, on Norman's own desk he has access to over a dozen pens, not to mention books, bookmarks, pads, and numerous other objects.[10] This begs the question, why on a surface that never seems large enough do we place things other than the most functional?

Glancing at the advertising images, peering deeply into pictures in design books, looking at the content of furniture catalogues, taking in the background of a photograph profiling a CEO, perusing a selection of images of writer's desks, or staring at a design spread in a men's magazine—one's eye is often drawn to a desk in a room or an office. One's gaze is directed toward the objects on a man's desk. Why are the things present selected?[11]

The room where a man's desk is situated is either an office, at a place of work, or in the home environment, in a den, a study, library, or home office. It becomes a personal space, even within a public environment when one puts selected possessions on the surface. It may be one of the few areas where a man has total control over the contents and the display. In the case of the office, certain rules may dictate what is allowed and accepted, but in the home version, total latitude is available. The fact that this arena is all about complete freedom of choice makes the desk of particular importance as a barometer of masculine material culture. It differs significantly from the game room, "man cave," or ersatz sports lounge that are now finding their way into homes. This environment is free from the tackiness and open-ended expressions of the gung-ho masculine sphere. There is coolness here, dark and muted as opposed to the blinking pinball flashing neon of the sports zone. The private study or home library is the often-cited favorite room of men, a place where one can remove oneself, be alone, yet fuse with a unique and personal set of qualities.[12] The study can be designed to be the definitive masculine space, decorated with hyper-masculine décor that can range from stuffed animal heads to sports trophies and leather-bound books. Even odors can accentuate the maleness of the space; if *Cigar Aficionado* is to be believed, the scent of fine brandy mingled with superior cigars heightens the mannish quality of a room.

The freestanding desk evolved out of the more common, table desk and matured into its more familiar form in the eighteenth century. Made out of heavy wood—walnut, oak, mahogany—these "pedestal desks" were placed in libraries and were made to support large thick books as well as to serve as a place to write.[13] Not only has the desk evolved into a workstation, a platform for a computer, an area to phone from, or a surface to rest one's feet, the desk has become a space where one places specific and choice objects.

Whenever one looks at a desk or a photograph of a desk, one's eyes are drawn to the surface of the desk and then to the desk itself. This is because the surface contains objects that often obscure the plane. It is the objects that attract one's attention, not necessarily the desk—unless it happens to be particularly large, small, or extraordinary. Whether walking into someone's office or looking at a desk in the pages of a magazine, one is struck by the varied manner of how the desk is treated. Some desks are clean, clear of all but one or two objects, usually essential items. Others are cluttered in either a messy, overflowing manner or in an organized and methodical way. This latter group may seem to suggest that the chosen objects have been strategically placed, carefully angled, and thoughtfully selected. The items in the strategic category reflect the suggestion that time and consideration have been taken in selecting and placing the objects.

In material culture terms, objects can reveal a great deal about their owner's personality or how they wish to be perceived by others. Objects help sustain and define identity. They serve to represent "at least potentially, the endogenous being of the owner."[14] In their study of "things" and the self, Csikszentmihalyi and Rochberg-Halton suggest "household objects constitute an ecology of signs that reflects as well as shapes the pattern of the owner's self."[15] To the owner, the object stands for something subliminally, unconsciously, consciously, or overtly. It is there for a reason because of the perceived associations. The objects on a man's desk may serve as a bridge to aid the owner in making a transition to a particular condition, circumstance, or style.[16] It may be the role he plays in life, what he does for a living, what he wishes to exude, or even what he fantasizes himself as being.

The desk as container of objects can take on a museum-like aura. Just as museums are "repositories of objects which exist as special artifacts,"[17] the surface of the desk serves the same function to its owner. What a man chooses to place on his desk (and allow to be placed on his desk) is both defining and unique to him. The museum metaphor can be extended. What a museum desires to possess and in turn display is deliberate and calculated.[18] Someone funded the search or purchase and someone—a committee or a curator—made the decision to display. The owner of the desk purchased the object, found it, or received it as a gift. He allows it to remain on the desk, on display, for all to see. The objects chosen for viewing on the desk are deliberately placed there, otherwise they would be in a drawer or positioned somewhere else. Desk objects are most often considered to have some special significance in either personal or monetary terms.

Special objects that reside on desks are easily retrievable and of course, directly observable. They have been placed there for their usefulness, memory associations, beauty, or status. These descriptives imply that a variety of emotions and desires are at work. Taste, refinement, power, wealth, erudition, and acquisitiveness are all important motivations that factor into the objects residing on a man's desk.

Certain objects also seem to be magical in their placement on the desk, evoking something mysterious or serving to inspire the owner. Writers and thinkers in general have a tendency to place enchanted objects on their desks. Alberto Manguel has his own take:

> In my study I also require certain talismans that have washed onto my desk over the years, which I distractedly finger while I think of the next words to write. Renaissance scholars recommended keeping different objects in the study: musical and astronomical instruments to lend variety and harmony to the space, natural curiosities such as strangely shaped stones and colored shells, and St. Jerome, patron saint of readers. I follow their recommendations in part. Among the objects on my desk are a horse-shaped soapstone from Congonhas do Campo, a bone carved into a skull from Budapest, a pebble from Sibyl's cave near Cumae.[19]

A significant problem with most desks is the fact that they have a tendency to become extraordinarily messy. Stuff gets piled on top of other stop but usually the owner knows what's there. Many desks serve as what David Levy reports is a kind of "complex ecosystem" that demonstrates that a lot is happening. Like peering at a refrigerator door literally overflowing with everything from snapshots and coupons to old bills and stickers, the desk can contain both "personal and private" items, important current stuff, and piles that have been there for a long time. David Levy reports the following observation of his desk:

> On my desk right now I have three small images propped up against the wall, two photographs, and a postcard. In addition, I have drafts of various chapters of this book, some in colored file folders, some loose, some stapled, some clipped . . . I also have a handwritten to-do list, my Filofax (calendar), and a vertically arranged stack of bills and other correspondence still to be dealt with.[20]

Levy's description is typical of many desks and can serve as an interpretation of a common desk. The desk can be interpreted as a kind of material weigh station where a variety of objects reside until it is time to be used. There are a number of constants when viewing pictures of men's desks or when seeing them on television or in film. It is possible to classify the desks and the objects they contain into four unique categories.

THE DESK AS PODIUM OF POWER AND ACHIEVEMENT

The most common object found on the desks observed in advertisements and in photos is a selection of photographs in frames. These can reveal that someone special is directly linked or accessed—by looking. Susan Sontag has suggested that in contrast to movies, a still photograph makes the image an object of accumulation.[21] The act of capturing an image in a photograph transfers the living, breathing, moving subject into the confines of a border and reifies the image into an object to be possessed. What is within the photograph, be it a person, a loved one, or a landscape, becomes a "memento of the absent."[22] The use of the world memento is interesting for it means, according to the Shorter Oxford English Dictionary an "object serving as reminder, or something kept as a memorial of person or event." The emphasis here is on "object" and "thing," which is reinforced by the concept of the frame as container of memory. The quality of the frame reinforces the special place reserved for wives, lovers, and children. Heaviness seems to be a particularly common attribute of these frames, as does silver, both as color and material.

A second feature of this category is the fact that the "power" desk is more often associated with large size and fine material construction. This is in comparison to the plebian workstation, the drone-specific basic desk, or some rickety IKEA product. The significance of size is both accurate and stereotypical. Hollywood has made comedic hay out of the size of certain desks, the reality, especially when looking at *Forbes* or *Business Week*, often in line with the stereotype.

THE DESK AS PLAYGROUND

Another set of objects found on men's desks are toys. Toys, or if one prefers, collectibles or "antiques" such as model cars, hand-crafted trains, miniature airplanes—make up one common set of what were once playthings. There is also a subset of items, games, which are tactile and meant to be touched; heavy brass Xs and Os in a deep walnut base, gleaming clicker balls which swing back and forth, push pins designed to be imprinted with one's hand, and miniature Zen sand gardens, complete with a rake and stones. The employment of sand is interesting for it is meant to be moved, groomed, manipulated—without direct touch. Sand also makes one recall the definitive place of rest and tranquility—the beach. The popularity of desk toys has become so enormous that companies are now reissuing classic toys in miniature versions, often with adult components rather than gaudy plastic, in order to appeal to this segment of the market. One company produces sets of toys and playthings, "complete with pseudoscholarly booklets and faux-sophisticated touches" marketed under the Executive Set name. There are Tinker Toys made from cherry and ebony and the Barrel of Monkeys "recast in steely gray and housed in an attaché-black barrel." [23]

Sporting paraphernalia such as autographed baseballs, figurines of famous athletes, and encased cards reflect this playful and nostalgic side. These are now expensive items and significant enough to be off limits to touching. But one wants to touch them, hold them, and move them. Looking isn't satisfying enough. And this is part of the point. Only the owner is allowed to handle them. Like the famous Seinfeld episode, it is taboo for the visitor to indulge in contact.

Although oriented around leisure, entertainment, and playfulness, these objects connote something personal and evocative to their owners. Like the purchase of a souvenir on a vacation, which serves as a tangible reminder, this kind of paraphernalia can evoke the experience of memory. [24] Thus, these objects may mean something of grand importance to the individual, beyond their monetary value. They may represent a very important experience in the life of the individual and convey sentiments to the owner beyond what is visible or even accessible to the viewer or visitor. [25]

THE DESK AS AUTHENTIC WORKPLACE

In his fascinating book, *Cult Objects*, Deyan Sudjic makes the link between toys and utilitarian objects by suggesting that many objects that are functional become toys after a certain point. Of the matte black Braun ET 22 calculator, for example, he writes:

> It is a toy of course, but like all the best toys, it looks convincing enough to be taken seriously . . . Above all, it is good to touch. Running your fingers over the ultra-precise mouldings, and the shiny control buttons, bright as Smarties, is as soothing as playing with worry beads . . . Moulded out of decidedly uncissy grainy plastic, its hefty welts make it look like a cigar case. [26]

This icon of functionality has, according to Sudjic, become a fetish object that sits suggestively on one's desk and transmits "all kinds of flattering signals." [27] Many of the objects on men's desks do in fact transmit signals and to a great extent that is the purpose, to convey a series of messages to the owner and the viewer. [28] Purely functional items such as boxes, holders, storage trays, clip holders, ink blotters, and the like, carry messages and give off signs. These often apply to the initiated who can recognize a Tiffany clutter box or a Lancel leather tray.

One of the most-often-featured items on men's desks in magazine photographs for fashion and design spreads or in advertising is the pen. Big, thick, chunky styluses, often fountain pens, are a seemingly indispensable prop. In certain films and on news programs showing the signing of an important agreement, the pen still occupies a place of importance. Pens—a form of men's jewelry—Mont Blanc, Waterman, Parker— either placed on the surface of the desk or standing phallic, erect, in a holder made of marble, also complement the desk. Pens can be surrogates of adornment and after watches or cuff links, the pen stands as an attribute of taste even in a world where its importance as a functional item has been reduced. It is also something that is portable and moved from place to place as a constant reminder of luxury. Sudjic, in a recent book, discusses the pen's precarious state,

> the fountain pen is losing the attraction it once had. For a while the pen was presented as more than a practical writing implement. It was a possession that could be passed from father to son—the kind of industrial object that might form part of an atavistic coming-of-age rite. The protective cap could be unwound slowly and reverentially to reveal a sculpted gold nib. The proportions were satisfyingly commanding, and would be made even more so by placing the cap on the end of the barrel. There was a clip on the cap to discreetly signal the presence of the pen even when it was concealed in a jacket top pocket. [29]

Yet perhaps because of the associations that Sudjic describes and its almost archaic resonance as a luxury artifact, it is used so often to convey a series of signals. Phones on the desk no longer have the same impact that they once did. The bank of phones on the Hollywood movie mogul's desk is gone, replaced by one dominant type and a series of cell phones, PDAs, and Blackberrys. Clocks still remain—Seiko, Cartier—as do lamps such as the ubiquitous Tizzio or regal Waterford, and so too, surprisingly, magnifying glasses.

Magnifying glasses are a unique and interesting anachronistic feature. They serve the utilitarian function of enlarging the field of vision that limits us in looking at details. This is very much harmonious with the tools necessary for successful collecting and connoisseurship that became democratized in the nineteenth century. There was also a quasi-scientific patina associated with a magnifying glass, lending it a form of legitimacy and seriousness. For the close examination of stamps, coins, and other assorted antiquities, the magnifying glass became an essential staple of the masculine array of objects, just as the power drill is for the do-it-yourselfer today.

One of the more interesting desks was a photograph of Ralph Lauren's featured in a magazine spread a number of years ago. It was covered with beautiful objects such as a crystal decanter, a silver scissor, and letter opener, as well as a selection of antique toy cars. It was not exactly what one would call functional. It seemed decorative, almost museum-like in its display. The complete opposite of Lauren's desk is a writer's desk. Writer's desks are usually more utilitarian. The objects featured are purposeful and the desks, while cluttered in some cases, are usually free of adornment. Only the most vital and basic objects are present, such as pencils and pens stuffed in containers, pads of paper in various sizes and colors, things like scotch tape and Liquid Paper and matches, lighters, and ashtrays.

Leather goods such as agendas, diaries, blotters, and telephone books are also featured in many photographs and pictures and many are constructed from rare, possibly endangered species, such as ostrich and crocodile. Once again, these items provoke a desire to touch, which triggers a yearning for tactile satisfaction.

THE DESK AS MUSEUM DISPLAY

The final category is objects, which are overwhelmingly artistic. Unlike toys, these usually do not have exposed, moving parts and are not meant to invoke a caress. Busts of famous men, small sculptures, figurines, ceramics, cloisonné vases, glass paperweights, and assorted crystal creations can be included here.

There is also the idea of the personal museum, the one created haphazardly or by chance. These desks serve as places where important mementos rest, where items significant to the owner reside. They might not be valuable enough to reside in a museum but to the owners they mean a lot. Items that once served a completely different function now become statues or paperweights. Heirlooms trigger memories, ceremonial objects spark reflections. Like the "talisman" effect that Alberto Manguel mentioned, architect and writer Witold Rybczynski has similar feelings:

> On the desk, in addition to the mess of books and papers, are a heavy brass padlock used as a paperweight, a tin can full of pencils, a cast iron Sioux Indian head bookend, and a silver snuffbox with the likeness of George II on its cover. Did it once belong to my grandfather? I cannot remember. The plastic cigarette box next it must have—in addition to the prewar Polish marque, it carries his initials. [30]

One may dismiss objects on men's desks as trivial appurtenances of a society obsessed with things, yet as Rybczynski makes clear, for many men, they are more than that; they tell stories and evoke memories; they suggest and symbolize. They serve purposes, from the mundane to the profound.

Some desks are cluttered to the point that the surface is obscured. David Levy writes, "It is the rare person who isn't somewhat traumatized by the state of his or her desk." [31] Others are sparsely decorated with only the essential present in a minimalist way. Yet no matter why the object is there, it was placed for a reason.

Objects occupy a seminal place in western culture and society. As students, we read about the importance of objects in history and specifically in drama and in fiction. Works such as *The Glass Menagerie*, *The Catcher in the Rye*, or *Lord of the Flies* highlight the meaning of things.[32] In films, the sled in *Citizen Kane* or the statue in *The Maltese Falcon* suggest that it is possible to be completely attached to material possessions. We are taught to look for significance in these material props within the world of fiction[33] and their impact on masculine culture should be considered as well.

There are certain themes that can be harnessed to convey the potency of the masculine interior. Whether it is the bachelor bedroom or the masculine study, these are often composed of a pastiche of styles and colors designed to impart both a serious message and to elicit a coded response. Dark colors, usually black and brown, leather and wood, all suggest a luxurious, Spartan approach to living. The stereotypical template takes its cues from the hunting lodge motif. Darkness contrasted with light, simplicity juxtaposed with studied collections of things: a specific carpet, with references to animal skin, trophies and books are staples of this look. Accents of leather in chairs, couches, and other accoutrements, such as desk sets and blotters, round out the intended look. One of the reasons why certain luxury cars place a premium on the mixing of fine woods and plush carpets, well-appointed leather seats, and intricate instrument panels is to mimic the masculinity in a man's study.

The media room is a technological den combined with theater-like seating. Although by no way confined to males only, the big screen, the plasma, and soon the 3D television system with accompanying sound system is a trapping that, like a fancy car, speaks volumes to and about men. It is the single most important weapon in the male product arsenal. Talking to a group of young men, some of who have recently moved out of their parents' houses, it is the definitive object of desire. Most want a flat-screen television desperately; the larger and more clear, the better. Most also want to have the latest game system to play on it as well. The attraction to this is both individual and social. There is a desire to have the guys over to watch a major sporting event, to drink, and to hang out. It also serves as a prestige object, provoking coveting glances and longing sighs.

To a Tyler Durden, this is superfluous commodification and an excessive materialist environment. Yet, to many males, it is about asserting one's self upon a space. It is a far cry from the posters of athletes stuck on the walls, collections of Hardy Boys Mysteries, and groupings of Hot Wheels. At the higher end, it comes with the Eames chair, the big TV, and the best music player one can afford. Authentic sports memorabilia, such as signed posters and framed jerseys, is on the walls.

In the remake of *The Italian Job*, which starred *Fight Club*'s Edward Norton, there is a scene where the men who are about to become wealthy after a gold heist discuss what they will be buying. According to the tone of the scene, that is the point of being rich; not to become secure, but rather to celebrate consumption and surround oneself with the luxuries of material culture. One character talks in detail about an Aston Martin Vanquish, while another goes into a very comprehensive discourse about a state-of-the-art sound system—especially its extreme decibel level, which has the ability to "knock a woman's clothing off." Another character wants a room for first edition books and another for all of his shoes. Once they are double-crossed by Norton's character they discover that most of their dream purchases have been bought by him. This rankles them as much as being stolen from. No honor among thieves indeed.

In the movie *Tin Men*, Barry Levinson creates a character played by Richard Dreyfuss who is the ultimate hustler salesman. What is not necessarily focused on, but implied, is the apartment he lives in. It dovetails with the Hefner bachelor mystique, albeit in a germinal state. Levinson's creation has a unique and individual sense of style, a marked aura of autonomy and a bachelor pad of his own. One can surmise that this postwar recreation marks the first time that this option was affordable to men. It may have always been a possibility, especially for the well-to-do, but it is something that men aspire to have and decorate in their own image or with their own taste.

Most Hollywood films, when they do deal with masculine style, are very understated in this presentation. It is hard to think of a film that celebrates the male space in overt terms, unless one is thinking about a parody. Outward displays of associations with male space that go beyond architecture, sports, or other traditional male preserves are not part of the project—yet. These will, no doubt, change. The sloppiness of most male physical environments portrayed in film accentuates the frat boy mystique. As more of the metrosexual influence moves in, this will be reflected in film.

Men like objects. They approach their interest in and with them in a way that is markedly different from women. The attractions and tactile associations are much more subtle. Men gravitate toward objects that often reinforce traditional masculine associations. As noted above, heaviness and firmness, weight, and girth are often important in their choices. So too are technology objects which range from the scientific to the utilitarian. As Anna Lombardi writes, "Technology heightens his performance, and so he indulges in a passion for microscopes, telescopes, still cameras, and video cameras."[34] The first *Batman* movie, from 1989, capitalized on this attraction to technology. Tim Burton's recreation of the classic hero was submerged beneath an array of objects. From his suit to his belt, and to the car to the cavern, technological objects of innovation and coolness set the tone. Even the main villain, The Joker, played by Jack Nicholson, asks, "where does he get those wonderful toys?" implying both wonder and envy.

Gadgets of the technological kind and cool rooms to display them in—
like the bat cave—are almost juvenile in their appeal to men. But, no
matter how jaded and distant, there is always something supremely appealing to these things and places. Most men have fond memories of both
the James Bond knickknacks and the villains' fantastic hideouts, a process
that they try to create for themselves.

NOTES

1. James B. Twitchell, *Where Men Hide* (New York: Columbia University Press,
2006), p. 202.

2. James B. Twitchell, *Where Men Hide*, p. 67.

3. Streamerica, Tiffany & Company, pamphlet, 1993.

4. James B. Twitchell, *Lead Us into Temptation: The Triumph of American Materialism*
(New York: Columbia University Press, 1999), pp. 20, 21.

5. See Simon Schama, *The Embarrassment of Riches: An Interpretation of Dutch Culture in the Golden Age* (London: Fontana Press, 1987).

6. Thomas Hine, *I Want That! How We All Became Shoppers* (New York: HarperCollins, 2002), pp. 76, 77.

7. Leora Auslander, "The Gendering of Consumer Practices in Nineteenth-Century France," in *The Sex of Things: Gender and Consumption in Historical Perspective*, ed.
Victoria de Grazia, with Ellen Furlough (Berkeley: University of California Press,
1996), pp. 80, 85.

8. Maurice Rheims, *The Strange Life of Objects: Thirty-five Centuries of Collecting and
Collectors* (New York: Atheneum, 1961), p. 25.

9. Donald A. Norman, *The Design of Everyday Things* (New York: Doubleday, 1990),
p. 11.

10. Donald A. Norman, *The Design of Everyday Things*, p. 11.

11. See Nicholson Baker, "Books as Furniture," in *The Size of Thoughts: Essays and
Other Lumber* (New York: Random House, 1997). Baker examined books featured as
props in advertisements for catalogues. He took out a magnifying glass and read the
titles, then went to the library and checked out the books. He then speculated on why
those particular books may have been chosen.

12. Alvide Lees-Milne and Derry Moore, *The Englishman's Room* (New York: Viking,
1986), p. 7.

13. Judy Graf Klein, *The Office Book* (New York: Facts on File, 1982), p. 100.

14. Mihaly Csikszentmihalyi and Eugene Rochberg-Halton, *The Meaning of Things:
Domestic Symbols of the Self* (Cambridge, UK: Cambridge University Press, 1981), p. 17.

15. Mihaly Csikszentmihalyi and Eugene Rochberg-Halton, *The Meaning of Things*,
p. 17.

16. Grant McCracken, *Culture and Consumption: New Approaches to the Symbolic Character of Consumer Goods and Activities* (Bloomington: Indiana University Press, 1990), p.
110.

17. Alan Radley, "Artifacts, Memory, and a Sense of the Past," in *Collective Remembering*, ed. David Middleton and Derek Edwards (Beverly Hills, CA: Sage Publications,
1990), p. 7.

18. Alan Radley, "Artifacts, Memory, and a Sense of the Past," p. 53.

19. Alberto Manguel, *The Library at Night* (Toronto, ON: Knopf Canada, 2006), p.
178.

20. David M. Levy, *Scrolling Forward: Making Sense of Documents in the Digital Age*
(New York: Arcade, 2001), p. 122.

21. Susan Sontag, *On Photography* (New York: Farrar, Straus & Giroux, 1986), p. 3.

22. John Berger, *The Look of Things* (New York: Penguin, 1972), p. 80.

23. Christopher Noxon, *Rejuvenile: Kickball, Cartoons, Cupcakes, and the Reinvention of the American Grown-up* (New York: Crown, 2006), p. 116.

24. William L. Fox, *In the Desert of Desire: Las Vegas and the Culture of Spectacle* (Reno: University of Nevada Press, 2005), p. 147.

25. Joseph Pine II and James H. Gilmore, *The Experience Economy: Work Is Theatre and Every Business a Stage* (Boston: Harvard Business School Press, 1999), p. 57.

26. Deyan Sudjic, *Cult Objects* (New York: Paladin, 1987), p. 26.

27. Deyan Sudjic, *Cult Objects*, p. 27.

28. John Heskett, *Toothpicks and Logos: Design in Everyday Life* (New York: Oxford University Press, 2002), p. 125.

29. Deyan Sudjic, *The Language of Things: Design, Luxury, Fashion, Art* (New York: Penguin, 2009), pp. 95, 96.

30. Witold Rybszynksi, *Home: A Short History of an Idea* (New York: Viking/Penguin, 1986), p. 18.

31. David M. Levy, *Scrolling Forward*, p. 122.

32. Leah Hager Cohen, *Glass, Paper, Beans: Revelations on the Nature and Value of Ordinary Things* (New York: Doubleday/Currency, 1997), pp. 237, 238.

33. Leah Hager Cohen, *Glass, Paper, Beans*, p. 238.

34. Anna Lombardi, "Sex Objects," in *Material Man: Masculinity, Sexuality, Style*, ed. Giannino Malossi (New York: Abrams, 2000), pp. 94, 96.

TEN

Sports and Media Culture

Sports, in any manifestation—historical, social, or cultural—have traditionally been seen as a male preserve. As changes in North American society have impacted the way masculinity is portrayed in the media, sport has been elevated to one of the primary ways in which traditional forms of masculinity has been measured. Whether focusing on sports culture in the form of rabid fandom, participating in sport as a leisure activity, or casually watching the plethora of offerings, it has emerged as a significant barometer of defining masculinity. With satellite, cable, and regular broadcast offerings, not to mention the Internet, it is possible to watch a sporting event virtually all the time and there is no shortage of supplementary offerings from profiles in fashion magazines, autobiographies, and the sporting press. In essence, sport is one of the most consistently pervasive aspects of contemporary culture.

That being said, in the last fifty years, the presence of women in the public and private theaters of competitive sports has exploded. Some of the female presence in sport has to do, at least in the United States, with Title IX, which allowed equal funding for women in colleges.[1] Another factor has to be parents putting young girls into a variety of sports such as soccer and baseball that thirty years ago would not have been an option. A final consideration is oriented around the constant need for televised sport and the incessant demand for new sports. Women have been a part of everything from basketball to beach volleyball to a host of extreme sports that in many ways are part of the overall demand and resulting media saturation.

To some extent, the participation of girls and women in sports and their success in these endeavors puts added pressure on boys to participate and show an interest in sports. This is especially pronounced among boys who are not ready and willing to engage in sporting culture. Boys who don't show an interest in certain sports, either as spectators or participants, are suspect. "Jock" culture is still highly pronounced as a feature of most cultures and is very dominant in North American society.[2] Young men who do not gravitate in this direction have options but the rewards of being part of the cool athletic groups afford these boys more social currency than any other subgrouping. If not actually being a part of this highly prestigious class, being as close to it as possible is often essential for boys in high school. Even posturing as a jock prohibits boys from being labeled suspected. As C. J. Pascoe has observed,

> When athleticism is not an option for boys, they draw on the other masculine traits associated with the Jock, such as emphasized heterosexuality or dominance to "make up for" what they lack in claims on masculinity through sports. Sport can also function in contradictory ways in which it does provide a way to assert a masculine self while simultaneously facilitating a connection with other boys and men.[3]

Judging from the content of television shows and movies, from *Friday Night Lights* to *Rudy*, participation in sport is a seminal characteristic that defines masculinity. There are variations on the football theme, with hockey, baseball, and basketball offering up messages and morals. In the United States in particular, but also throughout the world, participation in sports and interest in viewing sports is equated with masculine indulgence. A man's or boy's masculinity is questioned if he does not embrace sports on some level. Team sports dominate, especially the rough-and-tumble world of contact sports, but as a surrogate, individual sports will suffice.

Sporting culture in all its variations is seen as a space that is male-focused and male-centered. Regardless of the advances in access and the influence of feminism, or perhaps, because of the influence of feminism, sport plays a significant role in allowing young boys to learn to be men and allowing men a chance to indulge in all-male activities. Whether symbolically or metaphorically, men getting together to watch or to play sports serves as a significant way for men to indulge in a relatively safe, all-male environment. The traditional association with sports as a masculine enterprise allows men to feel and to fulfill their masculine impulses. It is a place where they define their manhood and what they think of as vital for the display of masculine behavior. The specifics of this orientation are often honed during childhood. The focuses on the way boys play and watch sports is very different—physical, aggressive, and oriented on winning—than how girls play.[4]

Like so much that has been discussed in this book, the decade of the 1950s was decisive for sports for a number of reasons. From a visual, spectator point of view—the move to televise sporting contests became common, the massive expansion of professional sports came into being and the production of ancillary sports offerings became pronounced. It was in 1954 that *Sports Illustrated* was launched and quickly reached a huge audience.[5] One of the unique aspects of *Sports Illustrated* was its orientation around photography. A second and more interesting element was the broad appeal of the magazine. Virtually every sport was covered, which meant that its appeal transcended class.[6] The magazine profiled a diverse selection of athletes and events and allowed an up-close look at the personalities and the games. People could vicariously peruse the magazine to get an in-depth perspective, and this in turn solidified the connections between the athlete and the fan and provided for a series of masculine models that otherwise would not have been profiled.

No matter where men go and no matter what they do, sports and games often follow. The current popularity of big-stakes poker is just the latest manifestation of the connections between masculine culture and sports and gaming culture. Extreme sports of all kinds are constantly being invented; the more established or traditional sports seem to go on forever as far as their appeal, regardless of scandals, strikes, or steroids. The creation of television networks and Websites devoted to covering sports has reached unprecedented proportions. This was a trend that began with ESPN and was followed with numerous sports oriented programs and shows. What this suggests is that sports quite firmly occupy a seminal role in contemporary culture. Unlike so much of this work, it is not just confined to North American culture, but is in fact a worldwide phenomenon. Soccer in particular and David Beckham specifically are enormously popular on a global scale. One of the more unique trends over the past few years has been the close association of sports with fashion and style.[7] With Armani and Hugo Boss sponsoring team uniforms and providing clothing, the Canadian company Roots outfitting Olympic teams, Ralph Lauren and Tommy Hilfiger behind both athletes and teams, and athletes in general very aware of fashion, it is now part and parcel of the whole package. A number of athletes are designing their own lines and for years, sports figures have loaned their names to clothing manufacturers, Tiger Woods, Wayne Gretzky and Mike Weir to name a few. Because of the cameras, videos, and nonstop paparazzi presence, sports figures have to care and be interested in how they look. Magazines that profile athletes often ask what designers they favor and what clothes they prefer. Many can offer detailed with explanations and thoughts about clothing.[8]

Athletes are expected to play many roles. Some are successful in this multi-faceted slotting, while others are decidedly uncomfortable with this pressure and not very good at keeping out of trouble. On the one hand, this can advance a "bad boy image" but on the other, this can have enormous repercussions when it comes to endorsement contracts as well as public relations issues. Many athletes try to retain a clean image, one of wholesomeness and decorum. Yet even that can fall apart if private information is released and becomes glaringly public as with the 2010 Tiger

Woods scandal. With certain key figures, a form of retro-nostalgia kicks in with regard to their behavior and personas, which allows them to transcend and remain distanced from the ordinary fray. Some are constantly in the spotlight no matter what. Beckham and others are constantly pegged for micro-attention and thus everything they do is scrutinized by the press and the public, through blogs, and via Twitter.

The publication of biographies on sports figures and autobiographies seems to be a constant in the world of publishing. There is no end to the books by wrestlers, UFC fighters, baseball players, and snowboarders. Andre Agassi's 2009 autobiography quickly reached the bestseller list. In the fall of 2006, Stephen Brunt's biography on the legendary Bobby Orr was released and soared to the top of the bestseller list in Canada and was a brisk seller in Boston.[9] The almost hagiographical text on an athlete who had not played in over three decades indicates that the quiet and private demeanor of one who was truly outstanding still resonates with appeal to a mass audience. Some would argue that Orr was as great, if not greater, than Wayne Gretzky in skill and the ability to change the way the game was played.

In contrast to the quiet certitude of Bobby Orr—or a Sandy Koufax—there was the glamour of "Broadway" Joe Namath, the first true media darling of the modern sports age.[10] While Babe Ruth and Mickey Mantle had accepted and even thrived as sports idols, there were those such as Joe DiMaggio and Gordie Howe that during the post-war period were quiet and unassuming. Suddenly, in the late 1960s, the product of something new, television, came to the fore and bestowed attention on athletes in never-before-seen ways. Namath was, for a time, the most focused-on, given the fact that he was a Jet, but Mohammad Ali, Wilt Chamberlain, Bobby Hull, and a few others were often in front of the cameras and were comfortable with sharing their thoughts and being seen. The complex interplay between athletes who wished for privacy and those who could not get enough of the spotlight began to take on colossal proportions and was to initiate a celebrity scrutiny not seen again until the new century.

The ideal of the quiet sport celebrity is so diametrically opposed in contract to the show performer who seems to constantly bring attention. Deion Sanders, the enormously talented football and baseball player who has redeemed himself as a broadcaster, was savaged by fans and the media for his showy antics. As late as the 1980s, certain extreme forms of misbehavior could lead to firing or a hefty fine, but for the most part, it was tolerated because it generated significant interest in the sport. But one of the biggest concerns about the showboating, the dancing, and the stomping after the goal or the touchdown was that children began to mimic the antics of their idols. It was a far cry from the quiet sportsmanship of the past. Yet the bottom line was it attracted interest; buzz was generated and fans gravitated to whatever shenanigans were being tolerated.

The notion of fandom, of complete and utter absorption into the world of a professional sports team has grown from a modest arena confined to supporting a local franchise to absolute fanaticism. Some superfans, and these are overwhelmingly men, spend an inordinate amount of time and money cultivating their attraction to their favorite sports team. Rooms in the house are painted in team colors, cushions are embroidered with crests, and even lampshades and chairs come in team colors and logos. This suggests a fair amount of alienation from the real world and a tendency to indulge in compensatory collecting and emotional investment. These fans are very serious and in many cases literally live and die by their team's outcomes. "Male spectators," writes Douglas Hartmann, "are far more likely to watch events by themselves, follow sports close, and be affected by the outcomes of games and the performance of their favored teams and athletes."[11]

For many actively engaged sports fans, the problem of capriciousness invades the potential attachment to a particular team. Years ago, if a major player was traded, it was big news. Today, that potential exists as a regular feature—especially with baseball and hockey. This makes problems with prolonged attachment and identification especially problematic. Phone-in radio, as referenced earlier, provides a cathartic outlet for lessening the blows and for voicing concern over the future of the franchise. But what of the merchandise? If your favorite player is traded you now have to purchase a new team jersey that is a costly endeavor. No one should be wearing the shirt of a player who was traded. The same forces are also at work with the rare number change and the common uniform restyling. The sense of loss is particularly pronounced not just when a key player is traded but when the team moves to a different city. Although they have the Ravens, Baltimore is still reeling from the Colts' move to Indianapolis. The marketing and revenue potential is both huge and problematic for the loyal fan.

Fans are attracted to a team or a sport for a variety of reasons. When a team or a sport evolves into a brand, it accrues a number of key principles that marketers have surmised as essential in defining what the team or sport means. What is fascinating in this regard is the fact that these "values" resonate with masculine ideals and manly innuendo. As the authors of a book on this topic suggest, the common values are "power, ritual, heritage, respect, diligence, integrity, honor, loyalty, protection, and perseverance." The authors of *The Elusive Fan* propose that these values not only "define the brand but deepen and ensure the fan connection." They cite the Chicago Bears as a key illustration of this process.[12]

There is also the fact that this extreme form of identification provides an outlet or a safety valve while at the same time proffering up easy-to-digest interpretations for men. As journalist Robert Fulford observes,

Obviously, professional sports provide a place to which we can safely
shunt emotions that might otherwise be dangerous. It is an arena
where love and hate can flourish without danger of harm to the lives
we live when the TV set is switched off. More important, sport provides a structured, organized world that satisfies our need for meaning.[13]

The fact that sports now serves this purpose, at least for many men, is
both remarkable and rather sad. In his marvelous history of the pioneering magazine *Sports Illustrated*, Mark MacCambridge details the evolution of *Sports Illustrated* by suggesting that not only were editorial and
writing factors essential in the magazine's success, but so too was a pronounced awareness of who the readers were. The fact that the magazine
began by focusing on elite sports and graduated to profiling those with
huge television audiences is suggestive of the importance of the fan.
Readers throughout the 1970s and into the 1990s were especially attracted to profiles of major sports stars that often shed light on their
nonplaying lives.[14] *Sports Illustrated* ruled the roost until the advent of
sports broadcasting (through ESPN) usurped its role. The nightly broadcasts of ESPN and other networks became much more relevant and immediate in the world of sports.

ESPN has been one of the most remarkable creations in sports broadcasting. As with NFL Films, Monday Night Football, and a host of other
revolutionary media outlets, ESPN has changed how sports is perceived,
registered, and watched. It has become a surrogate for the analysis that
was once found in the sports section of the newspaper and in the pages of
Sports Illustrated. Although there is still an avid reader base for sports
reporting the seminal role that the sports pages once held has been
usurped. The sophisticated visual nature of television and the expansion
of sports behind the big four gives television an edge. As Michael Oriard
has observed, "ESPN has played a role in creating the rise of sports
celebrities and filling the day with constant sports coverage. Minor
events that were often ignored by sports writers or not covered by print
media, now take on a spectacle-like aura when they are featured on the
cable network. Importantly as well, because of its resources and blanket
coverage as well as its multiple stations, everyone else has to catch up to
what ESPN has done."[15]

One is forced to assume that since their inception and codification as
actual sports, these games and activities have always been a surrogate
outlet. Yet to a certain point in time, sports were played at a very local
level and in a limited way; either as an elite, upper-class endeavor or as a
pasttime during idle periods. It was not until the end of the nineteenth
century that professional, organized sport, located in large urban areas
and promoted heavily in the press, began to take on the capacity to
transcend life for its observers and participants.[16]

Modern sports, events, and participatory games began in the late nineteenth century and quickly spread to a wide array of places, becoming subsumed as leisure indulgences and full-blown staples of entertainment. Sports also evolved along class lines; in Britain and its colonies and in parts of the United States, only gentlemen played certain games while members of the other classes indulged in their own activities. Because certain sports were time-consuming and equipment-intensive, money was needed. As well, training was often required and so too were expensive venues on which to play. Most of these features made them out of reach for the common man and class bias was a key differential in designating who could play. By the end of the nineteenth century, certain sports had opened up but it took until the twentieth century for most to demonstrate full egalitarianism.[17]

Sport offered and continues to offer two main things among many to men. As has been discussed, it provides an arena and outlet to demonstrate masculine skill and the related attributes of strength and physical prowess. But for many boys, especially those living in urban areas, it offers a way up and out of their born place and time. Boxing, to cite one example, provided those from lower socioeconomic strata a way up and out of the confines of their class.[18] In the United States and in Canada, it was a pathway up the ladder and out of the proverbial ghetto. This is one of the reasons that so many Italians, Jews, and Irish were engaged professionally in the sport, especially during the first half of the twentieth century. This is also why so many African Americans and Hispanic Americans are so prominent within the sport today.

Men by and large have always retained a fascination for watching a fight. How does one explain the consistent attraction to boxing, schoolyard brawls, bar fights, and of course boxing, and by extension, the brutal UFC events? UFC is extraordinarily popular and generates huge revenues. It is a mixed martial arts base and is much more visceral than boxing. Why, one must ask, are so many young men drawn to the pugilistic model? How does one go about reconciling the context of boxing or UFC in a world that is supposed to abhor this kind of contact? Kath Woodward gives one answer: "Boxing is not just about men; it is about masculinity."[19] Expanded, what this may mean is that boxing is a whole world for men: train, fight, struggle, triumph, fail, do it again, all the while proving something to yourself and to others. This may even explain some of the reasons why it has become a popular form of exercise among the executive class. Joyce Carol Oates also comments on the core masculine association of boxing. "Boxing," she writes, "is a purely masculine activity and it inhabits a purely masculine world." Oates is quick to remark though that most men "are not defined by it" and she recognizes the world of female boxers with some claims to validity, which does upset the equation of appeal.[20]

Boxing is codified by rules and oriented around specific amounts of time. It is also somewhat nostalgic in its mechanics, and with the exception of the gloves, it harkens back to the past. On this key point, James B. Twitchell has observed "boxing returns male retaliation rituals to the more confined level of *sport* while still invoking honor and maintaining a definite ending."[21] One sees this in the highly staged big fights as much as on the schoolyard.

Baseball, like boxing, evolved during the nineteenth century. Because it is played on a field and moves at an almost glacial pace, it will always retain a pastoral set of associations.[22] It is the sport to which many men in North America (and Asia and South America) can relate. Unlike the skill and speed of hockey or the strength and vigor of football, baseball is something that is real in both its appeal and its orientation. To some extent, baseball is so appealing because it is anti-modern in a number of ways. It still conforms to most of its original rules and as it is played, has not become overly susceptible to technology, as has been the case in other sports. This makes watching it and playing it akin to eating comfort food. Baseball is also timeless in the sense that players from earlier eras would recognize it, it has no clock, and it is done when it is done.[23]

Baseball also holds appeal to men, many of whom are non-athletes, because of its fixation with statistics. The reliance on data, averages, percentages, and numbers in virtually every category imagined, actually appeals to those who are statistically minded. This originated as American culture was beginning to become more oriented around industry and commercial concerns and yet it did not erode the appeal of the game. By the last quarter of the nineteenth century, baseball became codified in rules and rationalized in specialization. The men and boys who played the game had to perform a specific task at a specific position, harmonious with a Fordist approach, and importantly, they could not be above the game. This made it very appealing as far as a pedagogic focus, especially for new immigrants, and for many, it served as a wonderful entertainment offering.[24]

Baseball has changed as a consequence of television and yet it still exudes a traditional series of hallmarks. The slow pace and the very key specifics do not lend the sport to variations that would allow the gait to quicken. There have been changes, such as the institution of the designated hitter in the American League and the arrival of free agency, but perhaps the most significant change to occur in baseball was the move of a number of major league teams to western cities, away from their crowded and popular eastern markets. The Dodgers' move from Brooklyn to Los Angeles is still discussed and written about.[25] Even with a few significant changes, baseball still seems wedded to the past and very much stable as compared to the changes and pace evident in hockey, basketball, and football. The beefy home-run hitter, the somewhat overweight pitcher, and the aging third baseman, still have a place in the sport where time seems to move slower in comparison with the other major sports.

Televised sports became huge business during the 1970s. Whether it was Roone Arledge and *Monday Night Football*, the Olympics, the Super-bowl, World Series, or the Final Four, the numbers of people viewing these events were enormous and the advertising revenue climbed each year. Television changed the way sports was seen and in turn affected how men watched. Videotape, the instant replay, compilations, and whole shows devoted to sports beyond actual events had a significant impact on male viewers. Since the advent of the home theater and the big screen/flat screen, this process has only accelerated. Multiple TVs and interactive capabilities are just the tip of the iceberg. A large part of this interest is not technological but rather the appeal of the drama.[26] Transferred from the arenas and stadiums to the world of television, the dramatic aspects of the contest are rebuilt and reconfigured in a way that most viewers understand. This means that many expect vicarious thrills, nonstop action, sudden changes, and a host of opportunities that make watching a heightened activity filled with the unknown, as if one was playing a video game.

In complete contrast to the tradition-based focus of baseball and boxing, and to some extent football and basketball, has been the rise of extreme sports. Beginning in the 1980s and abetted with the aid of television, a variety of very "modern" and dangerous sports, some of which were variations on older, more staid creations, started to become popular with young enthusiasts. These were sports that appealed to young people because in many cases, they were simply too demanding for anyone past a certain age. They required young bodies that were far more resilient to damage and to the impact that would inevitably be sustained. Spurred on by ESPN II, the Outdoor Living Network, Spike TV, and other newcomers to the visual scene, they were outside of the mold of anything previously shown. Unlike many of the now-corny offerings from the previous decades, these were well-thought-out, cutting-edge and filled with nonstop excitement. Many of these sports did not necessarily have formal uniforms but encouraged a display of sartorial and stylistic adoption that suggested nonconformity and rebelliousness. The colorful and highly personalized attire seemed more evocative of bicycle messenger subculture then professional sports. A focus on the individual as participant and as character is also a part of this trend.

According to Kyle Kusz, extreme sports also had appeal because they were "portrayed as sporting activities which have revived a set of traditional American masculine values and pursuits: rugged individualism, conquering new frontiers, and achieving individual progress."[27] For those too distanced from the traditional team sports, too disillusioned with the problems inherent in the politics and complaining of the established sports, and to those searching for something fresh and novel, the characteristics and sports that enshrine the attributes that Kusz mentions, either in participation or spectatorship, were all highly attractive.

Part of the appeal of mountain climbing and other proto-extreme sports has always been the risk element involved. Now, this same attraction is present in both the exotic variants as well as in closer-to-home versions such as skateboarding and snowboarding. Even more to the extreme end, street luge and BMX bike racing call for more risk and thus more visual excitement. These sports and activities are quick and fluid, with very little break in action and they are often filled with crashes, accidents, and danger. This accounts for their appeal to an audience that wishes to live vicariously through watching. Extreme sports participants do not abide by tradition and there are no boundaries in the comparable sense to older, established sports. Participants possess an on-the-edge mentality, which means they go all out without fear and worry. The courage displayed transcends normal day-to-day occupations and for some men this is enormously appealing. One commentator on this world has also remarked that many of these creations are constructed around an environment that does not feature women or men of color, in essence providing a space for white males to recapture some form of masculine equilibrium that is often not available in mainstream American culture.[28]

The rise of the voyeur in sports has become an accepted attribute of the masculine viewer. He must be a kind of connoisseur though, and in possession of the proper paraphernalia as far as viewing technology. This dovetails with a certain amount of sports knowledge, interest, whether real or feigned, and often, the adoption of a certain male posture. It seems that in some male subcultural groupings, watching is plainly enough. But one has to watch with a fair amount of attentiveness, for not knowing the rules, even in this visual universe, is as bad as not knowing how to play. If a man or a boy is not informed, he feels embarrassed, shamed, and out of place. Some men "bone up" on a particular sport before a meeting by reading the sports page in order to have something to contribute to a discussion. This is especially pronounced when one knows that a superior has a strong interest in cricket or rugby. *Esquire* editor-at-large A. J. Jacobs relates the following situation about not being that interested in watching sports all weekend. He feels that the "gap" between his inability to play and his lack of enthusiasm were related and left him with a marked feeling of disinterest:

> After twenty-one years it's gotten embarrassing. I go to meetings at *Esquire*, and they'll talk about the weekend's games, and I have to avoid all eye contact in the hopes I won't get called on. I'll be studying a particularly interesting floor tile, and my friend Andy, who knows that my sports awareness ended in 1982, will say, "Hey, A.J. did you see Craig Nettles hit a double this weekend?" And then everyone will crack up. I feel as emasculated as a crab after an encounter with a barnacle (barnacles consume crab testes)."[29]

A corollary to the rabid fandom and intense interest in sports spectator-ship and sports trivia is combined in fantasy sports leagues or rotisserie leagues. Originating in the early 1980s, participants would draft baseball players and thus become owners. It did not matter what team they actu-ally played for; they now became part of a fantasy team. Each morning, box scores published in the newspaper would allow owners to check on their players' progress and they would then tabulate their team's progress.[30] The participants in these leagues, which have now expanded beyond baseball to include hockey, football, and basketball, are over-whelmingly white, middle-class, and male. Research into this phenome-non suggests that it satisfies the masculine series of affirmations gleaned from watching sports and being involved with sports.[31] What is signifi-cant is the fact that there is a competition that is based on sports knowl-edge, not on actually playing the sport. According to the authors of a survey on this activity,

> Participants act as front office members of multimillion dollar sports teams, wheeling and dealing commodified players and allowing own-ers to experience the thrill of competition and victory.[32]

The point of the hobby is multi-faceted. It allows a tangible reason to pay attention to sports: it allows the participant to demonstrate his sports knowledge by forcing him to pay attention, to keep in the know. As well, this kind of activity allows for bonding through common interests and at the same time satisfies a love of competition. When large payouts are available to the winners, sometimes in the tens of thousands of dollars, the rewards add a level of substance that makes it much more real.

Whether an amount of sports capital is now necessary is not the point; it is crucial to be aware of key fundamentals. What often propels this knowledge and this interest is the rise of an athlete that transcends the sport, the game, and is beyond comparison. Tiger Woods, before his 2010 fall, had exceeded the norm and opened up interest in his sport that was not previously present. Yet his fall from grace had enormous repercus-sions for the game and for the person. As journalist Jonathan Mahler writes,

> Rarely has an athlete tumbled as far and as fast as Tiger Woods. In an era in which stories about athletes behaving badly—gambling, using drugs, carrying weapons—barely stand out in the news, the revelations of Wood's epic infidelities created a scandal of a whole different or-der . . . [33]

The popularity of golf as a spectator sport and a participant activity is soaring. And the main reason has to be Tiger Woods. Pressure for him to return so that the PGA could negotiate a lucrative television deal was enormous.[34] The culture of golf has spread far and wide and has been made immensely popular no doubt because of Tiger Woods.[35] Woods has soared to superstardom because of his talent and his appeal. He transcends race and class and his skills have elevated him to the top of his chosen sport as well as to being the most recognized athlete in the world. Woods also appeals to many because he is neat and clean, well-dressed, and properly attired, usually in Nike. Before his fall from grace and his antics became public knowledge he was known as a class act and an ideal ambassador for the game. His fashion sense had also carried the popularity of golf attire beyond the course, although not everyone has joined in.[36]

The democratization of golf has led, according to some, to a decline in the values that golf was once associated with. The decorum and deportment of playing on a private course that was a hallmark of exclusivity is gone. The subdued nature of the sport is banished to shouts and cheers, high fives, and wildly inappropriate attire. Cut-off shorts, muscle shirts, and in general a free-for-all as far as wardrobe goes, has provoked many clubs to reinstate a mandatory dress code. If anyone can now play, what was once so unique is no longer special. If seven-hour rounds are the norm, golf has changed. If fist-fights break out because of errant shots or slow play, then the nature of the game has truly evolved. Adam Sandler's *Happy Gilmore* is not too far-fetched.[37] Yet, there is one area of golf that is lauded today. Golf, unlike so many other sports, involves and invites women. This is not to say that mixed golf is embraced but rather that as couples, men and women can and do participate together. Only curling has as much of a co-gender appeal.

The competition, the drama, the action, the bonding, and the emphasis on strength, speed, and size coalesce around sport, becoming a tangible way that traditional aspects of masculinity are determined. Whereas more and more girls and women participate in virtually all the main sports, from boxing to hockey to baseball and soccer, certain realms remain the preserve of men. Women playing football is still uncommon and for men this is proper and fine. Whereas many fathers are thrilled to have their daughters playing soccer and softball, they do not want them engaging on the gridiron.

NOTES

1. Irving Rein, Philip Kotler, and Ben Shields, *The Elusive Fan: Reinventing Sports in a Crowded Marketplace* (New York: McGraw-Hill, 2006), p. 125, and Thomas Hine, *The Rise and Fall of the American Teenager* (New York: Perennial, 2000), p. 288.

2. See David Coad, *The Metrosexual: Gender, Sexuality, and Sport* (Albany: SUNY Press, 2008), pp. 3–6.

3. C. J. Pascoe, "Multiple Masculinities? Teenage Boys Talk about Jocks and Gender," *American Behavioral Scientist* 46, no. 10 (June 2003), pp. 1427–1428.

4. Douglas Hartmann, "The Sanctity of Sunday Football: Why Men Love Sports," *Contexts* 2, no. 4 (Fall 2003), pp. 14, 16. A number of aggressive incidents in soccer and basketball involving women are still considered anomalies.

5. Michael MacCambridge, *The Franchise: A History of* Sports Illustrated *Magazine* (New York: Hyperion, 1997), p. 4.

6. Patricia Vettel-Becker, *Shooting from the Hip: Photography, Masculinity, and Postwar America* (Minneapolis: University of Minnesota Press, 2005), p. 119.

7. See David Coad, *The Metrosexual.* Throughout the book Coad makes numerous connections between sports and fashion.

8. See David Coad, *The Metrosexual*, part II.

9. Stephen Brunt, *Searching for Bobby Orr* (Toronto, ON: Knopf, 2006).

10. See Mark Kriegel, *Namath: A Biography* (New York: Viking, 2004).

11. Douglas Hartmann, "The Sanctity of Sunday Football," p. 17.

12. Irving Rein, Philip Kotler, and Ben Shields, *The Elusive Fan*, p. 135.

13. Robert Fulford, "'Those Imbecilic, Stultifying Games': Notes on the Age of Sports," *Queen's Quarterly* 113, no. 1 (Spring 2006), p. 13.

14. See Michael MacCambridge, *The Franchise.*

15. Michael Oriard, *Brand NFL: Making and Selling America's Favorite Sport* (Chapel Hill: University of North Carolina Press, 2007), pp. 187, 188.

16. See David Whitson, "Circuits of Promotion: Media, Marketing, and the Globalization of Sport," in *MediaSport*, ed. Lawrence A. Wenner (London: Routledge, 2000), p. 60.

17. See Alan Metcalfe, *Canada Learns to Play: The Emergence of Organized Sport, 1807–1914* (Toronto, ON: Oxford University Press, 1987) and Peter Bailey, *Leisure and Class in Victorian Britain* (London: Routledge, 1978).

18. Kasia Boddy makes a number of references to this socioeconomic pattern. In particular, the often-cited choice that Barney Ross made regarding his career in the thirties is a standard example. *Boxing: A Cultural History* (London: Reaktion Books, 2008), pp. 260, 262.

19. Kath Woodward, *Boxing, Masculinity, and Identity* (New York: Routledge, 2007), p. 3.

20. Joyce Carol Oates, *On Boxing* (London: Bloomsbury, 1987), pp. 70–72.

21. James B. Twitchell, *Where Men Hide* (New York: Columbia University Press, 2006), p. 45.

22. Allen Guttmann, *A Whole New Ball Game: An Interpretation of American Sports* (Chapel Hill: University of North Carolina Press, 1988), p. 53.

23. LeRoy Ashby, *With Amusement for All: A History of American Popular Culture since 1830* (Lexington: University Press of Kentucky, 2006), p. 96.

24. Allen Guttmann, *A Whole New Ball Game*, pp. 53, 54, and LeRoy Ashby, *With Amusement for All*, p. 96.

25. Michael Mandelbaum, *The Meaning of Sports* (New York: Public Affairs, 2004), p. 98.

26. Michael Mandelbaum, *The Meaning of Sports*, p. 5.

27. Kyle Kusz, *Revolt of the White Athlete* (New York: Peter Lang, 2007), pp. 63, 74, 75.

28. See David Le Breton, "Athletic Ordeals: Extreme Sports, Heroism, and Virility," in *Material Man: Masculinity, Sexuality, Style*, ed. Giannino Malossi (New York: Abrams, 2000), p. 163.

29. A. J. Jacobs, *The Know-It-All* (New York: Simon & Schuster, 2004), p. 157.

30. Nikolas W. Davis and Margaret Carlisle Duncan, "Sports Knowledge Is Power: Reinforcing Masculine Privilege through Fantasy Sport League Participation," *Journal of Sport & Social Issues* 30, no. 3 (August 2006), p. 246.

31. Nikolas W. Davis and Margaret Carlisle Duncan, "Sports Knowledge Is Power," p. 247.

32. Nikolas W. Davis and Margaret Carlisle Duncan, "Sports Knowledge Is Power," p. 247.

33. Jonathan Mahler, "The Tiger Bubble," *New York Times Sunday Magazine*, March 28, 2010, p. 32.

34. Jonathan Mahler, "The Tiger Bubble," p. 32.

35. Leah R. Vande Berg, "The Sports Hero Meets Mediated Celebrityhood, " in *MediaSport*, ed. Lawrence A. Wenner (London: Routledge, 2000), pp. 150, 151.

36. Steven Skov Holt, "Notes on an Infinity of Sports Cultures," in *Design for Sports: The Cult of Performance*, ed. Akiko Busch (New York: Princeton Architectural Press, 1998), p. 6.

37. Steven Skov Holt, "Notes on an Infinity of Sports Cultures," p. 6.

Conclusion

Not a week goes by without a magazine, newspaper, journal, Website, television news show, or other media outlet offering a story, profile, or study on some aspect of contemporary masculinity. Segments on the news and in-depth analyses in magazines highlight trends and transitions. In numerous instances, the starting point is a product or a service that was once considered to be unmanly but that men are now indulging in. "Men are doing it now" is a familiar refrain, suggesting that whatever is in question or was in question regarding gender is now acceptable. The media authority has blessed this activity and men are given the thumbs up to use it, to try it, and to do it. Another staple is the profile of a famous man; the focus here is on his thoughts and impressions regarding fashion, style, and the presentation of the self. Much of this content often begins with an anecdote about one's father or grandfather, suggesting a parallel for comparison. Masculinity is often juxtaposed with time in order to make a point. A recent *Sartorialist* spread had people send in photographs of stylish family members and what they were wearing back in the day. The point usually focuses on how different or how similar certain masculine endeavors or actions are with the past.

The intention of this book has been to show how various masculine experiences have been conditioned, defined, or illustrated by different media. There are multiple templates that stand out as emblems for men to model themselves on. Many of these fluctuate depending on the time frame, but a host of them stay the same. The dominance of certain predilections and archetypes remain relatively cohesive even as variations come into being.

According to Kevin Alexander Boon, September 11 marked a watershed in the "return of the hero." Ordinary, everyday people demonstrated that heroic accomplishment and perceived heroic intent was very much a significant development in America recovering its social and cultural equilibrium. Boon—among others—suggests that the fracturing of the heroic "narrative" came as a result of the divisiveness of the Vietnam War, Watergate, and the malaise that plagued the United States throughout the 1970s and 1980s. Resurrected superficially with the Reagan years, and appropriated with varying degrees of success by Hollywood, it never got going until 2001. The notion of the hero had been in "hibernation" and resurfaced after 9/11. The hero, whether firefighter, policeman, or soldier was once again visible and present as an admirable and persuasive model.[1]

What made these men (and women) heroes was the fact that they were ordinary and everyday. Granted, a fair amount of popular mythology surrounds all three but they are easy for most to comprehend. Unlike the astronaut, the adventurer, the superstar actor, or the professional quarterback, these men could be your neighbor, your friend, your father, or your brother. The distance between them was and is comparably small compared to the mythologized heroes that transcend reality. The down-to-earth qualities of a contemporary mediated hero who does something to which most can relate—the pilot who landed the jet in the Hudson, "Sully"—carries enormous currency in a society that makes more and more distinctions between the regular and the out of the ordinary.

The search for heroes will always be part of the masculine experience and very significant in the mediated world. The templates, which have lasted for three thousand years, will continue in various forms to exert an enormous influence on boys and on men. What has changed though, especially over the past fifty years, has been the finiteness of these templates. No longer does *one* reign supreme as a dictate, but rather, there are many variations—often cut from the same cloth—for men to aspire to. In harmony with this has been the gradual validation of different form of masculine activity and enterprise. Many of these are still dependent upon a dominant template, but there has been an allowance for various permutations.

Like the ideas behind censorship, conceptions of masculinity are often being challenged and rewritten. What was significantly masculine in one period of time and in one particular place can suddenly or slowly seem anachronistic, silly, or out of touch. What was deemed hyper-masculine at one point may be the exact opposite today. As one commentator has observed,

> Masculinity is not an eternal and static object; masculinities change over time and the boundaries of masculinity are almost always the subject of redrawing, policing and contestation, as was the case in such diverse moments as Ancient Greece and Rome, the Renaissance, the Enlightenment, and the Industrial Revolution.[2]

On what may seem to some as a wholly trivial development, the rise of the metrosexual and its corollary, the übersexual, with its focus on appearance and shopping in the former and its "caring" aspect in the latter, may herald a paradigm shift in the masculine experience at least as far as the media are concerned. What this may evolve into is a much finer realization of emotion and felling as opposed to the winner-take-all aspect of historic masculinity.[3]

In her analysis of the detective film, Philippa Gates suggests that the evolution of masculine archetypes as pictured on the screen seems to change every decade. From the aggressive hard-boiled cop to the intellectual to the gun-toting vigilante to the physical enforcer, the variety of offerings is quite diverse. As an example of an archetype of masculinity, the detective on film, in television, and within the pages of books, responds to the perceived images that society deems appropriate. From the hyper-masculinity of Stallone to the boyishness of Keanu Reeves to the eccentric character *Monk* to sophisticated characters with special abilities, the performance of masculinity evolves. [4]

Even a casual analysis of media offerings of masculinity reveals that many forms are presented and flourish at the same time. As Robert Connell argues, from the standpoint of hegemonic masculinity, there has been "the emergence of an array of subordinated and marginalized masculinities" [5] which jockey for positions in the spectrum and within the media. James Twitchell suggests that masculinity and masculine culture have been redistributed in a way that is historically unparalleled. While keeping the consumption role in focus, he shows that the feminist movement has allowed for an expansion of the roles and of the masculine experiences:

> Today, an astonishing array of masculine identities compete for attention and their disposable income. A middle-class man of whatever color or religion can choose between rough-tough machismo or aching sensibility. Any man—whatever ethnic or racial background—who can afford it can mix and match masculine identities according to whim and situation. [6]

To a great extent, much of this is based upon both the compensatory consumption thesis and the role models available through media. To underestimate the power of consumption as well as both the media, marketing, and advertising is to completely evade some of the most seminal influences which condition on how men chose to be perceived and how they model themselves. Throughout this work, numerous examples have been chosen just for that reason: through film, television, advertising, literature, sports, hobbies, or décor, masculine experiences are heavily mediated and extraordinarily diverse.

NOTES

1. Kevin Alexander Boon, "Heroes, Metanarratives, and the Paradox of Masculinity in Contemporary Western Culture," *Journal of Men's Studies* 13, no. 3 (Spring 2005), pp. 301–312.

2. Garry Whannel, *Media Sports Stars: Masculinities and Moralities* (London: Routledge, 2002), p. 29.

3. While not directly addressing metrosexuals and confined to masculinity, two interesting articles in *Foreign Policy*, July–August 2009, are worth citing. "The Death of Macho" by Reihan Salam and "Good Riddance" by Valerie Hudson suggest that the

recession of 09/10 had a lot to do with the masculine attributes of bankers and politicians.

4. Philippa Gates, *Detecting Men: Masculinity and the Hollywood Detective Film* (Albany: SUNY Press, 2006), p. 41.

5. Robert W. Connell, *Masculinities*, 2nd ed. (Berkeley: University of California Press, 2005), p. 191.

6. James B. Twitchell, *Where Men Hide* (New York: Columbia University Press, 2006), p. 237.

Bibliography

Allister, Mark. "Introduction." In *Eco-Man: New Perspective on Masculinity and Nature.* Edited by Mark Allister. Charlottesville: University of Virginia Press, 2004.

Alterman, Eric. *It Ain't No Sin to Be Glad You're Alive: The Promise of Bruce Springsteen.* Boston: Little, Brown, 1999.

Aoki, Naomi. "Real Men Exfoliate." *Boston Globe*, April 19, 2005, online edition.

Ashby, LeRoy. *With Amusement for All: A History of American Popular Culture since 1830.* Lexington: University Press of Kentucky, 2006.

Aspesi, Natalia. "Military Style: The Reappearance of Uniforms in the Icon of Masculinity." In *Material Man: Masculinity, Sexuality, Style.* Edited by Giannino Malossi. New York: Abrams, 2000.

Atkinson, Claire. "He's Tough, He's Soft—He's Complex," *Advertising Age* 75, no. 19 (May 10, 2004).

Auslander, Leora. "The Gendering of Consumer Practices in Nineteenth-Century France." In *The Sex of Things: Gender and Consumption in Historical Perspective.* Edited by Victoria de Grazia, with Ellen Furlough. Berkeley: University of California Press, 1996.

Badinter, Elizabeth. *XY: On Masculine Identity.* New York: Columbia University Press, 1995.

Bailey, Peter. *Leisure and Class in Victorian Britain.* London: Routledge, 1978.

Baker, Carlos. *Ernest Hemingway: A Life Story.* New York: Collier/Macmillan, 1969/ 1988.

Baker, Nicholson. "Books as Furniture." In *The Size of Thoughts: Essays and Other Lumber.* New York: Random House, 1997.

Barbieri, Annalisa. "Bags of Masculinity." *New Statesman*, October 23, 2006.

Barthel, Diane. "A Gentleman and a Consumer." In *Signs of Life in the USA: Readings on Popular Culture for Writers.* Edited by Sonia Maasik and Jack Solomon. New York: Bedford/St. Martin's, 2003.

Belk, Russell W., and Janeen Costa. "The Mountain Man Myth: A Contemporary Consuming Fantasy." *Journal of Consumer Research* 25 (December 1998).

Bender, Jonathan. *LEGO: A Love Story.* Hoboken, NJ: Wiley, 2010.

Berger, John. *The Look of Things.* New York: Penguin, 1972.

Bernstein, Richard. "Shocked by the Printed Word." *Vancouver Sun*, January 19, 1991.

Best, Amy L. *Fast Cars, Cool Rides: The Accelerating World of Youth and Their Cars.* New York: New York University Press, 2006.

Bittar, Christine. "Men's Grooming: Past the Surface." *Brandweek*, December 13, 2004.

Blazina, Chris. *The Cultural Myth of Masculinity.* Westport, CT: Praeger, 2003.

Bloom, John. "Cardboard Patriarchy: Adult Baseball Card Collecting and the Nostalgia for a Presexual Past." In *Hop on Pop: The Politics and Pleasures of Popular Culture.* Edited by Henry Jenkins, Tara McPherson, and Jane Shattuc. Durham, NC: Duke University Press, 2002.

Bly, Robert. *Iron John: A Book about Men.* Reading, MA: Addison-Wesley, 1990.

Boddy, Kasia. *Boxing: A Cultural History.* London: Reaktion Books, 2008.

Boon, Kevin Alexander. "Heroes, Metanarratives, and the Paradox of Masculinity in Contemporary Western Culture." *Journal of Men's Studies* 13, no. 3 (Spring 2005).

———. "Men and Nostalgia for Violence: Culture and Culpability in Chuck Palahniuk's *Fight Club*." *Journal of Men's Studies* 11, no. 3 (Spring 2003).

Bordo, Susan. *The Male Body: A New Look at Men in Public and Private.* New York: Farrar, Straus & Giroux, 1999.

Boyer, G. Bruce. *Rebel Style: Cinematic Heroes of the 1950s.* New York: Assouline, 2006.

Boyle, T. C. *Talk, Talk.* New York: Viking, 2006.

Braudy, Leo. *From Chivalry to Terrorism: War and the Changing Nature of Masculinity.* New York: Knopf, 2003.

Breu, Christopher. *Hard-Boiled Masculinities.* Minneapolis: University of Minnesota Press, 2005.

Bribiescas, Richard G. *Men: Evolutionary and Life History.* Cambridge, MA: Harvard University Press, 2006.

Brinkley, Alan. *The Publisher: Henry Luce and His American Century.* New York: Alfred A. Knopf, 2010.

Brooks, David. "The Return of the Pig." *Atlantic Monthly*, April 2003.

Brown, Ian. "Introduction." In *What I Meant to Say: The Private Lives of Men.* Edited by Ian Brown. Toronto, ON: Thomas Allen, 2005.

Brown, Patricia Leigh. "The Return of Manly Men." *New York Times*, October 28, 2001.

Brownlie, Douglas, and Paul Hewer, "Prime Beef Cuts: Culinary Images for Thinking 'Men.'" *Consumption, Markets, and Culture* 10, no. 3 (September 2007).

Brunt, Stephen. *Searching for Bobby Orr.* Toronto, ON: Alfred A. Knopf, 2006.

Bruzzi, Stella. *Bringing Up Daddy: Fatherhood and Masculinity in Post-War Hollywood.* London: British Film Institute Publishing, 2005.

Burrill, Derek A. *Die Tryin': Videogames, Masculinity, Culture.* New York: Peter Lang, 2008.

Campbell, Colin. *The Romantic Ethic and the Spirit of Modern Consumerism.* Oxford, UK: Basil Blackwell, 1987.

Catano, James V. "Entrepreneurial Masculinity: Re-tooling the Self-Made Man," *Journal of American and Comparative Cultures* 23, no. 2 (Summer 2000).

Chabon, Michael. "I Feel Good about My Murse." In *Manhood for Amateurs.* New York: HarperCollins, 2009.

Chakraborty, Barmini. "Market for Men's Skin Care Grows." *Wall Street Journal*, April 20, 2005.

Cheever, Susan. *Home before Dark.* New York: Bantam Books, 1991.

Chudacoff, Howard P. *Children at Play: An American History.* New York: New York University Press, 2007.

Cicolini, Alice. *The New English Dandy.* New York: Assouline, 2005.

Clark, Michael J. "Faludi, *Fight Club*, and Phallic Masculinity: Exploring the Emasculating Economics of Patriarchy." *Journal of Men's Studies* 11, no. 1 (Fall 2002).

Clum, John M. *"He's All Man": Learning Masculinity, Gayness, and Love from American Movies.* New York: Palgrave, 2002.

Coad, David. *The Metrosexual: Gender, Sexuality, and Sport.* Albany: SUNY Press, 2008.

Cohen, Leah Hager. *Glass, Paper, Beans: Revelations on the Nature and Value of Ordinary Things.* New York: Doubleday/Currency, 1997.

Cohen, Robert. *Amateur Barbarians.* New York: Scribner, 2009.

Colomina, Beatriz. "Introduction." In *Cold War Hothouses: Inventing Postwar Culture from Cockpit to Playboy.* Edited by Beatriz Colomina, Annmarie Brennan, and Jeannie Kim. Princeton, NJ: Princeton Architectural Press, 2004.

Connell, Robert. *Gender and Power.* Palo Alto, CA: Stanford University Press, 1987.

———. *Masculinities.* 2nd ed. Berkeley: University of California Press, 2005.

———. "Studying Men and Masculinity." *Resources for Feminist Research*, Fall/Winter 2001.

Conniff, Richard. *The Natural History of the Rich.* New York: Norton, 2002.

Cornwall, Andrea, and Nancy Lindisfarane, eds., *Dislocating Masculinity: Comparative Ethnographies.* London: Routledge, 1994.

Cox, Meg. "More Protests Seen as Psycho Nears Release." *Wall Street Journal*, February 22, 1991.

Craig, S. *Men, Masculinity, and the Media.* London: Sage, 1992.

Crawford, Matthew B. *Shop Class as Soulcraft: An Inquiry into the Value of Work*. New York: Penguin, 2009.

Crewe, Ben. *Representing Men: Cultural Production and Producers in the Men's Magazine Market*. Oxford, UK: Berg, 2003.

Cross, Gary. *The Cute and the Cool: Wondrous Innocence and Modern American Children's Culture*. New York: Oxford University Press, 2004.

———. *Men to Boys: The Making of Modern Immaturity*. New York: Columbia University Press, 2008.

Csikszentmihalyi, Mihaly, and Eugene Rochberg-Halton. *The Meaning of Things: Domestic Symbols of the Self*. Cambridge, UK: Cambridge University Press, 1981.

Cuordileone, K. A. *Manhood and American Political Culture in the Cold War*. London: Routledge, 2005.

Davis, Nikolas W., and Margaret Carlisle Duncan. "Sports Knowledge Is Power: Reinforcing Masculine Privilege through Fantasy Sport League Participation." *Journal of Sport & Social Issues* 30, no. 3 (August 2006).

Deveau, Scott. "Lad Mags' Last Stand." *National Post*, February 24, 2007.

Dotson, Edisol Wayne. *Behold the Man: The Hype and Selling of Male Beauty in Media and Culture*. New York: Harrington Park Press, 1999.

Drummond, Murray J. "The Meaning of Boys' Bodies in Physical Education." *Journal of Men's Studies* 11, no. 2 (Winter 2003).

Dudink, Stefan, and Karen Hagemann. "Masculinity in Politics and War in the Age of Democratic Revolutions, 1750–1850." In *Masculinities in Politics and War: Gendering Modern History*. Edited by Stefan Dudink, Karen Hagemann, and John Tosh. Manchester, UK: Manchester University Press, 2004.

Dummitt, Chris. "Finding a Place for Father: Selling the Barbecue in Post-War Canada." In *Home, Work, and Play: Situating Canadian Social History, 1840–1980*. Edited by James Opp and John C. Walsh. Don Mills, ON: Oxford University Press, 2006.

Duncan, Margaret Carlisle, and Michael A. Messner. "The Media Image of Sport and Gender." In *MediaSport*. Edited by Lawrence A. Wenner. London: Routledge, 2000.

Ebenkamp, Becky. "The Uber-Measure of Man," "Out of the Box," *Brandweek* 46, no. 38 (October 24, 2005).

Ellis, Bret Easton. *American Psycho*. New York: Vintage, 1991.

Engelhardt, Tom. *The End of Victory Culture: Cold War America and the Disillusioning of a Generation*. New York: Basic Books, 1995.

Epstein, Joseph. *Snobbery: The American Version*. Boston: Houghton Mifflin, 2002.

Fairbanks, Rich. "The Boys' Trip." In *Eco-Man: New Perspectives on Masculinity and Nature*. Edited by Mark Allister. Charlottesville: University of Virginia Press, 2004.

Faludi, Susan. *Stiffed: The Betrayal of the American Man*. New York: Morrow, 1999.

Farrell, James J. "The Nature of My Life." In *Eco-Man: New Perspectives on Masculinity and Nature*. Edited by Mark Allister. Charlottesville: University of Virginia Press, 2004.

Farren, Mick. *The Black Leather Jacket*. New York: Abbeville Press, 1985.

Fillin-Yeh, Susan. "Introduction: New Strategies for a Theory of Dandies." In *Dandies: Fashion and Finesse in Art and Culture*. Edited by Susan Fillin-Yeh. New York: New York University Press, 2001.

Finch, Christopher. *Highways to Heaven: The Auto Biography of America*. New York: HarperCollins, 1992.

Fine, Lisa M. "Rights of Men, Rites of Passage: Hunting and Masculinity at REO Motors of Lansing, Michigan, 1945–1975." *Journal of Social History*, Summer 2000.

Fink, Thomas. *The Man's Book*. London: Wiedenfeld & Nicolson, 2006.

Flocker, Michael. *The Metrosexual Guide to Style: A Handbook for the Modern Man*. New York: Da Capo Press, 2003.

Flusser, Alan. *Dressing the Man: Mastering the Art of Permanent Fashion*. New York: HarperCollins, 2002.

Fox, William L. *In the Desert of Desire: Las Vegas and the Culture of Spectacle*. Reno: University of Nevada Press, 2005.

Freeman, Joshua B. "Hardhats: Construction Workers, Manliness, and the 1970 Pro-War Demonstrations." *Journal of Social History*, Summer 1993.

Fuchs, Cynthia J. "The Buddy Politic." In *Screening the Male: Exploring Masculinities in Hollywood Cinema*. Edited by Steven Cohan and Ina Rae Hark. London: Routledge, 1996.

Fulford, Robert. "'Those Imbecilic, Stultifying Games': Notes on the Age of Sports." *Queen's Quarterly* 113, no. 1 (Spring 2006).

Fussell, Samuel Wilson. *Muscle: Confessions of an Unlikely Bodybuilder*. New York: Poseidon Press, 1991.

Gallagher, Mark. *Action Figures: Men, Action Films, and Contemporary Adventure Narratives*. London/New York: Palgrave Macmillan, 2006.

Garcia, Guy. *The Decline of Men*. New York: Harper Perennial, 2008.

Gardaphe, Fred L. *From Wiseguys to Wise Men: The Gangster and Italian American Masculinities*. London: Routledge, 2006.

Garelick, Rhonda K. "The Layered Look." In *Dandies: Fashion and Finesse in Art and Culture*. Edited by Susan Fillin-Yeh. New York: New York University Press, 2001.

Gates, Philippa. *Detecting Men: Masculinity and the Hollywood Detective Film*. Albany: SUNY Press, 2006.

Gelber, Steven M. *Hobbies: Leisure and the Culture of Work in America*. New York: Columbia University Press, 1999.

———. "A Job You Can't Lose: Work and Hobbies in the Great Depression." *Journal of Social History* 24 (Summer 1991).

Ghamari-Tabrizi, Sharon. *The Worlds of Herman Kahn*. Cambridge, MA: Harvard University Press, 2005.

Gibson, James William. *Warrior Dreams: Paramilitary Culture in Post-Vietnam America*. New York: Hill & Wang, 1994.

Gilbert, James. *Men in the Middle: Searching for Masculinity in the 1950s*. Chicago: University of Chicago Press, 2005.

Giroux, Henry. *The Mouse That Roared: Disney and the End of Innocence*. Lanham, MD: Rowman & Littlefield, 1999.

Glazov, Jamie. "Men on Men: Intellectual Locker Room Talk." *American Enterprise* 14, no. 6 (September 2003).

Goldstein, Carolyn M. *Do It Yourself: Home Improvement in Twentieth-Century America*. New York: Princeton Architectural Press, 1998.

Goldstein, Richard. "Neo-Macho Man: Pop Culture and Post-9/11 Politics." *The Nation* 276, no. 11 (March 24, 2003).

Greenbaum, Andrea. "Brass Balls: Masculine Communication and the Discourse of Capitalism in David Mamet's *Glengarry Glen Ross*." *Journal of Men's Studies* 8, no. 1 (October 1999).

Grice, Samantha. "Boys Will Be Boys." *National Post*, April 10, 2004.

Gross, Michael. *Genuine Authentic: The Real Life of Ralph Lauren*. New York: HarperCollins, 2002.

Guttmann, Allen. *A Whole New Ball Game: An Interpretation of American Sports*. Chapel Hill: University of North Carolina Press, 1988.

Halberstam, David. *The Fifties*. New York: Villard Books, 1993.

Hall, Karen J. "A Soldier's Body: GI Joe, Hasbro's Great American Hero, and the Symptoms of Empire." *Journal of Popular Culture* 38, no. 1 (August 2004).

Hartmann, Douglas. "The Sanctity of Sunday Football: Why Men Love Sports," *Contexts* 2, no. 4 (Fall 2003).

Healey, Murray. "The Mark of a Man: Masculine Identities and the Art of Macho Drag." *Critical Quarterly* 36, no. 1.

Heron, Craig. "The Boys and Their Booze: Masculinities and Public Drinking in Working-Class Hamilton, 1890–1946." *Canadian Historical Review* 86, no. 3 (September 2005).

Heskett, John. *Toothpicks and Logos: Design in Everyday Life*. New York: Oxford University Press, 2002.

Higham, John. "The Reorientation of American Culture in the 1890s." In *Writing American History*. Edited by John Higham. Bloomington: University of Indiana Press, 1970.

Hine, Thomas. *I Want That! How We All Became Shoppers*. New York: HarperCollins, 2002.

———. *The Rise and Fall of the American Teenager*. New York: Perennial, 2000.

Hirschberg, Lynn. "Face Time." *New York Times Style Magazine*, Men's Fashion, Spring 2005.

Hollander, Anne. *Sex and Suits: The Evolution of Modern Dress*. New York: Random House, 1994.

Holt, Douglas B. "Jack Daniel's America." *Journal of Consumer Culture* 6, no. 2 (2006).

Holt, Douglas B., and Craig J. Thompson, "Man-of-Action Heroes: The Pursuit of Heroic Masculinity in Everyday Consumption." *Journal of Consumer Research* 31 (September 2004).

Holt, Steven Skov. "Notes on an Infinity of Sports Cultures." In *Design for Sports: The Cult of Performance*. Edited by Akiko Busch. New York: Princeton Architectural Press, 1998.

Howard, Hilary. "For Men: Rub In, Say 'Ahh,'" *New York Times*, November 19, 2009, online edition.

Hudson, Valerie. "Good Riddance." *Foreign Policy*, July–August 2009.

Hunter, Latham. "The Celluloid Cubicle: Regressive Constructions of Masculinity in 1990s Office Movies." *Journal of American Culture* 26, no. 1 (March 2003).

Hyman, Peter. *The Reluctant Metrosexual: Dispatches from an Almost Hip Life*. New York: Villard, 2004.

Hymowitz, Kay S. "Child-Man in the Promised Land." *City Journal*, Winter 2008.

Jacobs, A. J. *The Know-It-All*. New York: Simon & Schuster, 2004.

Jansz, Jeroen. "The Emotional Appeal of Violent Video Games for Adolescent Males," *Communication Theory* 15, no. 3 (August 2005).

Jarvis, Christina S. *The Male Body at War: American Masculinity during World War II*. Dekalb: Northern Illinois University Press, 2004.

Jeffords, Susan. *Hard Bodies: Hollywood Masculinity in the Reagan Era*. New Brunswick, NJ: Rutgers University Press, 1993.

Jenkins, Tricia. "James Bond's 'Pussy' and Anglo-American Cold War Sexuality." *Journal of Popular Culture* 28, no. 3 (September 2005).

Johnson, Paul. *Intellectuals*. New York: Harper & Row, 1988.

Jones, Thom. *The Pugilist at Rest*. Boston: Little, Brown, 1993.

Kaplan, Fred. *1959: The Year Everything Changed*. Hoboken, NJ: Wiley, 2009.

Kasson, John F. *Houdini, Tarzan, and the Perfect Man: The White Male Body and the Challenge of Modernity in America*. New York: Hill & Wang, 2001.

Katz, Donald. *Home Fires: An Intimate Portrait of One Middle-Class Family in Postwar America*. New York: HarperCollins, 1992.

Keen, Sam. *Fire in the Belly: On Being a Man*. New York: Bantam, 1991.

Kehler, Michael D., Kevin G. Davison, and Blye Frank. "Contradictions and Tensions in the Practice of Masculinities in School: Interrogating Embodiment and 'Good Buddy Talk.'" *Journal of Curriculum Theorizing* 21, no. 4 (Winter 2005).

Kelly, Ian. *Beau Brummell: The Ultimate Dandy*. London: Hodder & Stoughton, 2005.

Kilbourn, Russell J. A. "American Frankenstein: Modernity's Monstrous Progeny." *Mosaic: A Journal for the Interdisciplinary Study of Literature* 38, no. 3 (September 2005).

Kiley, Dan. *The Peter Pan Syndrome: Men Who Have Never Grown Up*. New York: Dodd, Mead, 1983.

Kimmel, Michael. *Guyland: The Perilous World Where Boys Become Men*. New York: HarperCollins, 2008.

———. *The History of Men: Essays on the History of American and British Masculinities*. Albany: SUNY Press, 2005.

———. *Manhood in America: A Cultural History.* 2nd ed. New York: Oxford University Press, 2006.

Kingston, Anne. "Too Many Cooking Shows . . . ." *National Post,* December 16, 2004.

Kirkham, Pat, and Alex Weller. "Cosmetics: A Clinique Case Study." In *The Gendered Object.* Edited by Pat Kirkham. Manchester, UK: Manchester University Press, 1996.

Klein, Judy Graf. *The Office Book.* New York: Facts on File, 1982.

Kriegel, Mark. *Namath: A Biography.* New York: Viking, 2004.

Kusz, Kyle. *Revolt of the White Athlete.* New York: Peter Lang, 2007.

La Cecia, Franco. "Rough Manners: How Men Are Made." In *Material Man: Masculinity, Sexuality, Style.* Edited by Giannino Malossi. New York: Abrams, 2000.

Le Breton, David. "Athletic Ordeals: Extreme Sports, Heroism, and Virility." In *Material Man: Masculinity, Sexuality, Style.* Edited by Giannino Malossi. New York: Abrams, 2000.

LeDuff, Charlie. *US Guys: The True and Twisted Mind of the American Man.* New York: Penguin, 2006.

Lees-Milne, Alvide, and Derry Moore. *The Englishman's Room.* New York: Viking, 1986.

Leland, John. *Hip: The History.* New York: HarperCollins, 2004.

Levenstein, Harvey. *Paradox of Plenty: A Social History of Eating in Modern America.* New York: Oxford University Press, 1993.

Levy, David M. *Scrolling Forward: Making Sense of Documents in the Digital Age.* New York: Arcade, 2001.

Lhamon, W. T., Jr. *Deliberate Speed: The Origins of a Cultural Style in the American 1950s.* Washington, DC: Smithsonian Institution Press, 1990.

Lienhard, John H. *Inventing Modern.* New York: Oxford University Press, 2003.

Lindsay, Greg. "Man vs. Man." *Advertising Age* 76, no. 24 (June 13, 2005).

Lombardi, Anna. "Sex Objects." In *Material Man: Masculinity, Sexuality, Style.* Edited by Giannino Malossi. New York: Abrams, 2000.

Lubin, David M. *Shooting Kennedy: JFK and the Culture of Images.* Berkeley: University of California Press, 2003.

Luciano, Lynne. *Looking Good: Male Body Image in Modern America.* New York: Hill & Wang, 2001.

Lupton, Ellen. "The Electric Carving Knife." In *Stud : Architectures of Masculinity.* Edited by Joel Sanders. New York: Princeton Architectural Press, 1996.

Lutz, Tom. *Doing Nothing: A History of Loafers, Loungers, Slackers, and Bums in America.* New York: Farrar, Straus & Giroux, 2006.

MacCambridge, Michael. *The Franchise: A History of* Sports Illustrated *Magazine.* New York: Hyperion, 1997.

MacDonald, Jake. *With the Boys: Field Notes on Being a Guy.* Vancouver, BC: Greystone/ Douglas & McIntyre, 2005.

Macinnis, Craig. "Macho, Macho Chef: I Want to Be a Macho Chef." *Toronto Star,* August 20, 2006.

Mackinnon, Kenneth. *Representing Men: Maleness and Masculinity in the Media.* London: Arnold, 2003.

Maguire, James H. "Fiction of the West." In *The Columbia History of the American Novel.* New York: Columbia University Press, 1991.

Mahler, Jonathan. "The Tiger Bubble." *New York Times Sunday Magazine,* March 28, 2010.

Malin, Brenton J. *American Masculinity under Clinton: Popular Media and the Nineties "Crisis of Masculinity."* New York: Peter Lang, 2005.

Malossi, Giannino. "Material Man: Decoding Fashion, Redefining Masculinity." In *Material Man: Masculinity, Sexuality, Style.* Edited by Giannino Malossi. New York: Abrams, 2000.

Mamet, David. "Conventional Warfare." In *Some Freaks.* New York: Penguin, 1989.

———. "Deer Hunting." In *Make-Believe Town.* Boston: Little, Brown, 1996.

———. "Practical Pistol Competition." In *Some Freaks.* New York: Penguin, 1989.

Mandelbaum, Michael. *The Meaning of Sports.* New York: Public Affairs, 2004.

Manguel, Alberto. *The Library at Night*. Toronto, ON: Knopf Canada, 2006.

Marwick, Arthur. *The Sixties*. New York: Oxford University Press, 1998.

May, Elaine Tyler. *Homeward Bound: American Families in the Cold War Era*. New York: Basic Books, 1999.

McCracken, Grant. *Culture and Consumption: New Approaches to the Symbolic Character of Consumer Goods and Activities*. Bloomington: Indiana University Press, 1990.

McInerney, Jay. "How Bond Saved America—and Me." In *Dressed to Kill: James Bond, the Suited Hero*. Edited by Jay McInerney et al. New York: Flammarion, 1996.

"Men Defy Stereotypes." *Global Cosmetic Industry* 170, no. 11 (November 2002).

Messner, Michael, and Jeffrey Montez de Oca. "The Male Consumer as Loser: Beer and Liquor Ads in Mega Sports Media Events." *Signs* 30, no. 3 (Spring 2005).

Metcalfe, Alan. *Canada Learns to Play: The Emergence of Organized Sport, 1807–1914*. Toronto, ON: Oxford University Press, 1987.

Micklewhait, John, and Adrian Wooldrige. *The Company: A Short History of a Revolutionary Idea*. New York: Modern Library/Random House, 2003.

Miller, Arthur. *Death of a Salesman*. New York: Viking, 1976.

Moody, Rick. "Against Cool." *The Best American Essays: 2004*. Edited by Louis Menand. Boston: Houghton Mifflin, 2004.

Moore, Roger, and Douglas Gillette. *King, Warrior, Magician, Lover*. New York: Harper-Collins, 1990.

Moran, Joe. *Star Authors: Literary Celebrity in America*. London: Pluto Press, 2000.

Mort, Frank. "Boy's Own? Masculinity, Style, and Popular Culture." In *Male Order: Unwrapping Masculinity*. Edited by R. Chapman and J. Rutherford. London: Lawrence and Wishart, 1988.

Moss, Mark. *Manliness and Militarism: Educating Young Boys in Ontario for War*. Don Mills, ON: Oxford University Press, 2001.

———. *Shopping as an Entertainment Experience*. Lanham, MD: Lexington Books, 2007.

Mosse, George L. *The Image of Man: The Creation of Modern Masculinity*. New York: Oxford University Press, 1996.

Mrozek, Donald J. "The Military, Sport, and Warrior Culture," in *The Columbia History of Post–World War II America*. Edited by Mark C. Carnes. New York: Columbia University Press, 2007.

Nathanson, Paul, and Katherine K. Young. *Spreading Misandry: The Teaching of Contempt for Men in Popular Culture*. Montreal, QC, and Kingston, ON: McGill–Queen's University Press, 2001/2006.

Neuhaus, Jessamyn. *Manly Meals and Mom's Home Cooking: Cookbooks and Gender in Modern America*. Baltimore: Johns Hopkins University Press, 2003.

Newell, Walter R. *The Code of Man*. New York: HarperCollins, 2003.

Newkirk, Thomas. *Misreading Masculinity: Boys, Literacy, and Popular Culture*. Portsmouth, NH: Heinemann, 2002.

Norman, Donald A. *The Design of Everyday Things*. New York: Doubleday, 1990.

Noxon, Christopher. *Rejuvenile: Kickball, Cartoons, Cupcakes, and the Reinvention of the American Grown-up*. New York: Crown, 2006.

Nylund, David Keith. "Have a Take: Masculinity and Sports Talk Radio," PhD diss., University of California, Davis, 2004.

Oates, Joyce Carol. *On Boxing*. London: Bloomsbury, 1987.

Oldstone-Moore, Christopher. "The Beard Movement in Victorian Britain." *Victorian Studies* 48, no. 1 (Autumn 2005).

Opie, Ioana. *The People in the Playground*. Oxford, UK: Oxford University Press, 1994.

Oriard, Michael. *Brand NFL: Making and Selling America's Favorite Sport*. Chapel Hill: University of North Carolina Press, 2007.

Osgerby, Bill. *Playboys in Paradise: Masculinity, Youth, and Leisure-Style in Modern America*. Oxford, UK: Berg, 2001.

Owens, Anne Marie. "Dads Are Always Good for a Laugh." *National Post*, June 19, 2004.

Owram, Doug. *Born at the Right Time: A History of the Baby Boom Generation.* Toronto, ON: University of Toronto Press, 1996.

Palmquist, Susan. "Handsome Ambitions." *Psychology Today* 37, no. 4 (July–August 2004).

Parini, Jay. *The Art of Teaching.* New York: Oxford University Press, 2005.

Pascoe, C. J. "Multiple Masculinities? Teenage Boys Talk about Jocks and Gender." *American Behavioral Scientist* 46, no. 10 (June 2003).

Pine, Joseph, II, and James H. Gilmore. *The Experience Economy: Work Is Theatre and Every Business a Stage.* Boston: Harvard Business School Press, 1999.

Pleck, Joseph H. "The Theory of Male Sex-Role Identity: Its Rise and Fall." In *The Making of Masculinities: The New Men's Studies.* Edited by Harry Brod. Boston: Unwin Hyman, 1990.

Polhemus, Ted. "The Invisible Man: Style and the Male Body." In *Material Man: Masculinity, Sexuality, Style.* Edited by Giannino Malossi. New York: Abrams, 2000.

Pollack, William S., with Todd Shuster. *Real Boys' Voices.* New York: Random House, 2000.

Pope, Harrison G., Jr., Katharine A. Phillips, and Roberto Olivardia. *The Adonis Complex: The Secret Crisis of Male Body Obsession.* New York: Free Press, 2000.

Postman, Neil. *The Disappearance of Childhood.* New York: Vintage Books, 1994.

Preciado, Beatriz. "Pornotopia." In *Cold War Hothouses: Inventing Postwar Culture from Cockpit to Playboy.* Edited by Beatriz Colomina, Annmarie Brennan, and Jeannie Kim. Princeton, NJ: Princeton Architectural Press, 2004.

Radley, Alan. "Artifacts, Memory, and a Sense of the Past." In *Collective Remembering.* Edited by David Middleton and Derek Edwards. Beverly Hills, CA: Sage Publications, 1990.

Raphael, Ray. *The Men from the Boys: Rites of Passage in Male America.* Lincoln: University of Nebraska Press, 1988.

Rein, Irving, Phillip Kotler, and Ben Shields. *The Elusive Fan: Reinventing Sports in a Crowded Marketplace.* New York: McGraw-Hill, 2006.

Remnick, David. "D.C. Postcard: Tyson's Corner." *New Yorker,* June 27, 2005.

Rheims, Maurice. *The Strange Life of Objects: Thirty-five Centuries of Collecting and Collectors.* New York: Atheneum, 1961.

Riemer, James D. "Rereading American Literature from a Men's Studies Perspective: Some Implications." In *The Making of Masculinities: The New Men's Studies.* Edited by Harry Brod. Boston: Unwin Hyman, 1990.

Riley, Tim. *Fever: How Rock 'N' Roll Transformed Gender in America.* New York: St. Martin's Press, 2004.

Robinson, Sally. *Marked Men: White Masculinity in Crisis.* New York: Columbia University Press, 2000.

———. "Men's Liberation, Men's Wounds: Emotion, Sexuality, and the Reconstruction of Masculinity in the 1970s." In *Boys Don't Cry?* Edited by Milette Shamir and Jennifer Travis. New York: Columbia University Press, 2002.

Rogin, Michael. *Ronald Reagan, the Movie: and Other Episodes in Political Demonology.* Berkeley: University of California Press, 1987.

Rombes, Nick. "Restoration, American Style." *C Theory* 23, no. 1 (May 31, 2000).

Ronson, Jon. *Them: Adventures with Extremists.* New York: Simon & Schuster, 2002.

Rose, Ava, and James Friedman. "Television Sports as Mas(s)culine Cult of Distraction." In *Out of Bounds: Sports, Media, and the Politics of Identity.* Edited by Aaron Baker and Todd Boyd. Bloomington: Indiana University Press, 1997.

Rybszynksi, Witold. *Home: A Short History of an Idea.* New York: Viking/Penguin, 1986.

Sabo, Don, and S. C. Jansen, "Prometheus Unbound: Constructions of Masculinity in the Sports Media." In *MediaSport.* Edited by Lawrence W. Wenner. London: Routledge, 2000.

Salam, Reihan. "The Death of Macho." *Foreign Policy,* July–August 2009

Salzman, Marian, Ira Matathia, and Ann O'Reilly. *The Future of Men.* New York: Palgrave Macmillan, 2006.

Sanders, Joel. "Introduction." In *Stud: Architectures of Masculinity*. Edited by Joel Sanders. New York: Princeton Architectural Press, 1996.

Sanford, Kathy, and Leanna Madill. "Resistance through Video Game Play: It's a Boy Thing." *Canadian Journal of Education* 29, no. 3 (August 2005).

Savage, Dan. *Skipping towards Gomorrah: The Seven Deadly Sins and the Pursuit of Happiness in America*. New York: Plume/Penguin, 2003.

Savran, David. *Taking It like a Man*. Princeton, NJ: Princeton University Press, 1998.

Schama, Simon. *The Embarrassment of Riches: An Interpretation of Dutch Culture in the Golden Age*. London: Fontana Press, 1987.

Schickel, Richard. *The Disney Version: The Life, Times, Art, and Commerce of Walt Disney*. New York: Touchstone/Simon & Schuster, 1985.

Schjeldahl, Peter. "American Abstract: Real Jackson Pollock." *New Yorker*, July 31, 2006.

Schor, Juliet B. *Born to Buy: The Commercialized Child and the New Consumer Culture*. New York: Scribner, 2004.

Schouten, John, and James McAlexander. "Subcultures of Consumption: An Ethnography of New Bikers." *Journal of Consumer Research* 22 (June 1995).

Segal, Eric J. "Norman Rockwell and the Fashioning of American Masculinity." *Art Bulletin* 78, no. 4 (December 1996).

Shannon, Brent. "Refashioning Men: Fashion, Masculinity, and the Cultivation of the Male Consumer in Britain, 1860–1914." *Victorian Studies* 46, no. 4 (Summer 2004).

Simpson, Mark. "Here Come the Mirror Men." *Independent*, November 15, 1994.

Sloan, Bob, and Steven Guarnaccia. *A Stiff Drink and a Close Shave: The Lost Arts of Manliness*. San Francisco: Chronicle Books, 1995.

Smalley, Andrea L. "'I Just Like to Kill Things': Women, Men, and the Gender of Sport Hunting in the United States, 1940–1974." *Gender and History* 17, no. 1 (April 2005).

Smith, Russell. *Men's Style: The Thinking Man's Guide to Dress*. Toronto, ON: McClelland & Stewart, 2005.

Solomon, Deborah. *Jackson Pollock: A Biography*. New York: Cooper Square Press, 2001.

Solomon-Godeau, Abigail. "Male Trouble." In *Constructing Masculinity*. Edited by Maurice Berger, Brian Wallis, and Simon Watson. London: Routledge, 1995.

"Sometimes It's Hard to Be a Man." *Economist*, December 22, 2001.

Sontag, Susan. *On Photography*. New York: Farrar, Straus & Giroux, 1986.

Spigel, Lynne. *Make Room for TV: Television and the Family Ideal in Postwar America*. Chicago: University of Chicago Press, 1992.

Sports Illustrated, November 26, 2007, vol. 107, no. 21.

Spufford, Francis. *The Child That Books Built: A Life in Reading*. New York: Metropolitan/Henry Holt, 2002.

Stanley, Alessandra. "Men with a Message: Help Wanted." *New York Times*, January 3, 2010.

Steinberg, Neil. *Hatless Jack: The President, the Fedora, and the History of an American Style*. New York: Plume, 2004.

Stimpson, Catherin R. "Foreword." In *The Making of Masculinities: The New Men's Studies*. Edited by Harry Brod. Boston: Unwin Hyman, 1990.

Storey, Mark. "'And As Things Fell Apart': The Crisis of Postmodern Masculinity in Bret Easton Ellis's *American Psycho* and Dennis Cooper's *Frisk*." *Critique* 47, no. 1 (Fall 2005).

Strangelove, Michael. *Watching YouTube: Extraordinary Videos by Ordinary People*. Toronto, ON: University of Toronto Press, 2010.

Streamerica, Tiffany & Company, pamphlet, 1993.

Sudjic, Deyan. *Cult Objects*. New York: Paladin, 1987.

———. *The Language of Things: Design, Luxury, Fashion, Art*. London: Penguin Books, 2009.

Sullivan, James. *Jeans: A Cultural History of an American Icon*. New York: Gotham Books, 2006.

Swofford, Anthony. *Jarhead: A Marine's Chronicle of the Gulf War and Other Battles.* London: Scribner, 2003.

Ta, Lynn M. "Hurt So Good: *Fight Club*, Masculine Violence, and the Crisis of Capitalism." *Journal of American Culture* 29, no. 3 (September 2006).

Tanenhaus, Sam. "Violence That Art Didn't See Coming." *New York Times*, February 24, 2010, online edition.

Taylor, Ella. *Prime-Time Families: Television Culture in Postwar America.* Berkeley and Los Angeles: University of California Press, 1989.

Thomas, Dana. *Deluxe: How Luxury Lost Its Luster.* New York: Penguin Press, 2007.

Tompkins, Jane. *West of Everything: The Inner Life of Westerns.* New York: Oxford University Press, 1992.

Traber, Daniel S. *Whiteness, Otherness, and the Individualism Paradox from Huck to Punk.* New York: Palgrave Macmillan, 2007.

Tragos, Peter. "Monster Masculinity: Honey, I'll Be in the Garage Reasserting My Manhood." *Journal of Popular Culture* 42, no. 3 (2009).

Troyer, John, and Chani Marchiselli. "Slack, Slacker, Slackest: Homosocial Bonding Practices in Contemporary Dude Cinema." In *Where the Boys Are: Cinemas of Masculinity and Youth.* Edited by Murray Pomerance and Frances Gateward. Detroit, MI: Wayne State University Press, 2005.

Twenge, Jean M. *Generation Me.* New York: Free Press, 2006.

Twitchell, James B. *Lead Us into Temptation: The Triumph of American Materialism.* New York: Columbia University Press, 1999.

———. *Where Men Hide.* New York: Columbia University Press, 2006.

Vande Berg, Leah R "The Sports Hero Meets Mediated Celebrityhood." In *MediaSport.* Edited by Lawrence Wenner. London: Routledge, 1998.

Vettel-Becker, Patricia. *Shooting from the Hip: Photography, Masculinity, and Postwar America.* Minneapolis: University of Minnesota Press, 2005.

Walker, Rebecca. "Putting Down the Gun." In *What Makes a Man: Twenty-two Writers Imagine the Future.* Edited by Rebecca Walker. New York: Riverhead/Penguin, 2004.

Watts, Steven. *Mr. Playboy: Hugh Hefner and the American Dream.* Hoboken, NJ: Wiley, 2008.

Waxman, Sharon. "The Next Action Heroes." *National Post*, July 2, 2004.

Weber, Brenda R. "What Makes the Man? Television Makeovers, Made-Over Masculinity, and Male Body Image." *International Journal of Men's Health* 5, no. 3 (Fall 2006).

Wees, Hans Van. "A Brief History of Tears: Gender Differentiation in Archaic Greece." In *When Men Were Men: Masculinity, Power, and Identity in Classical Antiquity.* Edited by Lin Foxhall and John Salmon. London: Routledge, 1998.

Weisman, Leslie Kane. "Prologue: Women's Environmental Rights—A Manifesto." In *Gender Space Architecture: An Interdisciplinary Introduction.* Edited by Jane Rendell, Barbara Penner, and Iain Borden. London: Routledge, 2000.

Whannel, Garry. *Media Sports Stars: Masculinities and Moralities.* London: Routledge, 2002.

Whelan, David. "Men, Their Motives, and Their Magazines." *American Demographics* 23, no. 10 (October 2001).

Whitson, David. "Circuits of Promotion: Media, Marketing, and the Globalization of Sport." In *MediaSport.* Edited by Lawrence A. Wenner. London: Routledge, 2000.

Willis, Gary. *John Wayne's America: The Politics of Celebrity.* New York: Simon & Schuster, 1997.

Wilson, Sara. "Oh Boy." *Globe and Mail*, August 28, 2004.

Winder, Simon. *The Man Who Saved Britain: A Personal Journey into the Disturbing World of James Bond.* London: Picador, 2006.

Woodward, Kath. *Boxing, Masculinity, and Identity.* New York: Routledge, 2007.

Zipes, Jack. *Fairy Tales and the Art of Subversion.* New York: Routledge, 1991.

Zukin, Sharon. *Landscapes of Power: From Detroit to Disney World.* Berkeley: University of California Press, 1993.

Index

About the Author

Mark Moss is the author of *Manliness and Militarism, Shopping as an Entertainment Experience*, and *Toward the Visualization of History*. After a career as a professor and administrator, he is currently engaged in a number of research projects and continues to write and consult from his home in Toronto.